MATTERS
THE ARTS AND AGING TOOLKIT

Creativity Matters: The Arts and Aging Toolkit
© 2007 by the National Guild of Community Schools
of the Arts, 520 8th Avenue, Suite 302, New York, NY 10018

All rights reserved. Published 2007
Printed in the United States of America

Evaluation: Performance Results, Inc., Laytonsville, Maryland
Editing: Ellen Hirzy, Washington, DC
Design: fuszion, Alexandria, Virginia

Photo Credits: Cover (top) and 14: PARADIGM, Solomons Company/Dance, Inc., New York, NY; cover (center): detail of work by Hang Fong Zhang, Center for Elders and Youth in the Arts, Institute on Aging, San Francisco, CA, Jeff Chapline, artistic director; cover (bottom) and 184: Concord Community Music School, Concord, NH, National Guild member since 1984; xxii, 32, 174, 178: Stagebridge Senior Theatre Company, Oakland, CA; 44: Amatullah Saleem (storyteller), *Pearls of Wisdom* program, Elders Share the Arts, Brooklyn, NY; 24: Alzheimer's Association Orange County, Irvine, CA; 70: detail of work by Celia Sacks, Center for Elders and Youth in the Arts, Institute on Aging, San Francisco, CA, Jeff Chapline, artistic director; 122: The Golden Tones, Wayland, MA; 146: Irv Williams and Carla Vogel (musician and dancer), Kairos Dance Theatre, Minneapolis, MN; 164: Jesse Neuman-Peterson and Moses Williams (dancers), Kairos Dance Theatre, Minneapolis, MN.

The author would like to acknowledge the support of Neil A. Boyer and the inspiration of the ladies on the garden level and her own well elder, Edward G. Misey. In memory of Rachel L. Misey.

To order, contact:
National Guild of Community Schools of the Arts
Phone: 212–268–3337
E-mail: guildinfo@nationalguild.org
Web: www.nationalguild.org.

CREATIVITY MATTERS
THE ARTS AND AGING TOOLKIT

JOHANNA MISEY BOYER

Sponsors

The National Guild of Community Schools of the Arts, National Center for Creative Aging, and New Jersey Performing Arts Center would like to thank the following funders for their visionary support:

MetLife Foundation

The National Guild of Community Schools of the Arts, the National Center for Creative Aging, and the New Jersey Performing Arts Center value lifelong learning in the arts. We believe that individuals and communities reap profound benefits from participating in arts programs, especially when those programs are led by professional teaching artists. In recognition of these shared beliefs, we joined forces in 2006 to explore how best to serve our respective members and audiences, particularly the growing population of older adults.

Thanks to the generous and enthusiastic support of our funders—MetLife Foundation, NAMM: The International Music Products Association, the Healthcare Foundation of New Jersey, and Roche—we are pleased to bring you *Creativity Matters: The Arts and Aging Toolkit*. Designed for both the arts and aging services fields, this resource offers detailed advice on, and examples for, designing, implementing, and evaluating professionally conducted community arts programs for older adults. The toolkit also is online at www.artsandaging.org. We look forward to releasing a Spanish-language edition and Web site in 2008.

As leaders of organizations that support the intersection of arts, education, and community, it is our hope that this toolkit will inspire readers to start or continue their work in the arts and aging field and to trumpet the importance of the arts to older adults' mental and physical health. We should encourage and support the continued creativity of older adults who have much to contribute to the quality of life in our communities.

Jonathan Herman
Executive Director
National Guild of
Community Schools
of the Arts

Susan Perlstein
*Founder and Director
of Education*
National Center
for Creative Aging

Lawrence P. Goldman
President and CEO
New Jersey Performing
Arts Center

Contents

Introduction — xvii

Chapter 1 Understanding the Context for Arts and Aging Programs — 1

Describing Normal Aging — 3
- The Language of Aging — 4
- Reality vs. Myth — 4

Changes During Aging — 4
- Physical and Biological Changes — 4
- Social and Emotional Changes — 6

The Demographics of Aging — 7
- Longevity — 7
- Diversity — 7
- Income — 7
- Education — 8
- Retirement — 8

Productive Aging — 8

Implications for Arts and Aging Programs — 9

Big-Picture Challenges to Arts and Aging Programs — 9
- Fear of Aging — 10
- Isolation of Older Adults — 11
- Communicating Value — 12
- Change — 12

Key Points about the Context for Arts and Aging Programs — 13

Chapter 2 How Arts Participation Benefits Older Adults — 15

Enhancing Community Quality of Life — 16
    Arts and Aging in Community Cultural Development — 16

Enhancing Individual Quality of Life — 20
    How Cognitively Fit Older Adults Benefit — 21
    How Older Adults with Dementia Benefit — 22

Key Points about the Benefits of Arts Participation to Older Adults — 23

Chapter 3 The Aging Services Field — 25

Understanding Key Issues — 26
    Increasing Costs — 26
    Emphasis on Home- and Community-Based Care — 26
    Consolidated Consumer Information — 27
    Reducing Residential Facility Staff Turnover
        and Increasing Morale — 27
    Addressing Family Caregiver Burnout — 27
    Implications for the Arts — 28

Exploring Infrastructure — 28
    Federal — 28
    State — 29
    Local — 29
    Foundations — 29

Making Connections — 29

Key Points about the Aging Services Field — 31

Chapter 4 The Arts Field — 33

Understanding Key Issues — 34
    Expanded Definition of Arts Education — 34
    Arts Participation — 34
    A Broader Definition of the Arts — 34
    Community Engagement — 34
    Demonstrated Impact — 34
    Scarce Resources — 35
    Professional Development for Teaching Artists — 35
    Special Issues for Creative Arts Therapies — 35

Exploring Infrastructure — 36
    Federal — 36
    Regional — 37
    State — 37
    Local — 37
    Arts Education — 38
    Creative Arts Therapies — 38
    Foundations — 38

Making Connections — 39

Key Points about the Arts Field — 41

Chapter 5 Effective Practices — 45

Defining Effective Practices — 46

Identifying Outcome Goals — 47
    Mastery — 47
    Social Engagement — 48

Influencing Others — 49

Understanding Adult Learning — 50

Program Examples — 52
   The Golden Tones — 52
   New Horizons Music — 54
   Luella Hannan Memorial Foundation — 57
   Kairos Dance Theatre — 59
   Elders Share the Arts — 62
   Osher Lifelong Learning Institute, University of Southern Maine — 64

Key Points about Effective Practices — 68

Chapter 6 Program Design — 71

Planning the Program — 72
   Conducting Internal and Eternal Assessment — 73
      Internal Assessment — 73
      Eternal Assessment — 74
   Creating an Advisory Committee — 78
   Establishing Purpose — 80
      Determining Mission, Vision, and Values — 80
      Setting Goals and Objectives — 81
   Designing Activities — 82
   Applying Andragogy and Instructional Design — 83
      Establishing Trust — 85
      Setting Challenges — 88
      Ensuring Success — 89
      Accommodating Diversity — 89
      Encouraging Participation — 90
      Setting Session Length and Frequency — 90
      Facilitating a Learning Community — 91
   Evaluation — 92
   Reminiscence — 93
   Community Sharing of Art — 94
   Key Points about Program Planning — 95

Finding and Working with Partners — 96
   Understanding Partnerships — 96
   Planning Partnerships — 97
   Identifying and Securing Partners — 100
   Training Partners — 102
   Implementing the Partnership — 103
   Key Points about Partnerships — 104

Securing Resources **105**
    Exploring Revenue Sources   105
    Creating a Budget   108
    Developing a Plan   109
    Making the Case   112
    Understanding Challenges   113
    Key Points about Resource Development   114

Marketing to Participants **115**
    Getting the Word Out   115
    Motivating Participants   117
    Using Your Assets   117
    Creating Materials   118
    Key Points about Marketing to Participants   119

Summary **120**

Chapter 7 Program Implementation   123

Setting the Stage **124**
    Ensuring Physical and Programmatic Accessibility   124
    Setting Group Expectations   126
    Key Points about Setting the Stage   127

Keeping on Track **128**
    Assessing Progress and Process   128
    Planning Community Sharing of the Art   129
    Key Points about Keeping on Track   134

Supporting Teaching Artists **135**
    Assessing Qualifications   135
    Making the Hire   137
    Conducting Training   138
    Providing Support   140
    Train the Trainer Programs   141
    Key Points about Supporting Teaching Artists   144

Chapter 8 Evaluation — 147

Defining Terms — 148

Understanding Benefits — 149

Planning the Evaluation — 150
- Determining What You Want to Learn — 150
- Assessing Costs — 153
- Identifying Audiences — 153
- Creating Communication Tools — 154
- Seeking Help — 155

Implementing the Evaluation — 156

Evaluating People with Dementia — 162

Key Points about Evaluation — 163

Chapter 9 Public Awareness — 165

Defining Terms — 166

Identifying Audiences — 167

Developing Messages — 167

Selecting Messengers — 169

Developing Methods — 169

Key Points about Public Awareness — 172

Chapter 10 Looking to the Future — 175

Notes	**179**
Glossary	**185**
Contact Information	**195**
Appendixes	**201**
1. Program Logic Model Example	202
2. Project Timeline Formula and Curriculum Planning Format	204
3. Fundraising Tools	205
4. Marketing Tools	216
5. Policies and Procedures Example	218
6. Teaching Artists Tools	220
7. Evaluation Tools	225

Acknowledgments

Project Partners

Kenneth Cole, Program Director, National Guild of Community Schools of the Arts, New York, NY

Susan Perlstein, Founder and Director of Education and Training, National Center for Creative Aging, Washington, DC

Gay P. Hanna, Executive Director, National Center for Creative Aging, Washington, DC

Desiree Urquhart, Former Vice President of Arts Education, New Jersey Performing Arts Center, Newark, NJ

Donna Bost-White, Director of Arts Education, New Jersey Performing Arts Center, Newark, NJ

Advisory Committee

Gene Cohen, M.D., Director, Center on Aging, Health, and Humanities, George Washington University, Washington, DC

Roy Ernst, Professor Emeritus, Eastman School of Music, and Founder, New Horizons Music, Rochester, NY

Beverly Ferry, Executive Director, Wabash County Council on Aging, Inc. (representing the National Institute of Senior Centers), Wabash, IN

Maria Genné, Artistic Director, Kairos Dance Theatre, Minneapolis, MN

John McEwen, Executive Director, New Jersey Theatre Alliance, Morristown, NJ

Robin Middleman, Arts Education Coordinator, New Jersey State Council on the Arts, Trenton, NJ

Harry R. "Rick" Moody, Director of Academic Affairs, AARP, Washington, DC

Patricia A. Polansky, Assistant Commissioner, Division of Aging and Community Services, New Jersey Department of Health and Senior Services, Trenton, NJ

Lisa Shaw, Former Director of Adult Programs, Levine School of Music, Washington, DC

Interviews

Unless otherwise noted, all quotations are from phone interviews conducted with leaders in the arts and aging field between November 2006 and January 2007 and in July and August 2007. The project partners would like to thank the following individuals for their time and advice:

Alzheimer's Poetry Project
Gary Mex Glazner, Director
Santa Fe, NM

Arts for the Aging
Janine Tursini, Executive Director
Bethesda, MD

ArtAge Publications
The Senior Theatre Resource Center
Bonnie Vorenberg, President
Portland, OR

Center for Elders and Youth in the Arts/Institute on Aging
Jeff Chapline, Administrative and Artistic Director
San Francisco, CA

Creative Aging Cincinnati
Mary Kay Morris, Former Executive Director
Cincinnati, OH

Donovan Scholars Program, University of Kentucky
Michael D. Smith, Director, Council on Aging, School of Public Health
Lexington, KY

Drum Circle Facilitators Guild
Nelli Hill, Secretary
Founder, Playful Spirit Adventures
Fulton, MD

Elder Craftsmen, Inc.
Janet Langlois, Former Executive Director
New York, NY

Elders Share the Arts
Carolyn Zablotney, Executive Director
Brooklyn, NY

EngAGE: The Art of Active Aging (formerly More Than Shelter For Seniors)
Maureen Kellen-Taylor, Vice President
Burbank, CA

Evergreens Senior HealthCare System
Janie Johnson, Renaissance Director
Greensboro, NC

The Golden Tones
Maddie Sifantus, Founder and Director
Wayland, MA

Foundation for Quality Care
Ed Graham, Former President
Albany, NY

The Intergeneration Orchestra of Omaha
Chris Gillette, Co-Founder
Director, Community Services Division, Eastern Nebraska Office on Aging
Omaha, NE

Kairos Dance Theatre
Maria Genné, Artistic Director
Minneapolis, MN

Levine School of Music
Lisa Shaw, Former Director
of Adult Programs
Washington, DC

Liz Lerman Dance Exchange
John Borstel, Humanities Director
Takoma Park, MD

The Luella Hannan Memorial Foundation
Pam Halladay, Senior Program Officer
Detroit, MI

Memories in the Making
La Doris "Sam" Heinly,
National Program Consultant
Newport Beach, CA

**National Coalition of Creative
Arts Therapies Associations**
Laura Greenstone, Chair
Silver Spring, MD

National Institute of Senior Centers
Beverly Ferry, Delegate
Executive Director, Wabash County
Council on Aging, Inc.
Wabash, IN

National Center for Creative Aging
Susan Perlstein, Founder,
Director of Education and Training
Washington, DC

National Endowment for the Arts
Barry Bergey, Director,
Folk and Traditional Arts
Washington, DC

New Horizons Music
Roy Ernst, Founder
Corning, NY

**New Jersey Office of Area Agency
on Aging Administration**
Tina Wolverton, Director
Trenton, NJ

**New Jersey Department
of Health and Senior Services**
Pat Polansky, Assistant Commissioner,
Division of Aging and Community Services
Trenton, NJ

New Jersey Intergenerational Orchestra
Susan Peterson, Vice President
and Administrative Director
Cranford, NJ

The OASIS Institute
Marcia Kerz, President
St. Louis, MO

**Osher Lifelong Learning Institute
National Resource Center**
Kali Lightfoot, Director
Portland, ME

Roland Corporation U.S.
Lynda Smith
Los Angeles, CA

The Seasoned Performers
Martha Haarbauer, Executive Director
Birmingham, AL

SPIRAL Arts, Inc.
Jean Badran, Director of Elder Arts
Priscilla Dreyman, Executive Director
Portland, ME

Stagebridge Senior Theatre Company
Stuart Kandell, Director
Oakland, CA

TimeSlips
Anne Davis Basting, Founder and Director
Milwaukee, WI

Yamaha Corporation of America
Mike Bates, Director, Institutional and Commercial Services, MMG
Buena Park, CA

Introduction

Creativity. According to the *Random House Unabridged Dictionary*, it is "the ability to transcend traditional ideas, rules, patterns, relationships, or the like, and to create meaningful new ideas, forms, methods, interpretations, etc." A more concise definition is "bringing something new of value into existence." The etymology of "creativity," however, is what resonates for those of us who are passionate about embedding the arts—or creativity—in the lives of older adults and the communities in which they live. The word comes from the Latin *creatus*, which means "to have grown." Older adults have grown in knowledge and experience, and we should value them for what they contribute to each of us individually and to our communities.

The arts are the key. They enable us to communicate effectively within and between generations, making sense of and reconciling life experiences, understanding and celebrating the present, and creating a legacy for the future. They also allow us to experiment without fear of failing—to be challenged—and to succeed in learning new skills and discovering latent ones. Strengthening connections among older adults, family, friends, residents, and caregivers, the arts create a sense of community in which each person's contribution is respected. In sum, the arts enhance quality of life.

No matter what their age or their physical or mental ability, older adults can and should participate in the arts. And not just any arts, but high-quality, participatory arts programs conducted over a significant period by professional teaching artists.

The National Guild of Community Schools of the Arts, the National Center for Creative Aging, and the New Jersey Performing Arts Center believe that the arts are of vital importance to the lives of current and future generations of older adults. Many leaders in the arts, healthcare, and aging services industries share this belief, but too few have created or sustained effective arts and aging programs. Now is the time to be part of the process, part of the solution: the "beyond bingo" generation is here.

This resource is designed for leaders and program staff in public, nonprofit, and for-profit arts and humanities organizations and institutions and in healthcare and aging services organizations, corporations, and institutions. It is intended to increase the expertise of those who direct existing community arts and aging programs and to give others in the community the tools to take the first step—and keep going.

This information will also benefit:

- Teaching artists who want to work with older adults
- Leaders and staff of lifelong learning organizations and programs (such as higher education) who are interested in intentionally including the arts in their curriculums
- Private- and public-sector funders who need to define effective practices before creating or revising guidelines

The *Arts and Aging Toolkit* will help you:

- Appreciate why this is a pivotal time for arts and aging in the United States
- Understand that older adults continue to learn and benefit from education
- Learn about the aging services field
- Learn about the arts field and community arts
- Discuss the benefits of professionally conducted, participatory arts and aging programs with a variety of stakeholders (elected officials, funders, partners, and policymakers)
- Design, implement, market, support, evaluate, and sustain these programs for older adults
- Find and train teaching artists who are directly responsible for delivering programs
- Locate advice, training, and assistance

Enhancing quality of life by embedding the arts in the lives of older adults and the communities in which they live is more than a goal. It is one facet of a broader movement in the arts and aging services fields: a push toward designing or redesigning community so that the infrastructure works harmoniously to support everyone's needs as defined by *all* community members.

How to Use This Toolkit

If you are reading this resource, chances are you want to develop a new arts and aging program or enhance an existing one. You may be an experienced program designer or someone just starting out. You probably identify with or work in the arts or aging services fields. You may be hoping for answers—knowledge, rationales, tips, models, and resources—and this toolkit is intended to provide them. Your commitment and passion for older adults and the arts will help you face the challenge and make the difference between success and failure.

Chapters 1 through 5 provide the background to help you design and implement an arts and aging program. These chapters explain the context for arts and aging today; the benefits of arts participation for older adults; issues, infrastructure, and opportunities in the aging services and arts fields; and effective practices for arts and aging programs.

Chapters 6 through 9 offer practical, how-to guidance for program design and implementation; program evaluation; and public awareness. These chapters illustrate important concepts with concrete examples from successful programs. You can learn something from all of them, whether they are focused on well or frail elders, people who live in the community or in a residential facility, or older adults with dementia.

We have designed this toolkit for a variety of experience and interest levels. Many readers will find something of interest in every chapter, and others will browse the sections that are most relevant to them. Here is a roadmap to make the toolkit work for you:

If you are...	Read...
Just starting out or interested in this subject	The entire toolkit
An older adult who wants to learn how to age productively	Chapters 1, 2, and 6, which explain normal aging and the benefits, challenges, and outcome goals of effective arts and aging programs
Experienced in the arts and aging field	Chapter 2 to refresh your existing arguments about benefits and chapter 8 to understand the value of outcome evaluation
Working in the aging services or arts fields and want to convince others of the value of arts and aging programs	Chapters 1 through 5
A teaching artist	Chapter 1 to understand normal aging and chapters 6 and 7 to understand program design and implementation
A private- or public-sector funder	Chapters 1, 2, and 5 for background on arts and aging programs and an explanation of effective practices
A family member of an older adult	Chapter 1 to understand normal aging and chapter 2 to learn about rationales that can convince senior centers, adult day programs, and long-term care facilities to offer professionally conducted participatory arts programs

Basic Terms

Before you begin, it is helpful to learn these definitions:

Aging services field—Organizations, corporations, institutions, and individuals such as the Administration on Aging, state units on aging, local-level area agencies on aging, senior centers, continuing care retirement communities, corporations or foundations that own these communities, healthcare-focused community organizations (such as the Alzheimer's Association and the Visiting Nurse Association), family and professional caregivers, adult day programs, and hospitals (see chapter 3).

Arts field—Public, nonprofit, and for-profit arts organizations and institutions, such as the National Endowment for the Arts, state and local arts agencies, regional arts organizations, community schools of the arts, individual artists, arts education organizations, organizations focused on the literary arts, community-based organizations, musical instrument manufacturers, artist materials manufacturers, performing arts centers, presenting organizations, museums, symphonies, and dance, opera, and theater companies (see chapter 4).

Arts and aging field—Organizations and individuals in the arts and aging services fields who are focused full-time or part-time on providing sustained, high-quality, professionally led, participatory, community arts programs to older adults.

Community—A physical and social construct that includes cities, neighborhoods, apartment buildings, condominiums, residential facilities (for example, independent living, assisted living, skilled care/long-term care), and a group of people who interact and share certain things such as values or proximity.

Lifelong learning—A process of accomplishing personal, social, and professional development throughout the lifespan of individuals in order to enhance the quality of life of individuals and their communities. Lifelong learning also refers to educational classes, usually affiliated with a college, community college, or university, designed by or for older adults, and often taught by older adults.

The glossary at the end of this toolkit contains additional definitions.

Creativity Opens Doors

If you're looking for a reason to start an arts program for older adults, the older adults quoted throughout this toolkit offer eloquent testimony. By her own description, Suzanne could not string three sentences together before she moved into an EngAGE: The Art of Active Aging community (formerly known as More Than Shelter For Seniors). After she began participating in writing and visual arts programs, she wrote a screenplay for a 10-minute film. Her story of reinvention, including the making of the film, was featured in the Showtime series *This American Life*. She is now working on several other film and stage projects.

Suzanne's enthusiasm speaks volumes about why creativity matters to older adults:

> I couldn't believe that there would be a community for me at this time in my life. I didn't think I would be able to find something new inside of me. You know that same feeling when you got out of school and the whole world was open to you? Now, all over again, the whole world is open to me.

I feel blessed to have found something at this juncture of my life—something that not only fills my heart and soul and challenges me, but something I can do for the rest of my life. It was the turning point in my life.

Storyteller, Stagebridge Senior Theatre Company

1

Understanding the Context for Arts and Aging Programs

Today, we have an opportunity to advance the arts and aging field. Susan Perlstein, founder of the National Center for Creative Aging (NCCA), describes the state of the field in the first years of the 21st century:

> Professionals in gerontology, social work, education, and the arts have developed a keen interest in the theory and practice of creative work with elders. I attribute this in part to biomedical advances against some of the more debilitating physical conditions of old age. We can now expect to live longer, healthier lives. I also think interest has increased as our baby boomers [born between 1946 and 1964] reach retirement.[1]

Building on theories developed over 40 years by psychologists and gerontologists, the arts and aging field has grown slowly but steadily. Psychoanalyst and human development expert Erik Erikson hypothesized in 1967 that human development continues through the lifespan. In old age, integration of our past failures and successes is our main psychological task. Reminiscence—the process or practice of thinking or telling about past experiences—had been considered an unhealthy preoccupation until gerontologist Robert Butler linked it with Erikson's ideas about integration and recommended that reminiscence be encouraged. Butler's theory—published in 1975—paved the way for a blossoming of reminiscence models in gerontology. But until the late 1990s, creativity and the arts were missing from the big picture even though, in the mid- to late 1970s, artists were already working with older adults.

By 2005, there was clear evidence that participation in the arts enriches the lives of older adults in multiple ways, though awareness of the potential was limited. At the third conference on creativity and aging, sponsored that year by the National Endowment for the Arts in partnership with NCCA, AARP, and NAMM: The International Music Products Association, arts leaders sought to move the arts onto the agenda of the 2005 White House Conference on Aging. Participants submitted resolutions for review by the conference's policy committee, which forwarded one to delegates for consideration. Ultimately, the delegates did not include an arts resolution among the 50 that were approved for further action, but the issue made progress; it was ranked 58th.

The resolution states:

> Research suggests that active participation in the arts and learning promotes physical health, enhances a sense of well being among older Americans, improves quality of life for those who are ill, and reduces the risk factors that lead to the need for long-term care. Even though there is an interest and participation in the arts by many older Americans, there is a general lack of awareness in the public, healthcare, and social services communities about the positive physical and psychological impacts of arts participation. However, there is a valuable untapped resource of older artists who could be teachers or mentors in expanded arts programs for seniors. Older Americans may be encouraged to participate in dance, music, and visual arts activities and may choose to expand their horizons through art appreciation programs. Participation in arts activities may lead to intergenerational exchange of values and knowledge. For example, seniors may work together and with younger populations to preserve the value of older adults' memories and life experiences by recording their experiences and life histories in various mediums.
>
> Resolution: Increase awareness of the positive physical and psychological impact that arts participation can have on older Americans.[2]

To explore the potential for advancing the arts and aging field, this chapter examines:

- Language and attitudes we use to describe normal aging
- Physical-biological and social-emotional changes that occur during aging
- Shifting demographics of aging in the United States
- Productive aging as a concept that alters our view of growing old
- Big-picture challenges that affect the arts and aging field

Arts and Aging Policy: A Chronology

1961
The first White House Conference on Aging sets the stage for Medicare, Medicaid, and the Older Americans Act of 1965. Conferences are convened every decade: 1971, 1981, 1995, and 2005.

1981
The National Endowment for the Arts brings together experts to articulate the importance of arts and humanities for older adults. The group delivers a resolution to the White House Conference on Aging.

1995
The National Endowment for the Arts, National Endowment for the Humanities, and National Council on Aging sponsor a second conference on the arts, humanities, and older Americans. Jane Alexander is the first Arts Endowment chairman invited to keynote a White House Conference on Aging.

2001
The new National Center for Creative Aging (NCCA) receives funding from the Arts Endowment to create a database of programs for older adults and to network, train, and advocate for the field of creative aging.

2005
The Arts Endowment in partnership with NCCA, AARP, and NAMM: The International Music Products Association sponsors a conference on creative aging. Participants prepare a resolution for the White House Conference on Aging that delegates consider but do not formalize.

2006
The National Conference on Arts and Aging: Creativity Matters—the first conference of its kind—is presented by NCCA and the New Jersey Performing Arts Center. The 235 community-based artists and representatives of healthcare, aging, education, and cultural organizations; foundations; corporations; and government agencies explore the intersections among research, policy, and practice.

Describing Normal Aging

Aging is a progressive and cumulative process of change occurring throughout our lives and affected by many factors. Learning to walk as a toddler is an example of an age-related change. We perceive these changes as negative only as we grow older.

Most theories of aging have a common theme: It's in your genes. Another major factor is everyday wear and tear. While there is no one simple explanation, aging is affected by intrinsic factors, such as heredity and age-related changes, and extrinsic factors, such as environment, disease, and lifestyle.

We do slow down as we get older, but our ability to function isn't necessarily affected. And each of us ages at a different rate. In the absence of disease, many limiting effects of normal aging are often not even felt until sometime after age 75. Even then, an older adult can adapt his or her normal routine to accommodate these physical-biological and social-emotional changes.

The Language of Aging

We use a variety of terms when referring to the large and diverse demographic of people who are older, including:

old	senior
young-old	retiree
old-old	institutionalized
emerging elder	community-dwelling
elder	older adult
frail elder	well elder
older adult with dementia	

Notice that our choice of words often suggests disability. It's important to focus instead on ability, which is not necessarily related to age or mental capacity. An 80-year-old woman with dementia who uses a walker and lives in a long-term care facility moves her hand to the music. A 65-year-old man waltzes once a week at the senior center. They are both dancing.

Reality vs. Myth

Emphasizing ability instead of disability represents an evolution in attitude about what it means to be old. Thirty years ago, older adults were seen primarily in terms of their diseases. In a shift from a deficit model to an asset model—from looking at older people as medical objects to seeing all their vitality and wisdom—we have acknowledged that no matter how frail or cognitively fit, they have something to contribute.

Older adults' assets include:

- A range of life experiences
- The ability to recognize what is important and enduring
- Objectivity and an even temperament
- Fewer inhibitions
- More time to devote to civic engagement
- An understanding of how they learn best and the ability to shape their own learning processes

But many still believe the myths about aging:

- To be old is to be sick.
- You can't teach an old dog new tricks.
- The secret to successful aging is to choose your parents wisely.
- The lights may be on, but the voltage is low.
- The elderly don't pull their own weight.

Changes During Aging

One way to help dispel the myths of aging is to understand how people change during the aging process.

Physical and Biological Changes

- The transmission of messages in the nervous system—the body's communications superhighway—slows down, often resulting in balance problems and slower reflexes.

- Sensory losses affect our ability to interact with our environment. By age 65 or 70, 90 percent of adults have some vision loss, and some have significant hearing loss.

- There is little change in intellectual ability if we remain healthy. Cognitive changes affect memory, reasoning, and abstract thinking. We need more time to learn new things, and some loss of short-term memory may occur.

- The efficiency of the heart muscle decreases, and susceptibility to hardening of the arteries increases. As a result, we are less able to respond to physical or emotional stress, and blood pressure may increase.

- Changes in bones, muscles, and lung tissue can result in decreased lung efficiency. Shortness of breath and fatigue may lead to inactivity, which results in further declines in overall function and fitness.

- Nutritional status and enjoyment of food are often affected. We need fewer calories, but not fewer nutrients, so ensuring a healthy diet while avoiding excessive weight gain is a challenge.

- Normal age-related changes result in skin wrinkles, dryness, and thinning; diminished skin resiliency and an increase in "liver spots"; increased susceptibility to hypothermia and hyperthermia; and loss, thinning, and graying of hair. Nail growth slows, and nails become thicker and more brittle.

- Ligaments, joints, and bones undergo structural changes. Bone loss occurs, and there is decreased muscle bulk, strength, speed, strength, and endurance.

- While incontinence is not a normal part of aging, there are changes in kidney function and bladder capacity. The message that "you have to go" can be slowed, resulting in greater urgency.

- Prostate gland problems in men are more common.

- Though there are some changes in both sexual function and response in males and females, people retain the capacity for sexual activity well into old age.

- The greater the number of medications, the greater the risk of adverse side effects. Changes in kidney and liver function mean that drugs are not metabolized in the same way as in younger people, and changes in the digestive system may affect the absorption of drugs.

Dementia

Dementia is a general term characterized by serious memory loss, difficulty with concepts of time and space, problems with speech and hearing, and severe shifts in mood. The two most common types are multi-infarct dementia caused by strokes and dementia caused by Alzheimer's disease. The latter accounts for more than 60 percent of the cognitive function disorders in the aging population.

Not surprisingly, increasing age is the greatest risk factor for Alzheimer's disease. Statistics show that:

- Someone in America develops Alzheimer's every 72 seconds; by midcentury, someone will develop the disease every 33 seconds.[3]

- In 2007, an estimated 5.1 million Americans have Alzheimer's disease. This number includes 4.9 million people age 65 and older and at least 200,000 individuals younger than 65 with early-onset Alzheimer's. By 2030, the total number could soar to 7.7 million.[4]

Social and Emotional Changes

- As life expectancy increases, so does the period following the end of paid employment. For many, this new phase of life is a time to enjoy more freedom, explore options, spend more time with family and friends, and develop new skills. For others, not working can affect their sense of identity and leave them feeling lost, bereft, and useless.

- Those who retire from paid employment may have less money, depending on whether they have saved over the years or have an adequate pension. Social security income alone is seldom sufficient. It may be difficult for an older adult to change his or her lifestyle to accommodate changes in income. Worry over medical expenses and long-term care makes the situation worse.

- As we get older, so do our friends and family. Death may occur at any time, of course, but mortality increases with age. In addition to sadness and anger, people who experience loss typically feel lonely and overwhelmed.

- Once the limiting effects of normal aging begin, older adults may have to give up driving. Reductions in hearing or vision may make it more difficult for us to do routine tasks such as grocery shopping, read the newspaper, go to doctors' appointments, or go out with friends to the theater. Cognitive changes, too, may make us reluctant to interact with friends and family. None of these limitations has to result in a loss of independence, but the perception of loss and the thought of figuring out accommodations can be daunting.[5]

Salt & Pepper
Samuel Menashe

Here and there
White hairs appear
On my chest—
Age seasons me
Gives me zest—
I am a sage
In the making
Sprinkled, shaking

This poem is published in *Samuel Menashe: New and Selected Poems*, published by the Library of America in 2005.

The Demographics of Aging

Shifting demographics have catalyzed new priorities, policies, and plans.[6] Americans are living longer and staying healthy into their later years. The expanding over-65 population reflects the increasing diversity of our society. And older Americans live on both sides of an economic gap—some in financial comfort and others on limited incomes. Consider these demographic trends:

Longevity

The population worldwide is aging due to falling fertility (fewer births per woman) and rising longevity (longer lives). In the United States:

- Average life expectancy at birth rose from 47.3 in 1900 to 76.9 in 2000.

- In a 2006 study, 80 to 90 percent of participants age 65 to 75 and approximately 60 percent of those over age 85 reported excellent or good health.[7]

- The over-65 population numbered 35.9 million in 2003, an increase of 3.1 million (9.5 percent) since 1993. Among this population, 18.3 million people were age 65 to 74, 12.9 million were 75 to 84, and 4.7 million were 85 and older.

- The number of centenarians (age 100 and older) has increased in the past several years, from about 37,000 in 1990 to more than 50,000 in 2000. About 80 percent of centenarians are women.

- The over-65 population is projected to be twice as large by 2030 as in 2000, growing from 35 million to 72 million, or nearly 20 percent of the total population.

- The over-85 population is projected to increase from 4.7 million in 2003 to 9.6 million in 2030.

Diversity

In 2003, 17.6 percent of the over-65 population was African American, of Hispanic origin, or Asian or Pacific Islander. This percentage is expected to increase to 26.4 percent in 2030:

- African-Americans—from 8.2 percent to 10 percent
- Hispanic origin (of any race)—from 5.7 percent to 11 percent.
- Asian or Pacific Islander—from 2.8 percent to 5 percent.

In 2000, 13 percent of the over-65 population spoke a language other than English at home; among them, more than one-third spoke Spanish.

Income

Statistics on the current and projected wealth of older Americans indicate a continuing chasm between the "haves" and the "have nots":

- The median income of people over 65 in 2003 was $20,363 for males and $11,845 for females. For one-third of Americans over 65, social security benefits constitute 90 percent of their income.

- Households maintained by people over 65 have a higher net worth ($108,885 in 2000) than all other households, except for those maintained by people in the 55-to-64 age group.

- People age 50 and older control more than 50 percent of the total U.S. discretionary income.[8]

- The estimated annual spending power of baby boomers (born between 1946 and 1964) is more than $2 trillion. Each household spends about $45,000 a year.[9]

Education

Older adults are better educated than they were in the past, and this trend is expected to continue:

- In 1950, 17 percent of the over-65 population had graduated from high school, and 3 percent had at least a bachelor's degree. By 2003, 72 percent were high school graduates and 17 percent had at least a bachelor's degree.

- The future older population is likely to be even better educated, especially when baby boomers start reaching 65. Increased education levels may lead to better health, higher incomes, and more wealth, and consequently higher standards of living in retirement.

Retirement

People now in their 50s are predicted to work longer than members of prior generations.

- In 2012, more than 60 percent of men age 60 to 64 are projected to be in the workforce, up from about 54 percent in 1992.[10]

- A 2005 study revealed that more than three-quarters of baby boomers expect to keep working past age 65,[11] in part to increase their retirement income but also because they know they will live longer.

Productive Aging

Leaders in the aging field are using the term *productive aging* to celebrate older adults' capabilities, potential, and social and economic contributions. (Other terms include vital, creative, successful, optimal, active, or healthy aging.) Productive aging means continuing to live life. At age 20, 40, or 80, we want to

- achieve a sense of control and feel empowered through mastery of a technique or topic;
- be socially engaged;
- exercise our bodies and brains to ensure high physical and mental function;
- be healthy by reducing the risk factors for disease and disability;
- have a positive attitude and zest for life; and
- express ourselves creatively.

In a 2006 study of 205 adults over age 60 and living in the community, 92 percent rated themselves as aging productively despite having chronic illnesses and some disability. Findings showed that productive aging is not related to age, ethnicity, level of education, marital status, or income, but rather to

- greater participation in activities;
- having more close friends;
- visiting with family; and
- spending time reading and listening to the radio.[12]

Older adults who are frail can also experience the six characteristics of productive aging, but in a different context. Exercise for someone who is frail may be raising an arm as opposed to doing push-ups. Productive aging is no less relevant for people with dementia, though mastery is deemphasized because developing skills is often not possible.

Implications for Arts and Aging Programs

The stars are aligned for arts and aging programs to be part of the process and part of the solution. Our understanding of aging shapes today's arts and aging field. Evolving conditions for older adults in our society—including new knowledge about the aging process, demographic shifts, and increasing enthusiasm for the concept of productive aging—offer significant potential to advance the arts and aging field. Organizations that provide participatory arts programs for older adults will discover

- more demand for intellectually challenging lifelong learning programs;
- increased competition from the other activities that fill busy adults' lives;
- stronger interest in arts programs that bridge cultural and communication differences; and
- greater focus on tailoring activities and instructional design to the interests and capabilities of participants.

> *I'm glad I got to know the Puerto Rican children. I learned something new from them. We both had to learn a new language—English—at the same age.*
>
> Participant, Generating Community (ESTA)

Big-Picture Challenges to Arts and Aging Programs

Despite the positive climate for arts programs that enrich the lives of older adults, some lingering challenges affect the arts and aging field and present psychological or physical barriers to effective programs:

- Fear of aging
- Isolation of older adults
- Communicating the value of work in the arts and aging field
- Change—from individual to community to societal

When planning, designing, and implementing programs, success will depend on our ability to understand, accommodate, and overcome these challenges.

Fear of Aging

A fear of growing old pervades our society. Advertising proclaims the wonders of plastic surgery, herbal extracts, anti-aging lotions, and drugs to enhance or suppress bodily functions. Middle-aged actors have difficulty finding meaningful roles. Older adults don't want to see themselves portrayed as "old" — living in nursing homes or sitting on park benches.

Erik Erikson and his coauthors describe this long-term preoccupation in *Vital Involvement in Old Age*:

> Young is beautiful. Old is ugly. This attitude stems from a stereotyping deeply ingrained in our culture and in our economy. After all, we throw old things away — they are too difficult to mend. New ones are more desirable and up-to-date, incorporating the latest know-how. Old things are obsolete, valueless, and disposable.[13]

Ageism, the authors conclude, has a devastating impact on older adults:

> The cruelest aspect of this cultural attitude is the elders' vulnerability to the stereotype. Some feel themselves to be unattractive, dull and, quite often, unlovable, and this depressing outlook only aggravates the problem. One response is to avoid looking or acting your own age at all costs. The result is, of course, humiliating failure. Another attitude is to let go, renouncing even rewarding interests and pleasures as unseemly. The acceptance of the stereotype then actualizes the stereotype itself.[14]

A fear of aging contributes to a variety of negative perceptions:

- Older adults have negative reactions to words or concepts. For example, some won't go to a senior center because it is labeled senior.

- Healthcare personnel assume that an older man or woman is incapable of understanding medical terms.

- Adults have a serious fear of dementia and Alzheimer's disease. According to a 2006 report, U.S. adults worry about having Alzheimer's disease more than heart disease, stroke, or diabetes.[15]

- Older adults in early- to mid-stage dementia may be in a state of denial about their illness, pushing a caregiver away just when help is needed most.

- There may be mutual wariness, distrust, and fear among older and younger generations, particularly when cultural differences are involved.

Ageism can affect the arts and aging field:

- Board members of arts and aging organizations may be reluctant to see programs in action because they are afraid of their own aging process.

- Teaching artists or other program facilitators may not understand that participants are just older versions of themselves.

- Leaders of partner organizations or schools may be apprehensive because they don't have any experience with older adults.

- Those who don't understand normal aging may view all older adults as frail or prone to falling, and therefore liability risks.

- Children and young adults who do not have older adults in their lives may have negative perceptions.

Program Example: Overcoming Ageism Barriers

A before-and-after survey of kids' attitudes toward older adults showed how Pearls of Wisdom (ESTA) changed perceptions. Pearls of Wisdom member Amatullah Saleem explains that before interaction with the program, words and phrases used to describe older adults included "walk slowly," "grouchy," "mean," "they have money," and they "put their teeth in a glass." After the students spent time with Pearls of Wisdom, their descriptions included "good people," "not grouchy," "good storytellers," and "they are pretty for old ladies." In fact, older adults, through effective intergenerational programs, become role models to younger participants.

Isolation of Older Adults

Isolation results from living in a community that isn't designed to support aging in place. A 2006 study of 1,790 communities in nine regions of the United States revealed critical shortcomings in healthcare, nutrition, exercise, transportation, public safety and emergency services, housing, taxation and finance, workforce development, civic engagement or volunteer opportunities, and aging and human services.[16] Older adults who experience normal aging may eventually have difficulty leaving their homes. They may no longer drive, which limits their ability to interact with others.

This situation sets off a chain of negative effects: "Loss of mobility, especially when combined with spatial barriers to an active social life, can provoke a downward spiral. Social isolation increases the danger of depression, disease and decline, particularly for surviving members of marriages and long-term relationships."[17]

Ironically, over-55 and continuing-care retirement communities may contribute to the problem because residents are segregated from intergenerational civic life and even from their families. The community within long-term care facilities may not be elder-friendly, either, if the care philosophy is not person-centered—attuned to individual preferences, perspectives, and abilities. For people with dementia, the isolation is exponentially greater.

Communicating Value

Leaders of organizations and programs in the arts, aging services, and arts and aging fields all struggle with communicating the value of their work to funders, policy makers, and the public. This challenge affects recruiting and retaining staff and board members, securing resources, marketing to participants, and attracting media attention.

One explanation for why many people don't understand the value of arts and aging work is that the field lacks compelling, outcome-based arguments to make the case—or is not making the case effectively. Another reason is that too few family members, caregivers, funders, policy makers, and community leaders understand the definition of community arts—which draws on the cultural meaning, expression, and creativity that reside within the community—and the importance of context to quality and excellence. They may attend an intergenerational living history performance at a school or an exhibit at a senior center and think that what they are seeing is not "good art." They may not appreciate the process and, consequently, may question the value of the overall program.

Change

The arts and aging field must deal with the challenge of change both externally and internally. The communities in which we work are often in transition thanks to factors such as the diversity of residents and the actions of government and private interests. Demographics, new funding opportunities, resource shortfalls, community demands, and public policy shifts are among the external factors that affect our organizations. Internally, the departure of key staff members is typically a time to reconsider how you do business.

Whether change is positive or negative depends, in part, on individual and organizational response. All organizations—not just arts and aging services—need to prepare themselves to be appropriate and relevant service providers to older audiences and participants. Residents can also join to effect change through political action or volunteerism. Organizations can design arts programs designed to facilitate communication among and knowledge of disparate groups.

For individuals throughout the lifespan, moving from the familiar to the unknown may be daunting. In general, trying something new is both exciting and intimidating. Because older adults are perceived through ageism as being resistant to change, they are not given the opportunity to try new activities, have new experiences, and learn new information. While some may be afraid of aging, they are also liberated from fear of failing or the opinions of others.

Key Points about the Context for Arts and Aging Programs

- People continue to develop and learn throughout the lifespan.
- The physical, biological, social, and emotional changes associated with aging are normal and do not affect a person's ability to function.
- It is important to emphasize ability—and not disability—in language describing older adults.
- Older adults should be appreciated as assets to a community.
- Shifting demographics in the United States are affecting the aging services and arts fields: the population is growing older, more diverse, and better educated, and people are working longer.
- Older adults can age productively by celebrating their capabilities, potential, and social and economic contributions.
- The challenges to arts and aging programs include ageism, isolation of older adults in our communities, and the challenges of change and communicating value.

Before they started the creative writing and storytelling classes at Villa Azusa, I had been depressed to the point of being suicidal. I didn't feel I even had a reason to get out of bed in the morning. With writing class, I have a purpose. I'm able to laugh more now, and I feel respected because not only does somebody think I have a brain, they make me use it.

Lucy, resident of Villa Azusa,
an EngAGE: The Art of Active Aging
community

How Arts Participation Benefits Older Adults

Art is the transformation of the tangible (bodies, instruments, paper, ink, clay, fabric) and intangible (words, sounds, memories, emotions, ideas) into something new, such as sculpture, living history theater, musical performances, stories, paintings, dance, quilts, or poems. The process of creating, as well as the art that is created, transforms the participants and the people around them: other participants, family members, professional caregivers, and everyone who experiences the art. The artistic discipline, specifically in the performing arts, is transformed by the inclusion of older adults. And older adults in the audience benefit when they see themselves reflected in the artists.

Enhanced quality of life is a distinctive benefit of participation in the arts. Quality of life has many components. Aristotle used the term *eudaimonia*, often translated as happiness. For most of us, quality of life is synonymous with well-being. The arts are known to enhance the quality of life in different but parallel ways for communities and for individuals.

This chapter looks at transforming lives through the arts by:

- Enhancing community quality of life
- Enhancing individual quality of life

Enhancing Community Quality of Life

The arts help all residents of a community

- develop a sense of communal identity;
- bond socially;
- communicate with each other across generations, income, abilities, and cultures; and
- contribute to preserving or restoring social capital.

The arts can have a powerful role in elder-friendly communities, which have the characteristics shown in figure 2-1.[18]

As the illustration suggests, the social structures that help define community are no less important than the physical structures. The concept of aging in place involves more than the ability to remain in one's home; it includes the ability to continue functioning and thriving in one's community. Marc Freedman, founder of the think-tank organization Civic Ventures, refers to "aging in community." This concept "encourages a proactive strategy to create supportive neighborhoods and networks. Thus, the well-being and quality of life for elders at home becomes a measure of the success of the community. Aging in community advances the concept of being 'a darn good neighbor'—and, as a result, promotes social capital, a sense of trust and mutual interconnectedness that is enhanced over time through positive interactions and collaboration in shared interests."[19]

Arts and Aging in Community Cultural Development

Arts and aging programs often find a good fit with community needs in the context of community cultural development, which involves "a range of initiatives undertaken by artists in collaboration with other community members to express identity, concerns, and aspirations through the arts and communications media, while building cultural capacity and contributing to social change."[20]

The concept of community cultural development has seven guiding principles:

1. Active participation in cultural life is an essential goal of community cultural development.
2. All cultures are essentially equal, and society should not promote any one as superior to the other.
3. Diversity is a social asset, part of the cultural commonwealth, requiring protection and nourishment.
4. Culture is an effective crucible for social transformation, one that can be less polarizing and create deeper connections than other social-change arenas.
5. Cultural expression is a means of emancipation, not the primary end in itself; the process is as important as the product.
6. Culture is a dynamic, protean whole, and there is no value in creating artificial boundaries within it.
7. Artists have roles as agents of transformation that are more socially valuable than mainstream art-world roles—and certainly equal in legitimacy.[21]

Addresses basic needs

» Provides appropriate and affordable housing

» Promotes safety at home and in the neighborhood

» Assures no one goes hungry

» Provides useful information about available services

Promotes social and civic engagement

» Fosters meaningful connections with family, neighbors, and friends

» Promotes active engagement in community life

» Provides opportunities for meaningful paid and voluntary work

» Makes aging issues a community-wide priority

Elder-Friendly Community

Optimizes physical and mental health and well being

» Promotes healthy behaviors

» Supports community activities that enhance well being

» Provides ready access to preventive health services

» Provides access to medical, social, and palliative services

Maximizes independence for frail and disabled

» Mobilizes resources to facilitate "living at home"

» Provides accessible transportation

» Supports family and other caregivers

fig. 2-1

Design for Elder-Friendly Communities

Universal design—also called inclusive design, design-for-all, and lifespan design—is an orientation to any design process that starts with a responsibility to the experience of the user. Universal design is not a design style, but a framework for the design of places, things, information, communication, and policy to be usable by the widest range of people operating in the widest range of situations without special or separate design. Quite simply, it is human-centered design of everything with everyone in mind. Illustrations include Oxo kitchen implements, walk-don't-walk signals that chirp or talk when it is safe to cross the street, signs that have large type and high contrast against the background, and at-grade building entrances without doorsills.

Universal design is a nondiscriminatory response to barriers faced by older adults who wish to age in place in an elder-friendly community. It empowers people by allowing them to remain independent longer, and it advances human dignity by enhancing independence. It makes the physical structures usable to all, the community accessible to all. For more details, visit the Center for Universal Design at North Carolina State University, www.design.ncsu.edu/cud.

Community Arts

Arts and aging programs mesh well with community cultural development because they are community arts programs, which are based on the premise that cultural meaning, expression, and creativity reside within the community. The artist's task is to collaborate with community members so that they can free their imaginations and give form to their creativity. Liz Lerman uses dance as an example:

> For me, an excellent dance performance includes the following: the dancers are 100 percent committed to the movement they are doing; they understand why they are doing what they are doing. And something is being revealed in that moment: something about the dancer or about the subject, about the relationship of the dancers or about the world in which we live. Something is revealed.[22]

This fluid definition doesn't imply that community arts are unprofessional or amateurish; they should be of high quality, led by professional teaching artists. Understanding how context relates to quality and excellence is particularly important when program participants have dementia. In this case, any validated self-expression and successful communication with others is excellent; however, the more the art created by people with dementia resembles art, the more professional caregivers identify it—and the person—as valuable.

A hallmark of community arts is the importance of the process of making art. Don Adams and Arlene Goldbard describe the relationship between process and product: Although projects may yield products of great skill and power (such as murals, videos, plays, and dances), the process of awakening to cultural meanings and mastering cultural tools to express and communicate them is always primary. To be most effective, projects must be open-ended, leaving the content and focus to be determined by participants.[23]

> *Seeing a 70-year-old man falling as part of a dance is amazing, and seeing him succeed gives audience members a different perspective when they see younger dancers completing the same movement.*
>
> John Bostel, Humanities Director, Liz Lerman Dance Exchange

Chapter 6 looks at the equally transforming effects that the process and the art created have on older adults' quality of life.

Culture Change

Culture change facilitated by the arts has a great many commonalities with community cultural development. Some facility-based communities (such as assisted living or skilled care) are creating a resident- or person-centered paradigm in which the environment is one of community rather than medicine. Adopting this asset-based model over a deficit-based approach "requires that long-term care providers respond to the values, preferences, and care needs of recipients while incorporating them into the fabric of their local communities.

Patient participation, client autonomy, and shared decision making are emphasized."[24] Older adults' potential is ignited, and staff members encourage them to give voice to their memories and wishes. Their quality of life is improved when they are heard, have options, and can make choices. And professional caregivers have greater job satisfaction when they *know* those in their care.

For an older adult with dementia, whether living in a residential facility or at home, art may be the only medium through which they can communicate their values, preferences, and care needs. Anne Basting and John Killick elaborate:

> Because arts activities do not have a "right" or a "wrong" answer, they can help solidify bonds between caregivers and people with dementia by giving them a space in which they can play together. In an arts session, caregivers don't need to correct the people for whom they care, and people with dementia don't need to anticipate being corrected. Together they can experience the joy of creating something new and of communicating on an emotional level….
>
> Because the arts open avenues to self-expression, arts activities can help staff to see the self still present and growing in people with dementia. Understanding that you are caring for a person, rather than an object, can make caregiving a much more rewarding and meaningful experience.[25]

Community Cultural Development Examples

- Generating Community, a program of Elders Share the Arts, used community cultural development principles to address intergenerational conflict. Organization founder Susan Perlstein explains that the program was created to help different groups find a meeting ground and a place to talk—"not just to complain at one another, but also to create and learn together. Instead of letting the groups face off… we turn everybody's head to face in the same direction, toward a common goal." The programs use living history community plays as a way to explore problems and find solutions together. "In the process," Perlstein says, "something new emerges." In one program in Spanish Harlem, for example, the seniors became surrogate grandparents for children whose grandparents had remained in Puerto Rico.[26]

- Other programs have incorporated community cultural development to connect types of communities—for example, residents of a long-term care facility who share their artwork with members of the broader community.

- In See Me! Training, Stagebridge Senior Theatre Company staff and actors work with nursing school staff at the Samuel Merritt College School of Nursing to create learning modules that address issues nurses face in working with older patients. Using improvisation, storytelling, role-playing, and other performance techniques, Stagebridge presents workshops that incorporate a senior voice and point of view, communicated with humor. The messages are reinforced through small group interactive discussion.

- Catalyzing Culture Change teaches staff at long-term care facilities a way of working that emphasizes and elicits the individual preferences, perspectives, and abilities of all participants—including people usually perceived as incapable of contributing to a group. Trainers from Elders Share the Arts (ESTA) teach facility staff the TimeSlips storytelling method, a ritualized group process in which an image elicits participants' sounds, gestures, word fragments, and whole sentences, all of which are validated and turned into story. The sessions highlight person-centered principles and skills such as emotional attunement, open-ended questioning, validation, and nonverbal communication. ESTA then works with caregiving staff to apply these principles to programs and activities throughout the facility.

- In Kairos Dance Theatre's Dancing Heart Caregiver three-day training program, caregivers learn how to engage older adults in the creative expression of dance and storytelling. Participants receive an introduction to the language of dance and the latest research on arts and aging, learn about best practices in arts and aging, and experiment with proven tools.

Enhancing Individual Quality of Life

Community arts programs run by professional artists have powerful positive results. Involvement in challenging, participatory programs has a positive effect on physical health, mental health, and social functioning in older adults. Art has true health promotion and disease prevention effects and helps older adults to maintain independence and reduce dependency, which drives the need for long-term care.

The first significant study of the individual benefits of arts participation was *The Impact of Professionally Conducted Cultural Programs on Older Adults*, initiated by the National Endowment for the Arts and conducted in 2001 by Dr. Gene Cohen, director of the Center on Aging, Health, and Humanities at George Washington University. Using a rigorously controlled experimental design, the study involved 300 participants at three sites: 150 in community arts groups and 150 in a control group matched in all major areas of functioning. The average age in both groups was 80—older than the average life expectancy in the United States. Both groups were identically active at the start of the project. Professional teaching artists led all the arts groups.

Cohen based his study design on established gerontology research focused on the connection between a sense of control and the immune system; social relationships and blood pressure/stress levels; aging and how the brain processes emotions; and aging and being able to use both sides of the brain simultaneously. (At younger ages, one side is dominant.) He found that by all measurements of physical health, mental health, and social functioning, there was stabilization and actual improvement for those in the arts groups, while in the control group there was a decline. The study found that participants in the arts groups

- used less medication;
- had fewer doctor visits;
- experienced elevated mood;
- showed an increase in the level of independent functioning, where normally decline would have been expected;
- did better on scales for depression, loneliness, and morale; and
- exhibited an increase in number of activities, while the control group members experienced a decrease.

How Cognitively Fit Older Adults Benefit

Other research into the connection between arts and quality of life has shown similar mental, physical, and social benefits for cognitively fit older adults:

Dancing
- Examining the relationship between leisure activities and the risk of dementia in 469 people older than 75 who resided in the community and did not have dementia at baseline, researchers found that participation in leisure activities is associated with a reduced risk of dementia. Among cognitive activities, reading, playing board games, and playing musical instruments were associated with a lower risk of dementia. Dancing was the only physical activity associated with a lower risk of dementia.[27]

- Responding to questions about Kairos Dance Theatre's weekly Dancing Heart program, most senior center participants said that their health was better and the dance and movement improvisation activities in the program helped them stay healthy by improving flexibility, coordination, balance, and endurance. They also agreed that the shared reminiscence and discussion increased their memory and socialization skills.[28]

- Assessing the motor and cognitive performance of 24 older social dancers compared with 84 age-, sex-, and education-matched older nondancers, researchers found that long-term social dancing may be associated with better balance and gait in older adults.[29]

- Italian researchers discovered using heart rate and artery imaging exams that dance, cycling, and treadmill training equally improved exercise capacity. Dancers also reported slightly more improvement in sleep, mood, and the ability to do hobbies, do housework, and have sex than the others.[30]

Playing music
- Assessing the health of 61 older adults taking group keyboard lessons, researchers measured levels of human growth hormone (hGH), anxiety, depression, and loneliness before the lessons and after each semester. Participants showed a dramatic increase in hGH levels (hGH is implicated in such aging phenomena as osteoporosis, energy levels, wrinkling, sexual function, muscle mass, and aches and pains) and a decrease in anxiety, depression, and perception

of loneliness, taking into account differences in life events and social support.[31]

- Measuring the effect of participating in Yamaha's Clavinova Connection keyboard program after a stressful situation, researchers found that playing an instrument—as opposed to relaxing by reading newspapers—reversed multiple components of the human stress response on the genomic level: six genes in the relaxation group reversed compared with 19 genes in the music group.[32]

Creating visual art

- Assessing the effects of the North Dakota Council on the Arts' Art for Life project on the negative feelings that often characterize life in institutional settings, researchers found that after eight months of folk arts activities, participants felt significantly less bored, lonely, and helpless. The project also distracted older adults, whose average age was 86, from their physical pain and stimulated their cognitive faculties.[33]

How Older Adults with Dementia Benefit

Older adults with dementia experience a better quality of life when they participate in the arts, according to research findings:

- Using an observational instrument that measured objective and subjective indicators of the affect state (feeling or emotion) and self-esteem of 41 participants in Memories in the Making programs conducted at adult day and long-term care facilities, staff of the Greater Cincinnati chapter of the Alzheimer's Association found that participation in the weekly sessions contributed to each individual's sense of well-being.[34]

- Using the Quality of Life in Dementia scale, Music for All Seasons and the New Jersey Neuroscience Institute at JFK Medical Center measured 23 nursing home residents before and after two live music performances given six weeks apart. Each set of measures was taken at two-week intervals. The principal result was a measured increase in quality of life. Scores increased significantly following each performance and stayed higher for as long as six weeks.[35]

- Observing 12 residents before and after the installation of a wall mural painted over an exit door, researchers discovered a significant decrease in overall door-testing behavior and in two of four distinct behavior types. Wall murals can be effective for cueing residents away from a situation that may evoke agitation and a situation of potential harm and litigation.[36]

- Studying the impact of the TimeSlips method in 20 nursing homes, researchers observed an increase in the number of meaningful interactions between staff and residents on the whole unit (not just among those involved directly in the storytelling). Staff attitudes toward people with dementia also improved.[37]

- Assessing the impact of caregiver singing and background music on interactions between caregivers and people with advanced dementia, Swedish researchers determined that, in the presence of background music, caregivers decreased their verbal instructing and narrating while the patient communicated verbally and behaviorally with an increased understanding of the situation. During caregiver singing, though verbal narration and description by the caregiver decreased, the patient implicitly understood.[38]

The arts and aging field can also learn from recent research into the effects of exercising the body, mind, and social ability. Notable findings include the following:

- Compared with a control group, healthy adults who received 10 memory training sessions did 75 percent better on memory tasks five years later; those who received reasoning training did 40 percent better on reasoning tasks; and those who received speed training did 300 percent better than the control group.[39]

- Researchers who reviewed 40 years of research on exercise and its effect on brain functioning in human and animal populations found that fitness training—an increased level of exercise—may improve some mental processes even more than moderate activity, and physical exercise in general might slow the effects of aging and help people maintain cognitive abilities well into older age.[40]

- Researchers from Rush University Medical Center in Chicago determined that social and emotional isolation in older adults increased their risk of developing dementia by about 51 percent. Among the 823 participants in the study, the risk of Alzheimer's was about twice as great in those reporting a high degree of loneliness.[41]

Key Points about the Benefits of Arts Participation to Older Adults

- The arts contribute to communicating, building a sense of identity, preserving or restoring social capital, and strengthening social networks in communities.
- The arts help create elder-friendly communities in which older adults are able to thrive and function, and therefore age in place.
- Arts and aging programs contribute to the cultural development of communities.
- Arts and aging programs are community arts programs in which cultural meaning, expression, and creativity reside within participants.
- The arts can effect community cultural development—culture change—within residential facilities so that professional caregivers and staff respect the wishes of residents and see them as assets.
- Scientific research demonstrates that involvement in challenging participatory arts programs has a positive effect on physical health, mental health, and social functioning in older adults, regardless of their ability.

The storytelling program gave me an opportunity to practice what I believed: that aging is not dull. You can stave off some of the effects of aging by being involved mentally. I think people age because they're not involved.

Storyteller, Stagebridge Senior Theatre Company

The Aging Services Field

The public dollars flowing through the aging services network in the United States total approximately $330 billion. It is a major industry replete with complicated and dynamic funding, policy and procedural issues, and federal, state, and local government and private entities and individuals. In this chapter, we will explore those most relevant to the arts and aging field.

- Understanding key issues
- Exploring infrastructure
- Making connections

Understanding Key Issues

Increasing Costs

As entitlement programs—social security, Medicare, and Medicaid—consume a larger and larger percentage of the nation's budget, discretionary programs—the source of most public arts and aging dollars—receive a smaller and smaller percentage. The costs of healthcare and long-term care are increasing as providers struggle to serve a growing population that demands more programs, better services, and up-to-date infrastructure. At a conference of the U.S. Administration on Aging in December 2006, speakers reported the following:

- Currently, $140 billion is spent a year on long-term care for the elderly. Of this amount, 60 percent is spent on institutional care.

- In 2005, the sources of financing for long-term care were Medicaid (38 percent), family (36 percent), Medicare (20 percent), long-term care insurance (3 percent), and other public sources (3 percent).

- The average monthly cost for a nursing home is $5,000. For private-pay residents (as opposed to Medicaid), the average cost per year is $74,095. In assisted living, the average cost is $34,860 per year, and the average cost of home healthcare is $19 an hour.

The long-term care system relies heavily on public funding. According to Matt Salo, director of the Health and Human Services Committee at the National Governors Association, Medicaid averaged 20 percent of states' budgets in 2006—more than the amount spent on K–12 education.[42] "By 2030, spending for Medicare, Medicaid, and social security alone will reach almost 60 percent of the federal budget."[43]

Emphasis on Home- and Community-Based Care

Trends in policy and funding favor home- and community-based care over long-term care provided in facilities. Several new initiatives from the Administration on Aging support the transfer of individuals from nursing homes to community settings and allow Medicaid enrollees to participate in cash and counseling programs in which they purchase long-term care services in the community using a predetermined budget. Another federal initiative is the Medicaid Home- and Community-Based Services Waiver for Older Adults. Administered by states, its goal is to enable older adults to remain in a community setting by allowing services typically covered by Medicaid only in a long-term care facility to be provided to eligible persons in their homes or in an assisted living facility.

> *Every performance we make makes me feel better and better. It makes me so joyous that I can make people feel happy. At this age, I've still got something in there.*
>
> Janie, 73, participant, Kairos Dance Theatre

Consolidated Consumer Information

Aging and Disability Resource Centers are one-stop shops that simplify information gathering for older adults, family caregivers, professionals seeking assistance on behalf of their clients, and adults planning for future long-term care needs. Center programs are also the entry point to publicly administered long-term support funded under Medicaid, the Older Americans Act, and state revenue programs. Most states have these centers up and running: www.adrc-tae.org.

Reducing Residential Facility Staff Turnover and Increasing Morale

Annual turnover among most paraprofessional long-term workers is about 50 percent. With a median hourly wage of $9.20 in 2003, they earn nearly one-third less than all U.S. workers.[44] Insufficient benefits, inadequate training, limited involvement in decision making, few opportunities for promotion, heavy workloads, and a high rate of injury also contribute to turnover. In addition, workers suffer from the widespread public perception that caring for older adults is unpleasant and unappealing. Not surprisingly, research has consistently demonstrated a relationship between staffing and quality of care in nursing homes.

Efforts to recruit and retain staff center on changing the workplace environment, increasing wages and benefits, and creating opportunities for career advancement and training. Long-term care facilities that have a person-centered approach have reorganized their caregiving process and management practices, resulting in lower turnover and higher-quality care. Though a number of states have attempted to implement policies or pass laws that increase wages and benefits or mandate more training, there are few systems in place to monitor compliance. Several states also support initiatives such as team building and peer mentoring.

Addressing Family Caregiver Burnout

Caregiver burnout is a state of physical, emotional, and mental exhaustion that may be accompanied by a change in attitude—from positive and caring to negative and unconcerned. Burnout can occur when caregivers don't get the help they need, or if they are physically or financially overextended. They may experience fatigue, stress, anxiety, and depression. Many caregivers also feel guilty if they spend time on themselves rather than on their older family members.

The aging service field addresses this issue primarily by offering support and information resources. Some residential communities, senior centers, and hospitals have caregiver support groups where family members share successes, challenges, and tips. Clearinghouses such as Aging and Disability Resource Centers direct caregivers to help, including facilities that provide respite services where an older adult lives for a weekend or a couple of weeks.

Implications for the Arts

- Plan for programs that serve older adults living at home as well as in facilities.

- Plan for programs that include a greater diversity of ages, ethnicities, and abilities.

- Provide transportation so that older adults can benefit from social interaction and programs at senior centers or adult day programs.

- Develop individualized programs delivered in the home to an older adult and his or her family and caregivers.

- Use centralized Aging and Disability Resource Centers to help locate older adults, aging service organizations and facilities, and potential funders.

- Design programs that help instigate culture change in long-term care facility settings, potentially reducing staff turnover and increasing morale.

- Design programs that help mitigate burnout among family caregivers by increasing the quality of life for the older adults receiving care.

Exploring Infrastructure

Led by the Administration on Aging, which is part of the U.S. Department of Health and Human Services, the aging services network consists of federal, state, and local agencies that work together to provide services and opportunities to help older adults lead independent and dignified lives at home and in their communities. This network serves 7 million older adults age 60 and above and anywhere from 325,000 to 800,000 caregivers (the number varies depending on the source.) It includes 56 state units on aging, 655 area agencies on aging, 243 tribal organizations, more than 29,000 local community service organizations, 500,000 volunteers, and a variety of national organizations.

Federal

Most federal aging funds flow through the Department of Health and Human Services under the Older Americans Act. The department includes the Administration on Aging, the Centers for Medicare and Medicaid Services, and the National Institutes of Health/National Institute on Aging. The Older Americans Act authorizes—or enables the existence of—programs and policies; the money primarily comes from appropriations legislation. It is not unusual for a federal agency to be directed by the authorizing legislation to do something new but have no new or additional dollars to support that mandate.

The Administration on Aging, the agency most relevant to the arts and aging field, heightens awareness of the needs of older adults, recommends policy, develops regulations, and disseminates money, including funds to state units (www.aoa.gov). Most funding for arts programs is available under Title III of the Older Americans Act; grants using Title IV funds, which support projects that develop, test, and disseminate best practices, may also be available.

State

State units on aging work with other state agencies and public- and private-sector entities on behalf of older adults (www.nasua.org). They receive funds from the Administration on Aging and state governments to support home- and community-based services and elder rights programs. State units award grants to area agencies on aging so that programs and services are tailored to meet the needs of older adults at the community level.

Local

Area agencies on aging address local needs and concerns. Each has an advisory council of providers and other stakeholders, such as healthcare foundations or veterans' associations. An area agency may be part of county or city government or a private nonprofit organization. Primary responsibilities include advocacy, planning and service development, and administration of funds to public and private service providers, such as senior centers, residential facilities, hospitals, faith-based organizations, foundations, and nonprofit community organizations. The Eldercare Locator helps find local aging services networks (www.eldercare.gov; 800-677-1116; TDD/TTY access and Spanish-language professionals available).

Foundations

More than funding sources, foundations are policy leaders actively involved in the aging services infrastructure of the field. Healthcare, family, and community foundations exist at the national, state, and local levels. A resource is the Foundation Center, www.foundationcenter.org.

Making Connections

Arts leaders and teaching artists who want to connect with the aging services field should focus primarily on the local level. The following organizations are good places to start when seeking participants, partners, and information:

Area agencies on aging

Resources: Aging initiatives and programs; information about aging services providers, programs, and key individuals. The National Association of Area Agencies on Aging (N4A) maintains a list of members and describes key policies on its Web site. Most area agencies on aging have an information hotline or toll-free number for ease of access.

For information: National Association of Area Agencies on Aging, www.n4a.org.

Senior centers

Resources: Frequent partners for arts organizations because they need to provide programming and offer fresh content. They also have accessible space and a pool of potential participants.

For information: Locate senior centers through the area agency on aging. At the senior center, contact the activities director or executive director.

Residential facilities (continuing care retirement communities, assisted living facilities, and skilled care facilities)

Resources: Needs and benefits are similar to those of senior centers: programs for older adults, accessible space, and potential participants

For information: The American Association of Homes and Services for the Aging, www.aasha.org. At the residential facility, contact the activities director (sometime called the resident services or lifestyle director).

Local Alzheimer's Association chapters

Resources: Educate arts leaders and teaching artists about dementia; manage and host programs and events that may benefit from the arts.

For information: Alzheimer's Association, www.alz.org. At the local chapter, contact the program director or executive director.

National organizations also offer specific expertise useful to arts and aging programs:

- **Education and training:** The American Society on Aging (www.asaging.org), an association of practitioners, educators, administrators, policy makers, business people, researchers, and students, provides educational programming, publications, and information and training resources.

- **Private funding:** Grantmakers in Aging (www.giaging.org) provides insights into what's on the mind of private funders. GIA presents key issues at an annual conference and through issue briefs and newsletters.

- **Policy and advocacy:** The National Council on Aging (www.ncoa.org) promotes understanding of national policy issues and how to make the case for increased public funding. Programs are targeted on improving the lives of older adults.

- **Program design and implementation:** National Center for Creative Aging (www.creativeaging.org) provides training and materials, an information clearinghouse, and a list of state-level member associations.

Many other national associations represent segments of the aging services field, including social workers, geriatric care managers, adult day services, ombudsman programs, and visiting nurse associations. For a list, visit the American Society on Aging Web site, www.asaging.org/links/national.cfm.

Key Points about the Aging Services Field

- The policy and funding emphases of the aging services field—containing the rising cost of healthcare and long-term care; providing home- and community-based care; consolidating consumer information and access to resources; reducing residential facility staff turnover and increasing morale; and addressing family caregiver burnout—have implications for the arts and aging field.
- Though the aging services field is composed of public and private organizations at the federal, state, and local levels of government, arts organizations that want to connect with aging services organizations should focus on those in communities, such as area agencies on aging, senior centers, residential facilities, and Alzheimer's Association chapters.

Acronyms in the Aging Services Field

AoA	Administration on Aging	LTC	Long-term care
AAHSA	American Association of Homes and Services for the Aging	NASUA	National Association of State Units on Aging
		NCCA	National Center for Creative Aging
AAA	Area agencies on aging		
ADRC	Aging and Disability Resource Center	NCOA	National Council on Aging
		NIA	National Institute on Aging
AL	Assisted living	NORC	Naturally occurring retirement community
ASA	American Society on Aging		
CCRC	Continuing-care retirement community	OAA	Older Americans Act
		PACE	Program of all-inclusive care for the elderly
CMS	Centers for Medicare and Medicaid Services		
		SNF	Skilled nursing facility
CNA	Certified nursing assistant	SUA	State units on aging
GIA	Grantmakers in Aging	WHCoA	White House Conference on Aging
HCBS	Home- and community-based services		
HHS	Department of Health and Human Services		

> *I didn't think I could act, sing, and dance—and I discovered I love it. It's never too late!*
>
> Participant, Generating Community (ESTA)

The Arts Field

Throughout the United States, individuals and communities engage in the arts. To support this participation, private and public organizations, businesses, educational institutions and government agencies, debate issues, create policies, and provide resources. Leaders of the aging services field who want to connect with the arts at the community level can benefit from this chapter, which looks at:

- Understanding key issues
- Exploring infrastructure
- Making connections

Understanding Key Issues

Expanded Definition of Arts Education

People of all ages—not just young people—make up the audience for arts education. Research shows that people want and need to learn, grow, and contribute to communities throughout their lives. With its focus on older adults' quality of life, the arts and aging field has the expertise, research, and evidence of impact to push for lifelong learning. One segment of the arts community that has long understood this concept is the folk arts field. The emphasis on passing traditions and skills from one generation to another, honoring elders, and preserving history provides a model for other arts disciplines that are just starting to think more broadly about arts education.

Arts Participation

The more ways people participate in the arts—and the more often—the more likely they are to engage in other activities that support community life. Increased participation, in turn, strengthens the case for providing political and economic support for arts and cultural institutions as valuable community assets. The Wallace Foundation, with its partners the RAND Corporation and the Urban Institute, has led efforts to understand why and how people participate in the arts. The foundation's intent is to give arts organizations insights and tools to increase participation.

A Broader Definition of the Arts

Arts leaders are exploring the implications of a definition of the arts that has broadened to include activities under the aegis of a variety of organizations, corporations, and community-based groups—activities such as singing in church, doing needlepoint, decorating pottery, viewing a Hollywood blockbuster, and attending a musical revue at Walt Disney World. Arts education is no longer only the purview of nonprofit organizations and schools. Yamaha, for example, not only manufactures musical instruments; it also develops music curricula aimed for the most part at older adults.

Community Engagement

Integrating the arts into community life benefits not only older adults, but all residents by facilitating lifelong learning, contributing to the economy, and building community. From the perspective of the arts field, community engagement means the continued growth of the artistic discipline, the opportunity to explore the value and relevance of the arts, and a forum to address community issues. Community schools of the arts, for example, are interested in expanding community beyond young people to older adults and others who have available time during the day.

Demonstrated Impact

Outcome evaluation measures the impact of programs on participants—what they learned and how they changed. Instead of asking, for example, "How many people took a singing class?" the question is, "How many people learned to sing?" This approach has gained currency in the public and nonprofit sectors since the early 1990s, and arts and aging programs must use it to apply successfully for public and private funds, market programs to older adults, and raise public awareness of the value of their work. Outcome evaluation has much in common with evidence-based research, a familiar concept in the aging services and medical fields.

Scarce Resources

Even though research demonstrates the value of the arts to individuals and communities and more arts organizations are evaluating outcomes, there is a gap between value and resources. Many policymakers—including public and private funders—are reluctant to allocate sufficient resources or implement supportive policies for the arts. A case in point is K–12 arts education. School, district, and state leaders are limiting or cutting arts instruction from the curriculum, in part because of testing requirements in the No Child Left Behind Act, the federal legislation that authorizes education programs and spending. In the arts and aging field, the challenge is greater because advocates have to demonstrate impact on two different audiences: arts and aging services.

Some public funders do not believe it is the role of government to fund the arts; see the arts as a frill instead of a way to help strengthen communities; or don't have available dollars. Closing the gap between value and resources requires assessing program impact and making a qualitative and quantitative case for resources.

It's also important to encourage program participants to serve as advocates.

Professional Development for Teaching Artists

Teaching artists not only teach and create art. They also administer programs, work in partnership with staff, and assess impact. They are at the heart of successful arts education programs for all ages. Like any professionals, they need continuing education to understand trends, implement new requirements, and improve techniques. Teaching artists might consider forming learning communities in which they can share ideas and solve problems together. Another strategy is to provide specific training on topics such as normal aging. In addition, arts organizations want to be certain that their teaching artists are of high quality. Partially in response to this concern, arts and education leaders in a few states and cities are discussing certification of teaching artists.

Special Issues for Creative Arts Therapies

The creative arts therapies include art, dance and movement, drama, music, poetry, and psychodrama. Therapists are licensed by states to use arts and creativity during intentional interventions in therapeutic, rehabilitative, community, or educational settings to foster health, communication, and expression; promote the integration of physical, emotional, cognitive, and social functioning; enhance self-awareness; and facilitate change.

In working with older adults, these therapists and professional teaching artists are complementary. The following description resonates with the same values found in arts and aging programs:

> Successful art therapy with older adults should stem from the belief that aging provides the opportunity to mine life's riches in the art-making process. As such, the hope is to empower older men and women through creative expression and to encourage them to draw from their wisdom and experience as valued members of society.[45]

Though complementary, there is a difference between creative arts therapies with older adults, which are primarily a medical intervention, and arts and aging programs, which are primarily about quality of life.

Relevant issues for creative arts therapies are:

Gaining official recognition
Licensing and credentialing are important for therapists for insurance reimbursement and standing within the medical community. With the exception of poetry and psychodrama, whose practitioners are already licensed because of their academic requirements, therapists typically need state licensing as counselors. (Just two states, New York and Wisconsin, have separate licensing for creative arts therapists.) The American Music Therapy Association, for example, lobbies states to recognize music therapy as a profession and music therapists as providers. The association also supports research to make the case for music therapy as a complementary and alternative medical intervention.

Determining ownership and dissemination of art created in therapeutic settings.
Since the creative arts therapies are a counseling profession with confidentiality requirements, the question of who owns the art created by clients is relevant. A similar concern is whether sharing the art with the community in some way puts the client at risk. A client must give permission since he or she owns the art—a challenge when the client has dementia. Though perhaps not a major issue within the creative arts therapies, the ownership question illustrates the sensitivity that those in the arts and aging field should have toward the community sharing of the art-making process.

Exploring Infrastructure

Federal

The National Endowment for the Arts, an independent federal agency, awards more than $100 million annually in every state and jurisdiction (www.arts.gov). Those dollars are estimated to generate more than $700 million in additional support. One distinctive feature of the grants process is peer review of applications. With a 2007 budget of $124.5 million, the Arts Endowment is the largest single funder of the arts in the nation. By law, the endowment allocates 40 percent of its annual program funds to states and regions, which use these funds to address local needs and broaden the reach of federal dollars across the nation.

Other federal agencies funding arts and culture include the National Endowment for the Humanities and the Institute of Museum and Library Services.

Regional

Six regional nonprofit arts organizations provide information and professional development to member state arts agencies and direct initiatives, such as touring performing artists and companies to communities. In 2006, their combined budgets were $21 million.

State

State arts agencies managed nearly $390 million in 2006. Ninety percent of this revenue came from annual or biennial state appropriations to state arts agencies. Some state arts agencies receive funding from private sources and other federal programs. State arts agencies provide an array of citizen services, including grant making, public information, partnership building, technical assistance, research, and planning. State arts agencies invest their funds in programs that foster

- educational success, through arts education opportunities for students;
- arts participation, through performances, exhibitions, and lifelong learning programs;
- accessibility, through programs that widen the availability of the arts, especially in rural areas and among underserved populations;
- cultural infrastructures, through operating support for cultural organizations and support for the development of grassroots arts networks;
- innovation, through support for individual artists and the development of new creative programs; and
- artistic heritage, through programs to preserve cultural traditions.[46]

Local

Local arts agencies, which are funded by state arts agencies, the National Endowment for the Arts, private donations, and municipal budgets, make grants to artists and organizations in the communities they serve. Like state arts agencies, they also provide advocacy and support services to artists and organizations, including professional development workshops for artists and print or online publications.

Another type of local arts agency is the united arts fund (UAF), which is the locus for corporate, business, and individual giving in a city or county. These organizations raise unrestricted, operating grant funds on behalf of three or more arts, cultural, and/or science organizations. Most UAFs were initiated by local business leaders seeking to minimize the number of individual funding requests and ensure that arts organizations meet standards of quality and fiscal responsibility.

Individual artists and arts organizations are the heart of the arts infrastructure. State and local arts agencies support a great diversity of individual artists primarily through services, fellowships, and grants to organizations that employ artists. Arts organizations— which may be dedicated to visual, performing, literary, folk, or media arts as well as arts education—receive roughly 56 percent of total funding from public and private sources and realize the rest through earned income (such as ticket sales and subscriptions). Exactly what they look like in any given community depends on the community. Typically, they include:

- Community-based arts organizations
- Community schools of the arts
- Museums
- Bands
- Visual arts centers
- Media arts centers
- Symphony orchestras
- Performing arts centers
- Chamber music groups
- Theater companies
- Dance companies
- Opera companies
- Choral groups
- Out-of-school arts programs (community-based education programs that occur after school, on weekends, or in the summer)
- Folk arts groups
- Literary centers and groups
- Photography centers and groups

Every community is also home to for-profit arts organizations, such as dance studios, art galleries, craft shops, and stores that sell music, instruments, and theatrical supplies. The artistic life of communities also includes what is sometimes called "informal arts" or "amateur arts," which include singing in houses of worship, quilting or sewing circles, scrapbooking, and creating Web pages.

Arts Education

A major partner of the National Endowment for the Arts is the U.S. Department of Education, which provided $13 million for arts education in FY2006. Its No Child Left Behind legislation includes arts as a core academic subject. State-level decision making—including teacher certification, high school graduation requirements, and standards for learning and assessment measures—guides much of what actually occurs in K–12 schools and out-of-school programs

Creative Arts Therapies

The infrastructure of this field is the National Coalition of Creative Arts Therapies Association (www.nccata.org) and the national associations devoted to specific disciplines:

- American Art Therapy Association (www.arttherapy.org)
- American Dance Therapy Association (www.adta.org)
- American Music Therapy Association (www.musictherapy.org)
- American Society of Group Psychotherapy and Psychodrama (www.asgpp.org)
- National Association for Drama Therapy (www.nadt.org)
- National Association for Poetry Therapy (www.poetrytherapy.org)

Foundations

Just as in the aging services field, foundations that fund artists, arts organizations, and arts programs are policy leaders as well as grant makers. Many smaller community and family foundations are involved in the arts at the local level. Nationally, two major players are the Wallace Foundation, which focuses on education leadership, arts participation, and out-of-school learning, and MetLife Foundation, which addresses arts education and access, among other areas. A resource is the Foundation Center, www.foundationcenter.org.

Making Connections

Leaders of aging services programs and organizations who want to connect with the arts field should focus on the local level, specifically on agencies that conduct community arts education programs, are experienced at working in partnership, and employ professional teaching artists. Americans for the Arts maintains an Online Field Directory of local, state, regional, and national arts organizations at www.americansforthearts.org (click E-Services). The following organizations are good places to start when seeking participants, partners, and information:

Community schools of the arts

Resources: These nonprofit, nondegree-granting, community-based institutions offer open access to quality arts instruction by professional faculty. Many are represented by the National Guild of Community Schools of the Arts, which promotes best practices, provides professional development, and develops policy. More than 40 percent of members offer programs designed for older adults; most enroll older adults in lessons or classes; and more than 15,000 professional artists are employed as teachers, making these institutions a good resource for teaching artists. Community schools of the arts are also adept at partnering with nonarts agencies to deliver arts programs.

For information: Click "Find a School" on the guild's Web site, www.nationalguild.org, and contact the program director.

Arts and aging programs

Resources: Potential partners and models for effective practices and program design, located nationwide

For information: Visit the National Center for Creative Aging's Web site, www.creativeaging.org.

> *Our seniors do things they have not done in years, never tried, or perhaps did not believe they could do…. Their cognitive abilities are challenged as they recall music from their past and have the opportunity to revisit those memories. As they move to the music or create a work of art, hand-eye coordination, balance, rhythm, and sequencing of instructions all contribute to feelings of accomplishment and well-being.*
>
> Amanda Frey, Director of Activities, Rockville Nursing Home (partner facility of Arts for the Aging)

New Horizons Music programs

Resources: Entry points to music making for adults, including those with no musical experience and those who were active in school music programs but have been inactive for a long period.

For information: To locate or start a program, consult the New Horizons International Music Association, www.newhorizonsmusic.org.

Local arts agencies

Resources: Links to arts organizations, arts programs, and individuals and teaching artists in a community.

For information: For a list of more than 3,000 local arts agencies, consult Americans for the Arts' Online Field Services Directory at www.americansforthearts.org (click E-Services). Contact the education, community, or program director.

For-profit music stores

Resources: Many stores have a commitment to music education and older adults and offer classes that follow a common curriculum.

For information: Two programs are the Roland Corporation's Music for Life (www.rolandus.com/community/musicforlife) and the Yamaha Corporation of America's Clavinova Connection (www.clavinovaconnection.com).

Community performing arts groups

Resources: Groups such as choruses and orchestras typically include teaching artists as performers or conductors and, like community schools of the arts, have a mandate to connect with all segments of the community. Community arts groups in dance, theater, the visual arts, and other disciplines are also potential partners.

For information: Consult a local arts agency, or visit the Web sites of Chorus America (www.chorusamerica.org) and the American Symphony Orchestra League (www.meetthemusic.org) for directories of members. Contact the executive director or artistic director.

National organizations

Various national organizations have expertise relevant to arts and aging programs:

- **Arts and healthcare programs:** The Society for the Arts in Healthcare (www.thesah.org) provides professional development, consulting, and grants that promote the use of the arts to enhance the healthcare experience.

- **Community livability:** Partners for Livable Communities (www.livable.com) has programs and initiatives that demonstrate how cultural resources can contribute to community design, among other livability issues. An aging in place initiative (www.aginginplaceinitiative.org) provides workshops, grants, and a guide to help state, local, and community decision makers better meet the needs of an older population.

- **Private funding:** Grantmakers in the Arts (www.giarts.org) has an extensive searchable database of articles, transcriptions from presentations and panels, and book reviews.

- **Advocacy, policy, and research:** The National Assembly of State Arts Agencies (www.nasaa-arts.org) also maintains a list of state arts agencies and regional arts organizations.

- **Arts education and various artistic disciplines (e.g., theater, media, dance, chamber music, performing arts centers, poets, writers, folk arts, and museums):** The National Endowment for the Arts (www.arts.gov/resources/disciplines/index.html) has a comprehensive list.

Key Points about the Arts Field

- The policy and funding emphases of the arts field—expanding the definition of arts education; increasing participation in the arts; understanding a broader definition of the arts; integrating arts into community life; demonstrating impact of arts programs on participants; making the case for increased resources; and supporting the professional development of teaching artists—have implications for the arts and aging field.

- The creative arts therapies and arts and aging programs have complementary goals.

- Though the arts field is composed of public and private organizations at the federal, regional, state, and local levels of government, aging services organizations that want to connect with arts organizations should focus on those in the community that have a track record of effective partnerships, that conduct arts education programs, and that employ professional teaching artists. These include community schools of the arts, New Horizons Music programs, local arts agencies, arts and aging programs, for-profit music stores, and community performing arts groups.

Acronyms in the Arts Field

AATA	American Art Therapy Association	NADT	National Association of Drama Therapy
ADTA	American Dance Therapy Association	NASAA	National Assembly of State Arts Agencies
AMTA	American Music Therapy Association	NCCA	National Center for Creative Aging
ASGPP	American Society of Group Psychotherapy and Psychodrama	NCCATA	National Coalition of Creative Arts Therapies Association
AE	Arts education	NGCSA	National Guild of Community Schools of the Arts
AEP	Arts Education Partnership	NEA	National Endowment for the Arts
AIE	Arts in education	NEH	National Endowment for the Humanities
ASOL	American Symphony Orchestra League	NCLB	No Child Left Behind
CPB	Corporation for Public Broadcasting	RAO	Regional arts organization
DOE	Department of Education	SAH	Society for the Arts in Healthcare
GIA	Grantmakers in the Arts	SAA	State arts agency
GOS	General operating support	SDOE	State department of education
IMLS	Institute of Museum and Library Services	UAF	United arts fund
LAA	Local arts agency		
NAPT	National Association for Poetry Therapy		

> There is something quite moving about watching 17 people of varying cultural and ethnic backgrounds, ages, and skill levels creating enjoyable, entertaining, and even profound dances together. It's as if you're watching a little working model of patience, care, and respect.
>
> Reggie, coordinator for community programs at an art center (Kairos Dance Theater)

5

Effective Practices

What are effective practices in an arts and aging program? Program leaders define them as: focusing on learning and cooperation; combining the latest learning in aging and art to benefit and build community; respecting the unique gifts of participants as artists in training and collaborators who can teach us about creativity and inventiveness; and meeting the needs of participants or constituents.

For a more comprehensive investigation of effective practices, this chapter looks at:

- Defining effective practices
- Identifying outcome goals
- Influencing others
- Understanding adult learning
- Examples of programs

Defining Effective Practices

Older adults receive the greatest benefits from an arts and aging program that exhibits these effective practices:

- *Shows intentionality.* The program is designed to accomplish one or more specific goals to enhance older adults' quality of life. The benefit to participants is not a byproduct or an afterthought. For example, the goal of the Foundation for Quality Care's Art from the Heart program is: "To qualitatively improve care and quality of life by offering nursing home residents the opportunity for creative expression and enhanced living."

- *Meets needs.* The program meets the self-identified needs of the participating older adults. Nothing is imposed upon the group, because this approach undermines the value of self-determination. Conducting a needs assessment—asking participants what they want—is a tenet of effective planning.

- *Demonstrates participatory, sequential learning.* The learning or instructional design takes into consideration the older adults' physical and mental abilities. For those who are cognitively fit, principles of adult learning are applied. For those with dementia, teaching artists focus on needs. Instruction is sequential, with each activity building on the one before it—much like learning the alphabet, then words, then sentences. Each step is challenging yet achievable. Finally, content must emphasize participation.

- *Includes professional teaching artists.* The program features a professional teaching artist, defined by *Teaching Artists Journal* as "an artist, with the complementary skills and sensibilities of an educator, who engages people in learning experiences in, through, or about the arts."[47] In arts and aging programs, the teaching artist is also grounded in community arts.

- *Evaluates impact.* Leaders of effective arts and aging programs are able to answer the question: How do you know that what you are doing is making a difference to participants? Are you accomplishing your goals? The Foundation for Quality Care, for example, would assess whether nursing home residents participating in the Art from the Heart program are receiving improved care and quality of life. Ideally, the answer would include both qualitative data (anecdotes) and quantitative data (statistics).

- *Demonstrates excellence and high quality.* The program has a high-quality process, which means that it demonstrates participatory, sequential learning. What is created during the process is also of high quality in context and honored as such regardless of context.

- *Engenders learning communities.* Participants are nurtured and supported by their own learning community— a group of people who share common values and beliefs. Those who manage the program—teaching artists along with administrative and program staff of the arts and aging services organizations— have a learning community as well so they can problem-solve and increase programmatic effectiveness.

- *Plans for sustainability.* The program leader plans for finding, sustaining, and increasing resources over the long term. A three-year record of accomplishment of growth is a good sign. Program partners aim for a permanent program that is an integral part of the community or institution. During the first three years, they engage participants, expand programming and activities, and involve stakeholders who are committed to the program's future. Ongoing evaluation is critical to sustainability.

- *Has circular program components.* The key program components—design, implementation, and evaluation—are circular, not linear (fig. 5-1). A successful and beneficial arts and aging program does not simply begin with design and end with evaluation. It constantly looks forward and backward so that decisions and actions are thoughtful and informed by reality.

fig. 5-1

Identifying Outcome Goals

The intent of arts and aging programs is to accomplish one or more of these goals—all aimed at enhancing quality of life:

- Older adults have a sense of control and feel empowered (i.e., mastery).
- Older adults are socially engaged.
- Older adults exercise their bodies and brains to ensure high physical and mental function.
- Older adults are healthy, with reduced risk factors for disease and disability.
- Older adults have a positive attitude and zest for life.
- Older adults express themselves creatively.

Research shows that these outcome goals are interrelated, with the older adult appropriately at the center (fig. 5-2, p. 48). Combined, the goals contribute to a positive quality of life for older adults. If the older adult has dementia, the emphasis is less on mastery and more on social engagement, because skill development and retention are not always possible for those with dementia.

Mastery and social engagement are particularly important for older adults, and they are two areas in which the arts have significant impact.

fig. 5-2 Outcome goals for older adults are interrelated.

Mastery

Mastery is skill or knowledge of a technique or topic. Older adults experience mastery when they overcome challenges successfully. Mastery relates to what is taught—program activities—and how it is taught—instructional design. The activities focus on teaching new skills, imparting new knowledge, and/or developing latent skills or interests. In the New Horizons Music program, for example, many participants had played instruments in their youth but stopped; others were learning instruments for the first time. The instructional design relates to the effective practice of participatory, sequential learning; each lesson or technique is challenging, yet achievable, and increases in difficulty. Success at each step is vital.

Almost all arts and aging programs involve reminiscence, which helps older adults make sense of and reconcile life experiences (see chapter 6). Organizing the past, much like pasting photos in an album, contributes to older adults' sense of control.

Social Engagement

Social engagement refers to active involvement in the community and with other people, not for the sake of being involved, but to accomplish something that is valued by the community and meaningful to the older adults. We all want to contribute to social capital—the collective value of social networks and the inclinations that arise from these networks to do things for each other. And we want to be remembered for making a positive difference, sometimes called legacy leaving. At a time of life when "old" connections may have disappeared, it is important for older adults to make new connections to other people; to the past, present, and future; and to their emotional lives.

In addition to community involvement, older adults benefit from a strong social support network of friends and family. John W. Rowe and Robert L. Kahn, the authors of *Successful Aging*, have a good metaphor:

> We like the term "convoy of social support" to describe the pattern of supportive relationships with which an individual moves through life. A convoy is a dynamic entity; the ships that make it up are in motion, en route to a destination. Being part of the convoy protects them, but each also provides a degree of protection to the others. The metaphor of the convoy seems to fit the personal networks of stability and change on which we depend for support as we move through the life course.[48]

Related to social engagement is communication, not just the ability to articulate ideas and feelings, but to be understood. Communication is particularly important in programs for older adults with dementia who may have lost the ability to speak. Memories in the Making, a program of the Alzheimer's Association, is a way to record expressions or feelings through art for people with dementia and limited verbal skills. The Orange County, California, chapter pioneered this program:

> Alzheimer's dementia brings with it a constant reminder of failures and losses. The Memories® art program is not about failure. Every picture is important and valid. Its value lies in the creative process of making the art and expressing feelings and emotions trapped inside. The ensuing sense of accomplishment brings renewed joy and self-respect to the patient.[49]

John is young, only 68, but has severe Alzheimer's disease. The title, "FA8," was not significant to the facilitator, until she showed the art to John's wife. John with his few words tried to explain, "It's going around those mountains down below." He circled with his finger tracing the swirling lines. When asked about the circle standing alone to the side, he said, "That one's calm because he is with God." John's wife, seeing the painting explained, "FA8 was our son's Navy jet and he was flying in formation with three other jets, two landed and two collided. Our son, Greg, 24, was one that died."

Source: LaDoris "Sam" Heinly, *I'm Still Here* (Newport Beach, CA: 2005)

Influencing Others

While outcome goals are focused on older adults, concentric circles of influence spread out from the participants to affect family members, professional caregivers, staff, and members of the public:

- Family members are amazed at the abilities of older adults and how much can be communicated through the arts.

- Family members seeing older relatives perform are also often inspired to do something they have not done before, such as attending more arts performances or taking up an artistic discipline of their own.

- Creative arts programs create a bond between older adults and caregivers in long-term care facilities. Staff may then see their jobs as a mission to take care of people, not just as employment.

- The quality of arts activities initiated by activities directors or other staff at residential facilities may improve as a result of the programs conducted by professional teaching artists.

- Artists bring the inspiration that other workers can use in their daily work with residents.

- Live performing arts events speak directly to people. During this era of alienation, they provide direct connection for audience members and performers.

These are, of course, just a few of the ripple effects of arts and aging programs.

> *Young people look through the windows of our memories and find assurances that life is worth living and striving for.*
> Amatullah Saleem, Pearls of Wisdom (ESTA)

Understanding Adult Learning

Adult learning is the educational philosophy that underlies effective arts and aging programs for cognitively fit older adults. Malcolm Knowles, who pioneered this field, identified the following characteristics of adult learners:

- Adults are autonomous and self-directed. Teachers are facilitators who involve adult participants actively in the learning process and guide them to their own knowledge rather than supply them with facts. Facilitators solicit participants' perspectives about what topics to cover; let them work on projects that reflect their interests; and allow them to assume responsibility for presentations and group leadership.

- Adults have accumulated a foundation of life experiences and knowledge that includes work-related activities, family responsibilities, and education. Facilitators draw out participants' experience and knowledge connected to the topic; relate theories and concepts to the participants; and acknowledge the value of their experiences to the learning process.

- Adults are goal-oriented. When joining a session or enrolling in a class, they usually have a goal in mind. They appreciate an educational program that is organized and has clearly defined elements. Early in the session facilitators should show participants how the class helps them attain their goals.

- Adults are relevancy-oriented and practical. They need to see a reason for learning something; learning has value if it applies to their lives. Facilitators identify objectives for adult participants before the class begins and relate theories and concepts to something familiar by letting participants choose projects that reflect their own interests.

- As do all learners, adults need to be shown respect. Facilitators acknowledge the wealth of experiences that adult participants bring to the classroom; treat them as equals in experience and knowledge; and allow them to voice their opinions freely in class.[50]

Tips for Facilitators

Stephen Lieb shares the following tips for effective facilitators:

- Learning occurs within each individual as a continual process throughout life. People learn at different speeds, so it is natural for them to be anxious or nervous when faced with a learning situation. Positive reinforcement by the facilitator and proper timing of the instruction enhance learning.

- Learning results from stimulation of the senses. In some people, one sense is used more than others to learn or recall information. Facilitators should present materials that stimulate as many senses as possible in order to increase success.

- If the participant does not recognize the need for the information (or has been offended or intimidated), all of the facilitator's effort to assist the participant to learn will be in vain. The facilitator should establish rapport with participants and prepare them for learning, thus providing motivation. Techniques include:

  » Establishing a friendly, open atmosphere

  » Adjusting the level of tension so that participants experience only low to moderate stress. If the stress is too high, it prevents learning.

  » Setting the degree of difficulty high enough to challenge participants but not so high that they become frustrated by information overload. The instruction should predict and reward participation, culminating in success.

  » Providing specific feedback

- Positive and negative reinforcement is necessary to encourage correct modes of behavior and performance; to teach new skills and information; and to help participants retain what they have learned.

- Participants need to retain information from classes in order to benefit from the learning, and they are more likely to do so if they see a meaning or purpose for the information, understanding how to interpret and apply it. Facilitators assist the learner with retention and application by ensuring that they learn and practice the information.[51]

Program Examples

Arts and aging programs are as individual as the older adult participants, reflecting their different abilities and needs, responding to partners and external events, and employing a variety of artistic disciplines. The following programs employ effective practices:

- The Golden Tones (Wayland, Massachusetts)
- New Horizons Music (in many communities)
- Luella Hannan Memorial Foundation (Detroit, Michigan)
- Kairos Dance Theatre (Minneapolis, Minnesota)
- Elders Share the Arts (Flushing, New York)
- Osher Lifelong Learning Institute, University of Southern Maine (Portland, Maine)

While these programs are successful, inspirational, and worthy of emulation, they are also constantly evolving in response to new research, life experiences, trial and error, and community and participant needs.

The Golden Tones

This senior adult chorus led by a professional artist is an example of a community arts organization that began as a program of a senior center initiated by the codirectors to serve the interests of attendees.

Planning

Observing that 10 older adults regularly meet to sing around the piano, the codirectors of the Wayland, Massachusetts, Senior Center, a program of the council on aging, decide to create a more formal singing group. One of the codirectors attends church with professional singer and church youth director Maddie Sifantus and asks for her help. Having an affinity for older adults from performing in nursing homes, she agrees to organize the group and recruits her mother, a concert pianist, to be the accompanist.

The singers, some of whom once appeared in amateur theater groups or plays at church, immediately express interest in performing. The rehearsal room at the senior center is also the home of the Wayland Senior Club, and the group performs for this audience twice in their first season. Thanks to these two performances and word of mouth, the number of chorus members doubles to 21 by the spring picnic, one of several social events during the year. As they perform more frequently in the community, their visibility and reputation attract new members. Older adults also join after participating in open rehearsals at other senior centers. Sifantus also contacts church choir directors in nearby communities, who then recommend the Golden Tones to older members who may benefit from a slower pace. No auditions are required.

Now, after 20 years, the Golden Tones has grown to 60 voices, and the more experienced singing group, the Golden Nuggets, has 20 members. Students from nursery school through college participate in intergenerational events with the Golden Tones, including rehearsing and performing with the chorus.

Through a verbal agreement (a written partnership agreement is in the works), the senior center donates rehearsal and storage space and the use of the piano. After the first couple of years, the chorus forms a steering committee, in part to develop revenue sources. They start charging a small fee to perform.

Then, the senior center offers Sifantus a small stipend using federal dollars distributed by formula through the local area agency on aging. In 1996, the chorus becomes a nonprofit with the help of a pro bono lawyer. Shortly thereafter, sources Sifantus has cultivated over the years make grants and contributions to launch a capital campaign and fund an endowment that is used to pay accompanists.

In 2005, the organization hires a part-time assistant director; receives capacity-building grants from two foundations and a local bank; initiates a strategic planning process; recruits new board members; and begins to transition from a working to a policy board. The Golden Tones receives 92 percent of its $60,000–$75,000 annual budget from individual donations (singers pay $25 per year), 5 percent from performance fees, and 3 percent from small grants. Sifantus plans to diversify revenue sources. Health insurance is provided through the local chamber of commerce.

Implementation
Members of the Golden Tones arrive 20 to 30 minutes early for their one-hour rehearsal held every Tuesday at 10:00 a.m. from fall to spring, less often during the summer. Some who no longer drive get a ride from those who do. After socializing and drinking coffee, the singers pick up music in large print and take their seats, with those who read music and are more able sitting next to less experienced or new singers or anyone who needs a little help.

Using a microphone, Sifantus leads the group through breathing, stretching, and vocalizing exercises, taking care not to stress the singers' voices. Once everyone is focused, she makes housekeeping announcements. The chorus then learns new music and reviews old music— all selected in collaboration with Sifantus. For some pieces, the Golden Nuggets sing harmony while others sing melody; for others, singers are free to add their own harmonies. Periodically, Sifantus explains terms and concepts using the blackboard. As always, the rehearsal ends with joining hands and singing "Till We Meet Again."

Sharing with the Community
Assisted living facilities, nursing homes, independent living communities, senior centers, schools, churches, and community leaders call Sifantus to request a one-hour Golden Tones performance for an average fee of $100. After a little direct marketing to ensure balance among types of facilities and perhaps to find a few family-related events with larger budgets, the schedule is set.

With 60 concerts a year in 25 towns, chorus members are always preparing for a performance. Typically, one member suggests a song to Sifantus who gets an idea for a theme, such as songs about music, dreams, or World War II, and brainstorms other relevant pieces with the chorus. Members learn the music; soloists and understudies rehearse the solos; and those who interact with the audience refine their timing, run lines, and check props.

At the facility, Sifantus reviews the performance space with the activities director and makes last-minute adjustments to chairs for the chorus, the piano, temperature, sound system, and lights. The audience arrives and picks up a program and sing-along sheets in large print that include the history of the Golden Tones and sponsor logos.

Sifantus welcomes them, introduces the theme, and serves as emcee throughout the concert. She turns around at the start of specific numbers to encourage everyone to join in. The singers' enthusiasm is contagious. After audience and chorus members conclude by singing "Let There Be Peace on Earth" and "Till We Meet Again," performers mingle with the audience, soliciting feedback and enjoying refreshments.

Evaluation

In addition to receiving informal feedback from concert audiences and chorus members throughout the year, Sifantus includes evaluative questions on the annual membership form that each singer completes. Audience, facility staff, chorus, and family members also send written testimonials. Using a raffle or other incentives, she entices the broader community to complete evaluation forms at the chorus' biennial gala. As an organizational grantee of the Massachusetts Cultural Council, she uses the preliminary assessment and panel review processes to gain insight into the chorus' administrative and board operations in comparison with other similarly sized nonprofits in the state.

New Horizons Music

With more than 140 band, orchestra, and choral programs in the United States, New Horizons Music is a proven example of an effective community-based performing arts program for well elders.

Planning

At an early spring retreat, the faculty and staff members of the local community music school brainstorm ideas on how best to serve all segments of the community, particularly older adults. One faculty member suggests exploring a New Horizons Music program, which is designed to contribute to the mental, physical, and social well-being of older adults and might have the added benefits of attracting new students of all ages to the school and enhancing the organization's visibility in the community.

New Horizons Music provides entry points to group music making for adults with no musical background and for those who were involved in music during their school years and have been away from it during their working years. Unlike most community bands and orchestras, which expect members to be able to read music and play their instruments, New Horizons groups provide beginning instruction. With the support of everyone present, several staff and faculty members form a small committee to pursue this idea. Meeting later in the spring, the group creates a timeline and divides assignments to complete before the planning session with community members in early June.

Guests at the planning session and lunch include the owner of the neighborhood music store; the director of the nearby senior center; and the older adult who chairs the activities committee at the continuing-care retirement community several miles from the music school. The faculty who will teach and conduct the music program are also at the meeting. The school's in-house New Horizons committee has already given the planning group information about New Horizons. After discussing the timeline and proposed budget, and creating a recruitment plan to kickoff the program with at least 30 members, the participants commit to moving forward and following through on their individual responsibilities.

The coordinator, who is a staff member at the school, joins forces with the senior center director and resident of the retirement community to recruit band members to attend the informational session scheduled for the end of July. Their "It's Never Too Late!" campaign features flyers in music stores and arts performance programs, along with announcements in the local newspaper and on several radio stations with classical music formats.

The program is budgeted to break even. Each band member will pay $150 for a semester, which includes a one-hour group lesson and one-hour rehearsal once a week. In addition, each will have to purchase music and music stands. The music store owner will rent and sell instruments to New Horizons members at a discount. The community school will provide the rehearsal room and enough space so that three or four group lessons can occur simultaneously.

Thanks to the success of the informational meeting, which included the New Horizons DVD, short introductions of the faculty who will lead and teach band members, and a lengthy question-and-answer session, 32 older adults enroll in the program. No auditions are required.

Implementation

On the last Tuesday of October, members of the New Horizons band begin to arrive at the community music school around 9:30 a.m. for coffee and conversation with their friends. Most drive, and others take the public bus or carpool. After six weeks of participation, the group has settled into a routine. By 10:00 a.m., section members (strings, brass, woodwinds, percussion) are in their circle of chairs for an hour of group instruction.

In the woodwinds room, the instructor welcomes her group and asks one of the musicians to lead the warm-up, which includes stretching, singing, and playing. She asks another to select a favorite song that they have rehearsed, and the musicians play. After helping a few members with finger positions and reminding everyone about posture, she suggests that they begin rehearsal with a familiar piece to build confidence; next, they work on a new piece. The instructor leads the section in tapping the rhythm. Then she asks them to hum the tune. Finally, they get to play. After demonstrating a few phrases on her oboe, she shares some specific techniques. She asks the musicians to try playing a favorite song by ear as they practice during the week.

After a short break, all band members meet in the rehearsal room. Musicians of different abilities share music stands, and, as they get settled, the room is filled with conversation about music. The director welcomes everyone, makes announcements, and leads a quick warm-up so members are aware of the larger group and the sounds of different instruments. Similar to the group lessons, he leads them in reviewing songs that they have learned and rehearsing several new numbers that they have selected together for the recital in December.

At the end of the two hours, the coordinator pops into the rehearsal room to encourage members to join a steering committee to help shape the future of the band. Responsibilities include recommending performance venues and community events; managing growth; forming and recruiting members for other committees as needed; and assisting with evaluation. She also distributes preliminary information about the New Horizons International Music Association's band camps next spring and summer. As the musicians pack up their instruments and music, several different groups make plans to share lunch.

Sharing with the Community

The small performance space at the community music school is filled with talking and laughter. Family members and friends of band members, other students at the school, and faculty members are excited to hear the New Horizons group play publicly for the first time. Applause greets the musicians as they take their seats and tune their instruments. Some have never performed; all are nervous.

The coordinator welcomes audience members and explains a bit about the program. She introduces the director, and the recital begins. At the end of the 40-minute program, musicians join audience members for a reception and celebration. Later in the month, the band will repeat their performance at the senior center and retirement community—two organizations represented during the initial program planning.

Evaluation

Since instructors do not administer formal assessments, they encourage musicians to reflect on their own progress and chart their own goals. The coordinator also distributes a three-page survey to band members toward the end of each semester (Appendix 7). The community music school's in-house New Horizons committee and the newly formed steering committee of members each review the results. Faculty members also contribute their observations to the meeting of the in-house committee. The evaluations are favorable and informative, and the school staff and faculty members adjust plans for the upcoming semester and start talking about recruiting new members and expanding the program over the next five years.

More Examples

In addition to the Golden Tones and New Horizons Music, the following organizations serve—or have programs that serve—well elders living in the community:

Baldwin-Wallace College Conservatory of Music

Clavinova Connection, Yamaha Corporation of America

Club Roland, Roland Corporation U.S.

Creative Aging Cincinnati

Elder Craftsmen, Inc.

Elders Share the Arts

EngAGE: The Art of Active Aging (formerly known as More Than Shelter For Seniors)

Levine School of Music

Liz Lerman Dance Exchange

Music for All Seasons

The Seasoned Performers

SPIRAL Arts, Inc.

Stagebridge Senior Theatre Company

Transitional Keys

Luella Hannan Memorial Foundation

The Hannan Foundation owns and operates a multiservice center infused with the arts for older adults in downtown Detroit. Foundation staff continuously assesses the interests and needs of Hannan House participants to create and grow their arts and lifelong learning programs.

Planning

After conducting a comprehensive needs assessment in 1993 of Detroit seniors living in the central city, the Luella Hannan Memorial Foundation converts its senior housing facility to an accessible and attractive nonprofit service center featuring a senior learning center, gallery, café, computer lab, and social service center. The latter includes free legal and tax advice, support groups, and access to a variety of community resources. Nonprofit tenants such as a disability resource center and the Brush Park Conservatory of Music and Fine Arts offer some services to older adults. In addition, the foundation coordinates services in several subsidized housing buildings, enabling residents to remain independent for a longer period.

To achieve its mission to enhance the quality of life for senior citizens in metropolitan Detroit, the foundation employs seven full-time and five part-time staff. The program budget is divided equally among senior learning, social services, and the gallery. Older adults pay $5 a semester to register for classes. The staff uses the reputation of Hannan House and its ability to access well and frail elders to attract community partners that donate time, services, and expertise to benefit participants throughout the facility.

From the beginning, foundation staff view Hannan House as a center for creative aging. The original activities program features arts and wellness activities, and it evolves in response to suggestions from participants into the senior learning center. Because of the facility's visibility in the community, people volunteer to teach. The mostly retired cadre of instructors includes practicing artists. Wayne State University also provides teachers. All are paid $25 to $75 per hour based on expertise and subject.

Soon after Hannan House opens, older adults begin taking classes in visual art and creating finished works. Noticing that the facility lacks a quality display space, the staff renovates a first-floor meeting room to also serve as the gallery. Under the curatorial guidance of a practicing artist, the Ellen Kayrod Gallery exhibits six to seven juried exhibitions a year of works by Detroit-area artists age 60 and older. Some take classes at Hannan House.

Works by older artists also hang in the Hannan House café.

Staff members locate adults over 60 through word of mouth, flyers in apartment buildings, ads in publications, and ongoing communication and information sharing with a network of aging services providers and partners. With an extensive invitation list, gallery openings bring first-time visitors to Hannan House who then return as participants or tell friends and family members about the array of services. The facility also offers limited transportation.

Implementation
Hannan House buzzes with activity. Throughout the week, students enrolled in the senior learning center sip coffee and chat with friends as they make their way to classes on opera, visual art, yoga, literature, history, nutrition, or chair aerobics. Others come weekly for lectures on environmental justice, a meeting of the quality of life group, or a drum circle.

Today, senior program officer Pam Halladay greets participants in one class and asks for a few minutes of their time to describe a request she received from NPR's StoryCorps to help engage Detroit seniors in telling their stories. The telling and recording of oral histories has been part of Hannan's mission for some time and, with StoryCorps and other Detroit organizations involved, this project has the potential to evolve into a multiyear theme for a variety of activities, from visual art and writing classes to oral history and discussion groups on historic and current topics. The students are enthusiastic and brainstorm ideas for how to connect with this project.

On the way back to her office, Halladay stops in the café for a cup of coffee and sits down with several older visitors. She describes the idea for the StoryCorps project, and they, too, offer support and suggestions. Next, Halladay works with a local committee to explore this collaboration. She lines up additional partners such as the Michigan Arts League and the Detroit Public Library, and engages other Hannan staff in finding people to help implement the six-week project and become part of the interview teams for the recordings.

Sharing with the Community
In the gallery, curator Mary Herbeck hangs an exhibit designed collaboratively with her visual art class that meets down the hall. The *Art of Aging Biennial* is presented to raise public awareness of the relationship between creative expression and healthy aging. For later in the week, she has scheduled a two-hour afternoon opening and reception, which will include a performance by the Hannan Choir, directed by a teaching artist with the Brush Park Conservatory.

Between now and then, the Hannan Foundation board of trustees is meeting in the room, and one of the tenants is holding a volunteer training. Next, Herbeck checks on the multimedia exhibit in the café by older Detroit artist Eric Mesko that explores patriotism through old-time baseball.

Later in the day, Herbeck and Halladay look through paintings donated to Hannan House by a former resident of the building. Several works are of good quality and in excellent condition, and they find appropriate display space in one of the halls. The paintings and antique quilts complement an adjacent mural conceptualized and created by an intergenerational art class led by a local teaching artist.

The invitations, produced in-house and mailed to everyone who has taken classes or obtained services at Hannan House, and distributed informally through the foundation's many contacts in the community, have generated a crowd at the exhibit opening in the gallery. Foundation staff circulate among guests, talking about ongoing services and soliciting input on new ideas. First-time visitors at this community celebration remark on the interesting and creative activities and promise to return.

Evaluation

A culture of open and safe communication pervades Hannan House. In addition to asking participants and visitors to comment on and brainstorm suggestions for new programs and activities, Halladay—often in the same conversation—asks for input on current services. Foundation staff also evaluate programs with partners, administer written satisfaction surveys, and convene focus groups several times a semester on specific topics. For some in-depth surveys, they may form a small group or use an existing advisory committee to test the questions before broader distribution. The foundation also collects basic quantitative information, such as how many people participate in programs and take advantage of social services—and why.

More Examples

In addition to the Luella Hannan Memorial Foundation, the following organizations provide an array of services to older adults:

Institute on Aging (the Center for Elders and Youth in the Arts is a program of this agency)

EngAGE: The Art of Active Aging (formerly known as More Than Shelter For Seniors)

Foundation for Quality Care

Kairos Dance Theatre

Kairos Dance Theatre, a community arts organization, created the Dancing Heart program to address the needs of frail elders and those with dementia. Led by teaching artists, the participatory, creative workshops combine opportunities for artistic expression and learning with the health-enhancing benefits of dance and music.

Planning

With a recent grant to expand the Dancing Heart program, teaching artist and artistic director Maria Genné contacts a nursing home director who expressed interest in the program many months ago after reading about it in the local newspaper. They meet at the facility. Referring to materials in an information packet, Genné cites research on the benefits of arts participation to the mental, physical, and social health of older adults, as well as to professional caregivers. She outlines the goals of Dancing Heart and shares Kairos' philosophy.

Though the program is developed with the facility to meet its specific needs, Genné explains that she has certain requirements before moving forward:

- A commitment by the partner to raise or provide 50 percent of the cost

- Ninety uninterrupted minutes once a week for a minimum of three months—ideally a year—in a private room or discrete space large enough for a circle of 12 to 17 participants

- An additional hour, ideally once a week and no less than once a month, to assess the artistic, cognitive, physical, and emotional changes among participants

- Fifteen to 30 minutes with staff after each session or later by phone to check in and fine-tune any details

- At least one staff member—the same person—who attends the Dancing Heart three-day training, workshops, and evaluative sessions and follows up with participants between workshops. Follow-up includes reviewing the storytelling concepts and continuing rehearsals with participants as the date for the informal performance nears.

- A letter of agreement or contract between the partner organizations

The nursing home director agrees, and over the next month the partnership is formalized. Activities staff post information about the Dancing Heart workshops on bulletin boards and use other established communication methods. Several members of Kairos Dance Theatre do a mini-performance for residents and describe the program.

Implementation

At the nursing home, residents assisted by a staff member form a circle of chairs. Genné and two other Kairos teaching artists greet each person individually and help with nametags. Genné starts the CD player or introduces the older jazz musician who will accompany the dancing, choreography, and storytelling. The music begins, and jazz, blues, Irish fiddle playing, Broadway songs, Cajun rhythms, or Andean melodies fill the room. Genné makes an arm movement and asks participants to follow. Gestures are at different heights, angles, and positions to warm up the body, focus and stimulate the brain, and create a sense of community.

Following Genné's cue, the group sings what has evolved over several months into their welcome song, which includes everyone's names. Then, names are paired with gestures, rhythms, and patterns as participants take turns leading the chair dancing. Or, seizing the moment, Genné and the participants choreograph a series of movements inspired by a woman's bright red shirt or the pouring rain. Since each group member chooses a musical theme for one workshop, they might dance to Russian folk songs or country-western.

Genné teaches the language of dance throughout, pointing out when a dancer illustrates a particular concept. The other teaching artists work one-on-one with frail elders to encourage and celebrate their movements. The foundation of the Dancing

Heart program is the artistic collaboration of each participant in the dance and story-making process.

After a break for water, the Kairos teaching artists facilitate storytelling, the topic of which varies from week to week. If the older musician is accompanying the workshop, his life story catalyzes participants' memories about music. Second- and third-graders join the group periodically, and all collaborate on creating stories or poems, cutting and pasting words from magazines and newspapers to document their work. From time to time, for groups with dementia, Genné uses an abbreviated TimeSlips process. Memories lead back to dancing: arms wave high to illustrate a poem about fishing or low to imitate waves. At the conclusion of the workshop, everyone sings the closing song, and the Kairos teaching artists thank and chat with each participant.

Sharing with the Community
Telling stories, writing poetry, or dancing in response to the rain suggest themes to Genné that she explores with participants. They consider "Storms We Have Weathered" and the musical "Oklahoma," and they decide on the former. Agreeing to perform in the facility for an audience of other residents and family members, the dancers and the Kairos teaching artists create a 30- to 45-minute program that includes dancing and storytelling set to the music of or inspired by their life experiences. They often honor the memories of friends, relatives, and perhaps group members who have died by incorporating their stories, movement gestures, or even a favorite waltz into the piece. Fortunately, several company members of Kairos Dance Theatre are able to perform with the Dancing Heart group and join them for rehearsals. All dancers enthusiastically work to make their artistic expression strong and clear.

The performance begins with a welcome from Genné, who provides background about the program. She encourages audience members to warm up with the dancers. At planned moments during the production, one or two participants lead everyone in dance movements. After the applause ends, dancers, friends, and family mingle at a reception and enjoy punch and cookies donated by the local bakery.

Evaluation
As part of planning, Genné and the nursing home director and staff discuss evaluation. They use a written survey to capture attitudes toward dance and the initial expectations of participants and staff involved in the program, and they ask similar questions at the end. They also administer the Survey of Activities and Fear of Falling in the Elderly as a pre- and post-test. For groups with dementia, the partnership team might decide to track cognitive change with the Mini-Mental State Examination and interview participants and family members about expectations and attitudes.

Conversations with staff following each workshop, and longer discussions weekly or monthly, also are opportunities to evaluate impact on participants. In addition, Genné and the other teaching artists ask participants periodically to provide feedback on the activities and teaching. At the end of the program, they check in for a final time with the group, exploring together what the participants learned, what was successful and what wasn't, and what Kairos Dance Theatre could do better. Last but not least, Genné asks each participant to write a letter of support. Those with trouble writing legibly dictate their comments to staff.

More Examples

In addition to Kairos Dance Theatre, the following organizations serve — or have programs that serve — frail elders or those with dementia:

Alzheimer's Poetry Project

Arts for the Aging

Center for Elders and Youth in the Arts

Creative Aging Cincinnati

Elder Craftsmen, Inc.

Elders Share the Arts

Evergreens Renaissance

Memories in the Making

Music for All Seasons

SPIRAL Arts, Inc.

TimeSlips

Transitional Keys

Elders Share the Arts

Elders Share the Arts (ESTA) is a community arts organization that fosters productive aging by using teaching artists to engage older adults in sharing memories, life experiences, and wisdom through the arts. ESTA's intergenerational programs enable older adults and K–12 students to explore their commonalities and differences through the arts, creating mutual understanding and strengthening community.

Planning

The Generating Community program of Elders Share the Arts engages elders and youth in transitional communities where they are divided not only by age, but also by ethnicity. For the past 15 years, ESTA staff have actively sought out partnerships to effect this goal. P. S. 24 and the Rosenthal Senior Center are neighbors in Flushing, New York (Queens).

After positive conversations about the program and its outcomes with the school principal and center director, ESTA executive director Susan Perlstein sends them information about her organization and requests support letters to use in fundraising (Perlstein has since founded the National Center for Creative Aging and become its director of education and training). She then tells a group of senior center attendees about the benefits of working with fifth-graders. Fifteen volunteer to participate.

With this level of interest, the senior center director donates space for the program. Perlstein and the director talk with the principal and special projects coordinator at P. S. 24, who agree that an intergenerational oral history project fits within the fifth-grade social studies curriculum. After obtaining approval from the district school board, the partnership is ready to move forward.

The partnership team — the principal, a coordinating teacher, a classroom teacher, the senior center program director, two members of the senior center staff who would function as senior representatives, the ESTA teaching artist, and the project coordinator

(Perlstein) — meets to hash out funding, logistics, and communication protocols. Fundraising is shared, the school matches revenues that ESTA raised dollar for dollar. Each person signs a contract that specifies responsibilities and a timeline. The team designs the program to meet weekly for 30 weeks.

Implementation
The seniors and the students meet separately with the teaching artist, Marsha Gildin, for the first five weeks to explore age stereotypes. Each session begins with breathing and moving exercises, an exchange of movements or ideas among group members, and chanting or complementary sounds. Next, Gildin leads acting exercises in which participants pretend to be someone or something different. Group members then learn how to uncover stories by asking questions, making timelines of important life events, and drawing a family tree. Each group considers what the word *neighborhood* means, listing likes and dislikes.

Together, the seniors and fifth-graders exchange stories, jokes, memories, and songs through exercises that Gildin facilitates; for example, she asks participants to move to a rhythm and stop when she says, "Freeze like you're happy to see someone!" or, "Freeze like you're in trouble!" Then, she asks them to interview each other to get at the stories "behind the freeze." Several teams of participants improvise and act out these stories, adding "freezes" at key moments to form tableaux.

Sharing with the Community
About halfway through the 30 weeks, Gildin identifies themes from her notes and the student's interviews with seniors to turn into a script for an intergenerational show. This year, the unifying theme is, "What makes up the flow of life in communities and neighborhoods?" At Gilden's request, each senior and student write one or two sentences about the meaning of home. She then creates dialogue for each scene as a guide for participants' improvisation.

Gildin divides the class into small groups of one or two seniors and five or six students, organized by personality types and traits (e.g., more reserved students with more articulate seniors). Gildin, the classroom teacher, an ESTA intern, and one or two seniors who have participated in ESTA programs each supervise a group as members develop a section of the script. Those who are not going to appear on stage learn how to run props or tech, organize costumes, or cue performers. Before the performance, the teaching artist leads several sessions with only the fifth-grade students to prepare them to cover for other actors. The entire group rehearses in the senior center and school so everyone is familiar with both stages.

Finally, it's show time. Gildin leads audience members in a brief warm-up exercise and explains the concept and benefits of intergenerational living history theater. The performance includes presentation-style pieces, group poems, movement, and dramatic scenes. After the cast bows and enjoys applause, Gildin leads an evaluative discussion with audience members about what surprised them, what they enjoyed, and what they learned. Actors, friends, family, and members of the public celebrate participants' accomplishments at a reception. Later, the students produce an anthology based on the show's theme and dedicate it to the seniors.

Evaluation

In addition to eliciting feedback from audience members immediately after each performance, school teachers and staff intentionally observe how students interact with seniors. Students write letters and cards to their partners after the program and volunteer to help at the senior center even though they are not old enough to do so. Gildin has recorded her impressions after each session throughout the year. The senior participants complete a written survey and share their reactions in a post-performance meeting with Gildin. The partnership team assesses the program and how they functioned as a team.[52]

More Examples

In addition to Elders Share the Arts, the following organizations are intergenerational or have intergenerational programs:

Center for Elders and Youth in the Arts

The Golden Tones

Intergeneration Orchestra of Omaha

Kairos Dance Theatre

Liz Lerman Dance Exchange

New Jersey Intergenerational Orchestra

Stagebridge Senior Theatre Company

Osher Lifelong Learning Institute, University of Southern Maine

The term *lifelong learning* is often used to describe the process of accomplishing personal, social, and professional development throughout the lifespan in order to enhance the quality of life of both individuals and communities. Lifelong learning also refers to educational classes, usually affiliated with a college, community college, or university, designed by or for older adults, and often taught by older adults. Generally, there are no tests, grades, or homework. The Osher Lifelong Learning Institute (OLLI) at the University of Southern Maine in Portland is an example of a program organized and managed almost entirely by the older adult members.

Planning

In 1997, a group of older adults in Portland, Maine, explore the possibility of learning opportunities with the University of Southern Maine. The result is the Senior College. With strong leadership and active members, it attracts the attention of the Bernard Osher Foundation, which awards the program its first lifelong learning grant in 2001.

The Osher Lifelong Learning Institute (OLLI) expands over the years in response to and with the leadership of its more than 900 members, who are age 50 and older. Member volunteers develop curriculum, teach classes, serve on committees, plan special events, market the program, staff the office, manage registration, and design extracurricular activities. The governance structure features a leadership council that operates like a nonprofit board of directors,

> OLLI was platinum when I hoped for silver. It has been as if I've come across treasure. I am fed intellectually and spiritually as well as welcomed into a community of friends. Most surprisingly and needed today, OLLI is a movement that affirms and demonstrates the worth of people in the latter third of their lives. We need it, and the larger community needs us. We have lived long enough and been through enough to know what counts and not settle for less or stop seeking it.
>
> Bill, member, OLLI-University of Southern Maine

but without financial, liability, or personnel supervision responsibilities.

The heart of OLLI is the curriculum. More than 700 students attend about 45 noncredit classes that meet for two hours a week on Friday morning and afternoon during the fall and spring semesters. Subjects are extensive—from music and art to history and science. Each winter and summer, shorter special-interest sessions introduce a variety of topics. Teachers are peers for whom a subject may be either a passion or a profession. OLLI also offers a lecture series, a special lecture each semester, a literary journal, an annual art show, the Senior Players, the Sixth-Age Puppet Opera Company, OLLI singers, a writers' group, and local and international educational trips.

Members pay an annual fee of $25 that enables them to participate in all activities, along with a $25 to $50 fee per course for tuition, books, and materials. Scholarships are available. Other funding sources include the Osher Foundation and the state legislature.

"Learn for the love of it!" is the message that OLLI members and staff convey as they recruit new members through community newspapers and local public radio stations. Members fill brochure stands in businesses and public facilities and mail newsletters with the class schedule to an extensive mailing list. Others speak at meetings and show a video developed by a professional videographer. Word of mouth proves the best marketing tool, and the staff rewards members for recruiting new participants.

Implementation

Though it is early spring in Maine, the 10 members of the curriculum committee are focused on next fall. After an update from the chair on a recent leadership council meeting, the committee reviews the preliminary topics for fall classes. For the most part, the list looks good, and the chair makes a note to follow up with two teachers whose topics appear similar. Next, she leads a discussion of three course proposals. Examining the balance of topics across all courses, the committee accepts most proposals. A new member who was recruited by the chair to fill a vacancy comments that the curriculum seems light on humanities courses, and the group brainstorms options. Remembering a popular class on Greek mythology from several years ago, the vice-chair agrees to contact that teacher.

After the OLLI leadership council approves the fall curriculum, the staff prepares the print and online course catalog. Volunteers help with logistical details of registration. Before the start of classes, the OLLI director orients faculty over lunch. She reviews administrative issues and the governance structure and reminds teachers about providing physical and programmatic accessibility; outlining course content and expectations in a syllabus; and distributing student comment forms toward the end of the semester. Even though most OLLI faculty members are experienced teachers, a professor from the university makes a presentation on adult learning.

Sharing with the Community
During the fall semester, the events committee and its subcommittees plan activities and prepare for the "ninth week" arts celebration that follows the conclusion of the eight-week semester. The Senior Players, which evolved from a play-reading class and now appear regularly in the community, have requested more time to perform, and the chorus class needs to sing in the morning instead of the afternoon. Everything is proceeding smoothly with the new writers' group, however, and several members will present original poetry.

Turning their attention to other events, the committee receives a report on OLLI Art, the annual exhibition of members' works. Another group reports on the *One Book, One Community* festival planned for February. Featuring a book group facilitated by a Maine author, the extravaganza includes a dramatic reading by the Senior Players and a chorus performance, poetry reading, and visual art exhibit all thematically linked to the book.

Elsewhere on campus, the Sixth-Age Puppet Opera Company members are sewing costumes, creating scenery, building puppets, and rehearsing for their third production, *Un, Deux, Trois*. The group was started by an OLLI member with a lifelong interest in puppets and inspired by a puppet production of Mozart's *Don Giovanni*. It performs for family members, community residents, and friends at OLLI and other venues— such as lifelong learning institutes, local libraries, and retirement communities— that invite the company to perform and publicize the production. OLLI provides space and funding with budgetary approval by the leadership council.

Evaluation
Since OLLI at the University of Southern Maine is member driven and peer taught, evaluation is routine, ongoing, and mostly informal. Those who design the curriculum and extracurricular activities are also participants and so are in constant communication with their classmates. While some teachers who are effective in a structured classroom setting are less effective at OLLI, most enjoy the high caliber of very engaged and active learners. In addition to informal evaluative mechanisms, the staff collects basic quantitative data.

Each teacher is encouraged to distribute one-page student comment forms that include questions about the teacher and about students' class preparation, attendance, and expectations. A subcommittee of the curriculum committee is currently developing a way to better analyze and use the evaluation results. The curriculum committee also encourages members to share comments and initiate discussion by means of a comment box in the OLLI office.

More Examples

In addition to the Osher Lifelong Learning Institute at the University of Southern Maine and in more than 100 other communities around the country, OASIS provides lifelong learning for more than 350,000 older adults at centers in 26 cities.

Reflect...

How do I start an arts program at the senior center in my community?

How can I encourage the aging services organizations in my community to be centers for creative aging?

How can I build assessment and evaluation into my day-to-day activities?

How can I seamlessly integrate fun and instruction in my artistic discipline?

How can I adapt my arts program to the needs of frail elders or those with dementia?

How can I involve older adults in every aspect of my program?

How can I apply these program examples to an intergenerational chorus or orchestra, a theater company, or a visual arts program?

Key Points about Effective Practices

- Older adults receive the greatest benefits from an arts and aging program that exhibits effective practices: shows intentionality, meets needs, demonstrates participatory, sequential learning, includes professional teaching artists, evaluates impact, demonstrates excellence and high quality, engenders learning communities, plans for sustainability, and has circular program components.

- The intent of arts and aging programs is to accomplish one or more outcome goals for older adults—all aimed at enhancing quality of life.

- Mastery—skill or knowledge of a technique or topic—and social engagement—community involvement and a support network—are particularly important for older adults, and they are two areas in which the arts have significant impact.

- Mastery is less important for people with dementia, for whom learning a new technique or topic may be difficult.

- Concentric circles of influence spread out from the participants to affect family members, professional caregivers, staff, and members of the public.

- Adult learning, which builds instruction around the experiences, interests, and goals of adults—is the educational philosophy that underlies effective arts and aging programs for cognitively fit older adults.

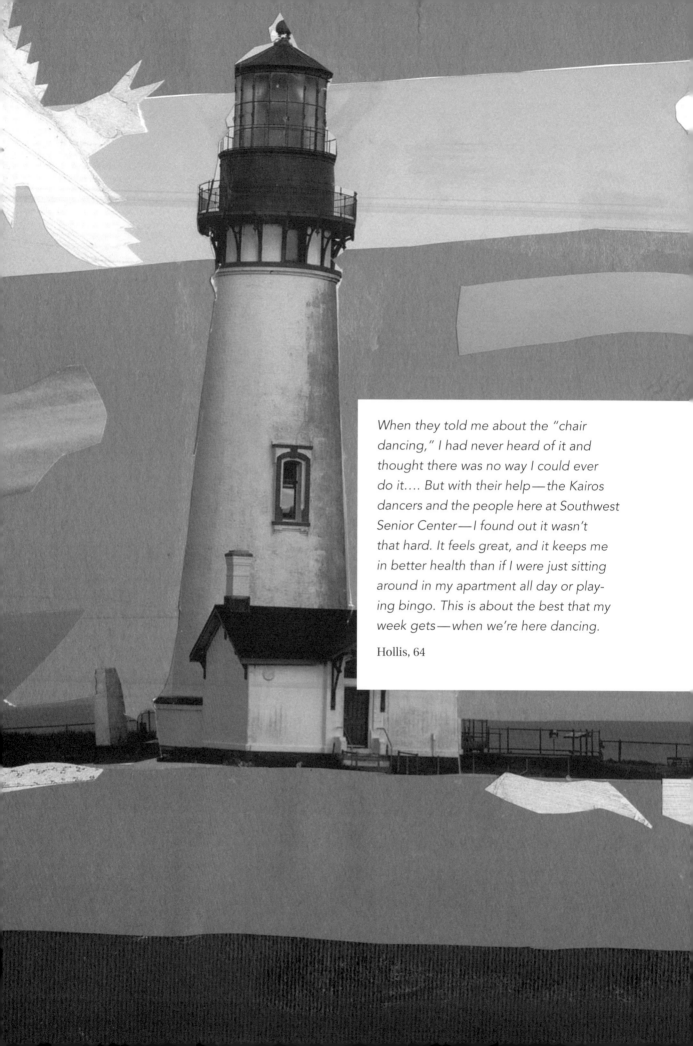

When they told me about the "chair dancing," I had never heard of it and thought there was no way I could ever do it.... But with their help—the Kairos dancers and the people here at Southwest Senior Center—I found out it wasn't that hard. It feels great, and it keeps me in better health than if I were just sitting around in my apartment all day or playing bingo. This is about the best that my week gets—when we're here dancing.

Hollis, 64

Program Design

So far, this toolkit has established the foundation for effective programs. Now you're ready to take the next step: program design. You may want to learn how to translate an idea into action. Or you may have created a program and find yourself at a crossroads: perhaps the founder has retired and you're stuck in status quo, or you're ready to move from an all-volunteer staff to a paid staff.

Whether you are already running with an idea or just starting out, pay particular attention to assessing the needs of participants, establishing a purpose, and creating the instructional design:

- If your program is not what potential participants want, they won't participate. "If we build it, they will come" doesn't always apply.

- A purpose—the vision, mission, goals, and objectives—is the destination. The purpose is the change that we want to effect in the lives of our participants and our communities.

- Through instructional design, you enable diverse participants to overcome challenges successfully. You help cognitively fit older adults achieve outcome goals of mastery and social engagement, and you help older adults with dementia be socially engaged.

Program design takes time. How much time depends on the organization. You may have conducted internal and external assessments, or you may have partners in place and be exploring effective programmatic options. An established organization with solid infrastructure and a strategic plan will be able to hit the ground running. But it is likely that you'll need to do some degree of planning. Remember that a successful and beneficial arts and aging program is not linear, beginning with planning and ending with evaluation. It is circular, so that our actions are thoughtful and generate positive outcomes for older adults. Program design is never set in stone, so you can respond to opportunities and help your programs evolve over time.

This chapter looks at:

- Planning the program
- Finding and working with partners
- Securing resources
- Marketing to participants

> *What do I know now that I wish I knew when I was starting out? To assess what people really want to do, to go to potential audiences and engage them in discussion.*
>
> Pam Halladay, Senior Program Officer, Luella Hannan Foundation

Planning the Program

Planning is the process of setting parameters for an organization or program. Through assessment and then developing a purpose, activities, an instructional design, and a plan for evaluation, you create the container in which partners, teaching artists, older adult participants, and community members come together to transform lives through the arts.

While you can just jump in and start working with older adults, a better idea is to begin with a roadmap—figuring out where you are, where you want go, and how you're going to get there. For those who are already managing programs, it is never too late to pause and consider the elements of effective planning.

This section explores steps in program planning:

- Conducting internal and external assessment
- Creating an advisory committee
- Establishing purpose
- Designing activities
- Applying andragogy and instructional design
- Planning for evaluation
- Reminiscence
- Community sharing of the art

Conducting Internal and External Assessment

Assessment is the process of documenting knowledge, skills, attitudes, and beliefs in measurable terms. There are two types of assessment: internal and external.

Internal Assessment

In planning as in life, it is a good idea to take a hard look at strengths and weaknesses. To "know thyself," as Plato recommended, improves the chances of connecting with partners, attracting participants, and achieving success. Refine your ideas by considering these questions. Ask people who know you or your organization to consider them, too:

- Values
  - What do we care so much about that we can't compromise?
  - What do we believe in?
  - Are we risk takers, or are we more cautious?
- Vision
  - What difference do we hope to make in this community?
  - What, ultimately, do we want to accomplish?
- Strengths
  - What do we do well?
  - What skills do we have among our board, staff, and volunteers?
  - What do we know a lot about?
- Weaknesses
  - What do we not do well?
- Resources
  - How much time and money do we have to devote to this program?[53]

Examining data and documentation—such as financial statements, evaluation reports, attendance statistics, and comments by past funders and grant panelists—is useful in internal assessment. Board members and other staff can provide input as well, perhaps through a brainstorming session around values, vision, strengths, weaknesses, and resources. Be sure that your program fits within the organization's mission: "Every program you choose to offer should reflect why you exist and whom you serve. As arts organizations strive to serve the needs of particular communities, memberships, and audiences, program planners should also resist the common compulsion to do more and more."[54]

Older adults are a good fit with the mission of the Levine School of Music, which includes these key phrases:

- Levine School of Music serves as a vital community resource by embracing two principles that are central to its mission: excellence and accessibility.

- Inside, the corridors are filled with people of all ages, skill levels, and economic and cultural backgrounds who come together to explore the universal language of music for lifelong learning.

- The school reaches out actively through its many community programs to bring music to the entire community.

- Levine strives to strengthen and enrich the life of any student who has the desire and commitment to learn.

External Assessment

Once you understand your organization, focus on the environment in which it operates. According to the *W. K. Kellogg Foundation Evaluation Handbook*, external assessment has these results:

- Identify existing community action groups and understand the history of their efforts
- Identify existing formal, informal, and potential leaders
- Identify community needs and gaps in services
- Identify community strengths and opportunities
- Understand [your] target population (both needs and assets) in order to improve, build, and secure project credibility within the community
- Create momentum for project activities by getting community input.[55]

Scanning the Environment

Conducting an environmental scan is a common technique to get a picture of your community. Consult board and staff on these key questions:

- What opportunities exist in the community that we might take advantage of? Opportunities could be related to resources (money, staff, facilities), change in political leadership, or a new awareness of an issue.

- What concerns or threats do we face (economic, political, social, technological, environmental)? Concerns might include an upcoming election, an industry moving out of town, the senior center closing for renovations, or new management at the long-term care facility or the performing arts center. Remember that change isn't automatically a threat. Often, new leadership in the community provides new allies and partners.

- What is our competition for providing this type of program to this population?

Assessing Community Members

Assemble a list of individuals and organizations to assess through interviews, focus groups, and/or surveys. Established arts, aging, and social services coalitions can also serve as focus groups. The purpose is to understand how community members take advantage of existing opportunities in the arts and services for older adults, identify barriers to participation, and determine community needs. If you plan focus groups, consider enlisting the help of an experienced facilitator to elicit responses and encourage participation.

Questions include:

- Are you familiar with arts activities and aging services in the community?
- Where do you get your information about arts activities and aging services?
- What performances do you currently attend?
- If you don't attend arts activities or performances, why not?
- In what arts activities do you currently participate?
- If you don't participate in any arts activities, why not?

- Which services for older adults do you or a family member use?
- If you don't use services for older adults, why not?
- What are the top three needs in our community in the arts? In aging services?
- Do you have older family members and friends living in the community?
- Are you familiar with the work of our organization/program?
- Do you have friends or colleagues who are involved in the arts? In aging services?

Some external assessment questions will be discipline specific. For example, in senior theater, you may ask:

- Are older actors dropping out of community theater because of the unrelenting demands on their physical and emotional energy?
- Do you see a smaller older audience because of physical limitations or because the theater today has left it behind?
- Are there older people who would like to participate in theater activities but who never had the time before or who lack the experience—or the nerve—to compete with other actors?
- Are there older people who need more opportunities for daytime activity?[56]

Program Example: External Assessment

In designing the Arts and Inspiration Center—an adult day program of the Great Plains and Heart of America chapters of the Alzheimer's Association—the staff conducted a three-step assessment to learn about needs for improving services and circumstances of people with Alzheimer's disease and their family members.

1. They assembled a group of key players, held a meeting, and interviewed those who couldn't attend the meeting. The group consisted of:
   » Professionals in the aging services field
   » Family members of individuals with the illness
   » Physicians
   » People in the early stage of Alzheimer's disease
   » Clergy
   » Individuals from the arts community
   » Leaders of community volunteer agencies, such as the Retired Senior Volunteer Project
   » Leaders of home health agencies
   » Individuals who are "motivators" in the community
   » Parks and recreation leadership
   » County extension staff
   » Representatives from academic institutions
   » Local media

2. The staff clarified, analyzed, and summarized all responses, which identified community-based respite care, education, and support programs as priorities.

3. The entire group discussed how best to address the priorities. One solution was the Arts and Inspiration Center.

CHAPTER 6: PROGRAM DESIGN

Consulting Stakeholders and Assessing Potential Participants

In addition to assessing community members, consult with those who care most about your work in the arts and aging field: your stakeholders. To identify this group, ask staff and board members questions such as:

- Who do we say we serve?
- Who do we really serve?
- Who should we be serving?
- Who would care if we went out of business?

The list of stakeholders doesn't have to be exhaustive. Most likely, you need to talk with funders, teaching artists, and potential partners and participants. In a residential facility, your stakeholders may include the residents, staff, and family members.

Explore with stakeholders questions similar to those you ask members of the broader community. This group, however, provides you with the opportunity to delve deeper into issues around needs and values. Funders in particular often have a good overview of the community, ideas about solutions, and specific outcomes in mind.

An assessment of potential participants' needs determines the where, when, and how of your program. You can use interviews, focus groups, and/or surveys, making sure that you are sensitive to individual abilities. Use a written survey, for example, for senior center attendees. Have a discussion with the residents' council or activities committee in a residential facility. For people with dementia, involve family and professional caregivers, keeping in mind the value of choice and self-determination.

If the proposed program is intergenerational, factor in young people's needs with similar questions. Pay attention to the curricular requirements of the school or organization that runs an out-of-school program. (For an example of an external assessment survey, see http://usm.maine.edu/olli/national/pdf/CSU_Sacramento-Survey.pdf. For an example of how to structure a focus group and questions to ask, see http://usm.maine.edu/olli/national/pdf/UU-Focus_Group_Guide.pdf.)

Devise questions that will elicit the following information:

Overall:

- What are your interests?
- What do you want to learn and do?
- Where do you live?
- What accommodations do you need: large print, Braille, sign language interpreter, written materials, reduced lighting to eliminate glare, accessible bathrooms, no stairs? Are you able to hold a paintbrush or pen?
- In what other activities are you involved, and what is the schedule?
- What is the ideal session length for you?
- How often should our sessions be scheduled?

For programs in a residential facility:

- When are the scheduled meals?
- Are you able to move independently to another room, or are you dependent on others?

For programs in a community facility:

- Can you drive, or do you need a ride? If you drive, can you drive at night? Can you afford to pay for parking? How far can you walk?
- Is convenient public transportation available?
- Will you feel safe?

Analyzing Assessment Findings

Two techniques that combine internal and external assessment are SWOT analysis and a modified Boston Matrix, which charts benefit to participants versus impact on organizational or individual resources.

Sample SWOT Analysis
Proposed program: Teaching older adults who live in a residential facility to write poetry.

	Helpful to achieving the objective	Harmful to achieving the objective
Internal (attributes of the individual or organization)	I know how to perform poetry. I have a passion for working with older adults. I have some available time.	I need to make a living. I am chronically late to appointments. I don't know if I can teach.
External (attributes of the environment)	There is an assisted living facility down the street from my house. I have some friends who are also poets whom I may enlist to help, and several of them also teach. The new director of the community foundation fancies himself a poet. There was recently a long article in the local newspaper about poetry.	The assisted living facility has recently been sold, and there will be a new administrator. The activities director says the residents don't like to participate in activities. Residents' meals and my schedule don't exactly mesh. A number of residents seem to have dementia.

fig. 6-1

SWOT is an acronym for:

- **Strengths:** Attributes of the organization or individual that are helpful to achieving the objective
- **Weaknesses:** Attributes of the organization or individual that are harmful to achieving the objective
- **Opportunities:** External conditions helpful to achieving the objective.
- **Threats:** External conditions harmful to achieving the objective.[57]

Once you complete the internal and external assessment phase, a SWOT analysis organizes the results so that you can make an informed decision (fig. 6-1, p. 77).

The modified Boston Matrix, which charts benefit to participants versus impact on organizational or individual resources, is a particularly useful technique when prioritizing among several programmatic options (fig. 6-2).

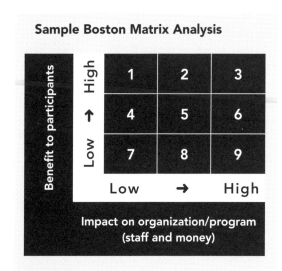

fig. 6-2

Consider two hypothetical program ideas:

1. Providing teaching artists in the visual arts to work with older adults and their caregivers in the home. This program has a high benefit to participants and a high cost, so it would be a 3 on the grid.

2. Working in partnership with a senior center to provide teaching artists in the visual arts to attendees. This program has a high benefit to participants and a low impact on staff and expenses, so it would be a 1 on the grid.

The smart choice is program 2.

Creating an Advisory Committee

One way to remain relevant to participants and other stakeholders and true to your mission and values is to form an advisory committee. Typically, committee members provide advice and guidance on program design and implementation. The external assessment process informs the selection of committee members who, in general, are potential partners, participants, and funders and are knowledgeable about some aspect of your program or the community to be served. If the proposed program is within another organization, the board of directors may serve this purpose; in a residential facility, the residents' council may be your advisory committee.

Just as program design is an ongoing process, your advisory group may exist indefinitely. As long as it is helpful to you and members feel that they are making a valuable contribution, there is no reason not to keep it.

You may want members to help plan programs or marketing, advocacy, or public relations campaigns, or be available when needed to provide expertise.

Before issuing invitations by phone or in person, create a mission for the committee and a job description for members. The mission can be as simple as providing expert advice from time to time and as complex as serving as a quasi-board. Be clear with potential members about expectations, roles, responsibilities, and the amount of time required. Figure out in advance how the group will operate:

- Will members meet as a group or be available to you for individual consultations?
- Will they meet by phone or in person? How often and for how long?
- Who will be the chair? Will the leadership rotate among members?
- Will members serve for a finite period?

Once the committee is established, keep members involved and take advantage of their expertise. Don't create it if you aren't going to use it.

Program Example:
Mission and Responsibilities—Advisory Committee

Mission

The Advisory Board, under delegated authority of the College for Lifelong Learning, is accountable for OLLI at Manchester program activities and operations. As representatives of the OLLI at Manchester membership, the Advisory Board is responsible for working to ensure that the program realizes its purpose. Advisory Board members articulate and represent OLLI program goals in their communities.

Responsibilities

1. Develop an agreement with the College for Lifelong Learning outlining lines of authority, roles, and responsibilities to ensure the effective governance, management, and operations of the OLLI at Manchester program.
2. Develop program policies and short-term and long-range program goals.
3. Monitor and evaluate effectiveness of program against the goals and plans.
4. Monitor program finances:
   » Review and approve the annual budget.
   » Review, approve, and participate in funding strategies and action plans.
5. Engage members in appropriate roles to achieve the program's short-term and long-range goals.
   » Appoint leadership of curriculum, publicity, and volunteer committees.
   » Participate on one committee.
   » Plan for the continued leadership of the Advisory Board.
6. Advocate for the program in the community.
7. Participate with Advisory Board members of other NH OLLI programs in the statewide network as appropriate.

Establishing Purpose

An organization's or program's purpose is derived from the information collected during the assessment process and the reflections or discussions catalyzed by the results. Like assessment, this planning component helps build the framework for your program. There are various ways to express purpose. Mission, vision, values, goals, objectives, activities — the terminology is confusing, and the how-to-plan literature doesn't always help. If you have an idea for a program, do you need a mission or a goal statement? What is the difference in wording? How does the purpose relate to the outcome goals we learned about earlier in the toolkit? And where does vision fit into the picture?

The short answer is: Don't get hung up on terminology. But a longer answer is more useful in program design. This section looks at:

- Determining mission, vision, and values
- Setting goals and objectives

Determining Mission, Vision, and Values

For organizations, the key concepts are mission (why you exist and what you hope to accomplish) and vision (what will happen if you accomplish your mission). Make your mission clear and concise enough to communicate your raison d'être to funders, policy makers, partners, and the community

---

Program Examples: Vision, Mission, and Values

EngAGE: The Art of Active Aging (formerly More Than Shelter For Seniors)
Vision: It is our vision to make aging a beginning.

Mission: By providing life-enhancing programs to low- and moderate-income seniors living in affordable apartment communities, they will be given the opportunity to continue to grow intellectually, creatively, and emotionally. Programming will focus on the combination of mind, body, and spirit to promote active engagement and independent living, and to provide seniors with a purpose.

Evergreens Senior Healthcare
Vision: The vision of the Evergreens Senior Healthcare is to become a model organization for long-term care.

OASIS
Mission: OASIS is a national nonprofit educational organization designed to enhance the quality of life for mature adults. Offering challenging programs in the arts, humanities, wellness, technology, and volunteer service, OASIS creates opportunities for older adults to continue their personal growth and provide meaningful service to the community.

Kairos Dance Theatre
Values: We believe there are many ways of dancing, and that each person has his or her own dance to share and story to tell.

Luella Hannan Memorial Foundation
Values: The Luella Hannan Memorial Foundation believes that caring for our elders is a central value of our community.

at large. Mission is grounded; vision is the dream, the desired future. Both should convey the spirit, if not the specific words, of one or more of the outcome goals described in chapter 5. Some organizations include a sentence about values or principles that permeate every aspect of the organization. Value statements typically begin with "We believe."

Setting Goals and Objectives
Programs generally have goals and objectives as opposed to mission and vision, which are organizational statements. One explanation is: "The vision expresses what could be, the assessment describes what is, and goals describe what it would be like if the gap between the vision and reality were bridged."[58]

Goals are future-oriented and results-oriented and answer these questions:

- What do you want to accomplish in the long term, and why?
- What difference are you trying to make in the lives of those served? Of family members? Of the community?
- What do you want this program to look like in three years?

A model goal is: Enhance older adults' physical and mental health by engaging them in participatory arts programs in the community.

Objectives describe what you are going to do to achieve your goals in the short term. They are specific and measurable and answer these questions:

- What specifically do you want to accomplish in the next year or during the length of the program?
- What specific changes or improvements do you want to see in place by the end of this year or at the end of the program?
- What observable outcomes should you be able to see if the program succeeds?
- What results could be measured or counted?[59]

Model objectives are:

- Over the next two years, create a partnership between the local senior center and a fifth-grade class at the local school that results in an original play written, directed, and acted by participants about a common community issue.

- Form a New Horizons Band with a target membership of 30 older adults at the beginning of the first semester and 40 at the beginning of the second.

- Expand the existing partnership with our local public library to include a book group on local authors and poets composed of no fewer than 10 older adults that meets once a month.

There can be a direct correlation between a specific goal and one or more objectives, or all of the objectives can work together to support one or more goals. A single, correct formula doesn't exist. Like mission and vision, goals and objectives touch on outcome goals for older adults.

CHAPTER 6: PROGRAM DESIGN

One technique to develop goals and objectives is to discuss the questions on the previous page with your staff, board members, advisory committee, and funders. Having an experienced facilitator is helpful. It is a good idea to devote focused time, perhaps a daylong retreat, to this component of planning.

Program Examples: Goals

Alzheimer's Poetry Project

Goal: The goal of the Alzheimer's Poetry Project is to enhance the quality of life for people with Alzheimer's disease, their families, and professional healthcare workers.

TimeSlips Project

Goals: The TimeSlips Project aims to

» inspire people with dementia to hone and share the gifts of their imaginations;

» inspire others to see beyond the loss and to recognize the strengths of people with dementia; and

» improve the quality of life of people with dementia and those who care for them.

Center for Elders and Youth in the Arts

Goal: Through creative expression, elders remain connected to the community and experience improved physical and emotional well-being.

Designing Activities

Activities are general approaches or methods used to fulfill objectives. The objective describes what you *want* to accomplish, and the corresponding activities outline *how* you will accomplish it. Consider these examples:

Objective
Legacy Works provides a platform for enhancing connections between elders and their caregivers.

> *Activity*
> Elders in the program are guided to retrieve memories of key life experiences that reveal their values and beliefs. Participants are encouraged to give form to their memories through visual arts—such as collage, photo essay, drawing, and painting—that are then shared in a community setting.

Objective
The Art from the Heart program is a means of qualitatively improving care and quality of life by offering nursing home residents the opportunity for creative expression and enhanced living.

> *Activity*
> The program features a juried competition of visual art works from nursing home residents created independently or in activities programs. Selected works are chosen for publication in a full-color annual calendar for distribution to a wide range of outlets and stakeholders. Additional selected works are chosen for a public exhibition in the Albany Institute of History and Art.

Create activities that are fun for all:

- For cognitively fit older adults, activities should focus on acquiring, rediscovering and retaining knowledge, skills, and talents in the arts.

- For people with dementia, activities should focus on using the arts to trigger memories and communicate with friends, family, and caregivers.

Start by sitting down with key stakeholders—partners, professional teaching artists, and participants. Review your goals and objectives, and brainstorm what you are going to do. You may be creating something new or expanding an existing program. Including older adult participants regardless of ability (cognitively fit, frail, or with dementia) is important because people learn from making artistic choices. Exercising self-determination contributes to their quality of life.

How Two Organizations Design Activities

At the Luella Hannan Memorial Foundation, older adults, community organizations, and staff get involved:

1. Older adults who participate in arts programs or lifelong learning classes—or who receive social services at Hannan House, a multiservice center—make suggestions for new activities to the foundation staff.

2. Community organizations also inquire about specific activities and/or working in partnership to explore relevant issues.

3. The staff brainstorms ideas with participants, typically taking a few minutes at the beginning of a class to solicit opinions and advice. They must have participants' endorsement to move ahead with planning.

4. The staff researches possible partnerships or contractual relationships that would provide expertise and resources for success and long-term sustainability.

The Osher Lifelong Learning Institute at the University of Southern Maine has a catalogue of courses designed by a curriculum committee composed of older adult members:

1. Interested instructors submit a 100-word course description and summary of their education and experience.

2. Committee members compare proposals with existing classes to ensure a balance of subjects.

3. They identify missing subjects and solicit proposals from previous instructors, retired teachers, or other community members with the requisite expertise and passion.

Applying Andragogy and Instructional Design

Activities are just activities unless you plan how they work together to effect learning. Understanding andragogy and instructional design is essential to enhancing older adults' quality of life.

- *Andragogy* is learner-focused education. The term typically describes the art and science of helping adults learn. It is closely related to the effective practices discussed in chapter 5, especially participatory, sequential learning and the learning community. Principles of andragogy inform instructional design.

- *Instructional design* is task oriented. It implies strategic solutions to specific situations. Other comparable terms are *lesson plan* and *activity sequence.* Instructional design supports principles of andragogy.

Together, these concepts are linked to the outcome goals of mastery and social engagement introduced in chapter 5. (Remember that mastery applies more to cognitively fit older adults than to those with dementia.)

- *Building mastery* through andragogy and instructional design involves introducing experiences gradually, beginning at the point at which the participant is confident and comfortable. Each new level of experience involves a slightly greater challenge. Along the way, participants see their success and receive positive feedback.[60]

- *Building social engagement* through andragogy and instructional design is more or less self-evident: all programs involve a group. Moreover, the arts engender a special sense of "stick-to-itiveness" and are particularly well suited for facilitating social connections among older adults.

Teaching artists need to understand the importance of encouraging participants rather than providing direct assistance. The outcome goals of mastery and social engagement are largely unattainable unless older adults make their own choices, explore their own creativity, and successfully overcome challenges by themselves, but with the support of others. John W. Rowe and Robert L. Kahn elaborate:

> An experiment in a nursing home compared mental performance under three conditions in which the kind of social support varied. Nursing home residents were assigned randomly to three groups, each of which had the same task—completion of a simple jigsaw puzzle. All three groups had four twenty-minute practice sessions, followed by a timed test session. People in the first group were given verbal engagement by the experimenter during practice—"Now you're getting it…. That's right…. Well done." People in the second group were given direct assistance—"Are you having a little trouble with the piece? Let me show you where it goes." People in the third group were given neither assistance nor encouragement during practice. In subsequent tests, people who had been encouraged improved in speed and proficiency. People who had been directly assisted did less well than in practice. And people who had been left alone neither improved or deteriorated.[61]

You can effect mastery and social engagement in an arts and aging program by understanding these components:

- Establishing trust
- Setting challenges
- Ensuring success
- Accommodating diversity
- Encouraging participation
- Setting session length, duration, and frequency
- Facilitating a learning community

Establishing Trust

Only in an environment of trust can older adults test their limits without fear of failure. One way to establish trust is through the sequence of activities. A familiar sequence or structure engenders trust. Even the basic arc of a session—beginning, middle, and end—builds trust, mirroring not only our earliest memories of stories, but also the life cycle.

In deciding how to sequence activities, focus on "scaffolding risk" by leading participants step by step through exercises in which they

---

Program Examples: Building Mastery and Social Engagement

Elders Share the Arts' Living History Program lasts 25 weeks, with each phase building on the preceding phase:

　　Phase 1. Trust building and skill building through improvisational theater, movement, and visual art or writing exercises

　　Phase 2. Oral history interviewing and storytelling exercises to elicit specific memories

　　Phase 3. Artistic development of a living history play

　　Phase 4. The culminating event— a living history festival

TimeSlips—a one-session program—uses storytelling to invite contributions from all participants.

1. Facilitators greet participants individually and then show the assembled "storytellers" whimsical, dramatic, provocative photographs.

2. Using open-ended questions, they elicit responses to the images that create a story, which is reread after every four or five answers to establish momentum and remind the storytellers of what they've created.

3. The telling format involves crediting individuals for their contributions as the tale builds. No narrative logic is necessary to express the participants' humor, desires, and sometimes sadness.

4. Facilitators record the story to share with staff and families.

increasingly reveal more of themselves to the group. For example,

- Do a movement warm-up, followed by group storytelling and then sharing selected stories with the broader community.

- Start with the familiar and move into the unknown. Place music or singing first, for example, and progress to activities that feature writing or dance.

When selecting topics for storytelling, writing, or movement, build trust by guiding newly formed groups in exploring less personal issues than may be discussed in established groups where there is already a high level of trust. In the former, participants may discover what they have in common; in the latter, they may focus on dreams or memories.

A trust-building exercise might be designed like this:

1. Each elder presents the person to his or her right with an imaginary gift that the giver thinks the recipient would like to receive—an object, an idea, or an emotion.

2. The giver should know exactly what the gift is and try to present it as if it were real, not imaginary.

3. After presenting the gift, the giver explains what it is. The recipient feels accepted, confident, and happy.[62]

Program Examples: How Sequence Builds Trust

Transitional Keys uses the elements of ritual to benefit the lives of older adults. This program has

» a beginning in which the intention and anticipated benefit of the ritual are stated;

» a middle in which an activity symbolically fulfills the intention; and

» an end in which there is a ceremonial closing that reflects back the intention and reinforces the benefit.[63]

Yamaha's Clavinova Connection suggests this sequence of activities for each session:

1. Arrival song—Played while the facilitator welcomes participants

2. Warm-up—Music, movement, imagery, and awareness

3. Drum circle—Each keyboard simulates a drum kit

4. Improvisation—Pentatonic-based exercises performed with dynamic soundscapes

5. Music insight—A discussion of musical concepts

6. Song of the day—Group and individual playing of a designated song to condition a sense of fulfillment, enthusiasm, and personal accomplishment

7. Mind-body wellness—A Clavinova cool-down that repeats the initial exercise

8. Reflection—A group discussion focused on awareness and progress

9. Farewell song—To inspire a light-hearted spirit in anticipation of the next class.[64]

"Icebreakers" or warm-ups are a typical beginning for a session. In effective instructional design, they establish trust, encourage participation, and help ensure success. Susan Perlstein explains why:

> Individuals arrive preoccupied with different thoughts and feelings. We need to channel these disparate energies into a unified group. This process of "centering"—moving from the world of daily activities into a creative world—enables people to experience heightened states of receptivity, spontaneity, and imagination. Warm-ups awaken the senses and unlock memories, preparing the group to become involved in creative expression.[65]

When you design icebreakers, keep in mind that they don't have to be complicated. They can be as simple as asking each participant to say his or her name and who named them. Make icebreakers authentic to the artistic discipline—for example, movement or gestures in dance or drama and vocal exercises in music. Ensure that they are appropriate to participants' abilities. People with dementia might breathe deeply; cognitively fit older adults might make a movement that symbolizes something personal or significant.

Icebreakers might be designed like this:

- Each person says his or her name with a gesture or movement and passes it to the next person or to a person across the room. The recipient can repeat the combination and pass it on or change all or part of it.

Acting is giving, and I still have a lot to give.

Cecil, 87, actor, Stagebridge Senior Theatre Company

- In an intergenerational group:

  1. Ask participants to arrange themselves in a line from youngest to oldest, which requires conversation.

  2. Starting at one end of the line, each person states his or her age.

  3. Recognize the oldest and youngest participants with applause, and calculate the age range.

  4. Tell everyone that they may now choose to move anywhere along the age line they would rather be.

  5. Discuss where people moved to and why, and why others chose not to move. What did people who moved have in common? What surprised people?

- The leader of the group makes different sounds, and the group repeats them. Begin with vowel sounds, which are easy to remember and tend to open the throat and mouth. Change leaders and experiment with different sounds.

Setting Challenges

Setting mental and physical challenges that older adults can overcome is another component of achieving mastery. It is closely related to establishing trust. Indeed, all of the exercises designed to build trust can also be challenging to participants.

To create achievable challenges, you need to understand what participants can do. Keep in mind that, in large measure, "challenge" is an individual concept; what is easy for one participant may be hard for another. Test the limits of a woman with arthritis, for example, by asking her to work with clay or make an arm movement. Ask a man who is hard of hearing to play an instrument; a woman who has had a stroke and slurs her speech to recite a poem that she has written; or a person with dementia to sing an old song.

The point is obvious: Challenge participants, *but* push them only as far as they want to go. Remember: It is always about older adults' abilities as opposed to their age or your perception of their abilities. Be attentive during your session. Watch for signs of frustration or boredom, and adjust accordingly.

This guidance is also true when working with people with dementia. Don't underestimate what they can accomplish. In fact, one challenge you might face is the perception of family members and professional caregivers that the person with dementia can't participate in a meaningful way or benefit from the experience.

Program Examples: Setting Challenges

Stagebridge Senior Theatre Company assumes that all actors will rise to the bar that is set, and the bar is generally high. Directors insist that actors learn their lines and teach them how to recover when there are problems during a performance. There are no understudies, so actors know that everyone is depending on them. The show must go on. The message is powerful: they are an integral part of something bigger than themselves. The rehearsal period for older adults may be longer than for younger actors, but once they learn the piece, they don't forget it.

As part of a story-quilt project at *Elder Craftsmen*, the teaching artist planned for participants to draw images for their templates. But the drawing task overwhelmed them. The artist switched to photography, and the older adults snapped pictures that she then enlarged. Participants traced the enlarged images to create the templates.

Gary Glazner, founder of the *Alzheimer's Poetry Project*, entered a small group home to engage the residents in reciting poetry. Staff steered him toward the one resident they judged to be more aware than the others. In spite of this direction, he worked with all four residents. At the end of the session, one of the "less aware" women blew him kisses. The staff was amazed.

Ensuring Success

Overcoming challenges and ensuring success are closely related. Develop techniques that are authentic to your artistic discipline, and don't make inexperience or failure obvious. No one wants to be singled out for lagging behind. In addition to the examples in the preceding section, try the following methods or use them to stimulate your own ideas:

- Allow people to participate without auditioning.

- Place experienced members of a music group next to those who are just learning to play or sing.

- Ask participants in an orchestra to sing before picking up their instruments so they aren't learning a tune and how to play it at the same time.

- Give older adults who lack specific theater experience small roles in a play or a support position that enables them to observe the rehearsal and production processes.

- Have various sizes of pens, markers, and pencils available in a visual arts session to accommodate participants whose hands may have lost dexterity.

Your job is not only to ensure that older adults succeed, but also to make sure they know that they are succeeding. Just as you think of a roadmap for planning—figuring out where you are, where you want go, and how you're going to get there—participants benefit from understanding how they are going to achieve program objectives.

Accommodating Diversity

Accommodating diversity is a critical component of a community arts and aging program. Indeed, the arts are an effective tool for bridging differences in ability, age, culture, and ethnicity because arts-based communication can bypass language that may interfere with mutual understanding. The participants in a performing group ideally should reflect the diversity of the audiences. Seeing people on the stage with whom they can identify because of ethnicity and age reinforces value and the message that you're conveying. Even among older adults, there are differences to accommodate in your program. Remember that this cohort is quite large. Maddie Sifantus of The Golden Tones, for example, notes that some of her younger 60s want to sing Elvis, while others want to learn music from the 1920s and 1930s.

Instructional design should treat diversity as an opportunity. Emphasize integration, not segregation. In a music ensemble, for example, give each person a task based on his or her skill level. The first step in learning how to play music is to be able to hear it, the next step is to listen and keep a beat, and the next step is to follow the sheet music and keep your place. Finally, you play. In a mixed-level ensemble, beginners follow along and play when they know their parts. A mixture of ability levels also provides one-on-one contact and mentorship. Facilitate these interactions by having players of different skills share music stands.

To enhance diversity in intergenerational programs, hold separate orientation sessions to explore age stereotypes, attitudes, and assumptions. Consider the ages of the young people; for example, structured music, dance, storytelling, and arts activities work well for preschool children. Fourth- to seventh-graders respond to questions about the community or neighborhood, while teenagers are more focused on jobs and careers. Well elders are better suited than are frail elders for programs that take place in schools.

Encouraging Participation
Follow the principles of adult learning and involve cognitively fit older adults in their own learning. Ask professional caregivers to participate, or just to observe. Even if older adults sign up to take a class, volunteer for a workshop at a senior center, or take part in a session at an assisted living facility, they may be initially reluctant to speak. Novelty can be intimidating.

Overcome self-doubt by starting each session with a warm-up or icebreaker at which participants can easily succeed. For older adults in the later stages of dementia, spark participation through the concrete, not the abstract: objects, photos, food, and music. For frail older adults, a little finger moving or glimmer of an eye shows involvement.

Sometimes, in spite of your best efforts, you aren't able to elicit any sound or action. "Patience," recommends Janine Tursini, executive director of Arts for the Aging. "Respect a person's boundaries, but keep going back. Maybe participation, for now, means just being in the room."

While your focus is on older adults as art-makers, pay attention to involving them as audience members. Participants in performance-oriented programs often appear before groups of their peers and/or those who live in residential facilities. Particularly in an intimate setting, these audiences benefit from interaction with the performers. The techniques are intuitive. Ask people to

- sing along with a familiar song or two, or join in on the chorus;
- make arm movements that complement the dance or tune;
- clap their hands to establish a rhythm; or
- play simple percussion instruments that you've brought along.

Those who are cognitively fit might enjoy a question and answer session with the performers and artistic staff after the show.

Typically, professional caregivers in a facility may be required to attend programs to provide assistance if necessary. Try to get them to join the residents in interacting with the performers or participating in the activities, but even if they just observe, they will learn. Helping them to respect and appreciate the older adults in their care as people is a good thing.

Setting Session Length and Frequency
Determining the optimum timing for a session requires balancing the desired outcomes, the abilities of the participants,

the complexity of the activities, the benefits of long-term participation and engagement, and reality. Older adults, like everyone else, can absorb only so much information at any one time. Unlike younger people, they may have physical issues such as arthritis that prevent them from sitting or moving for an extended period. Most current arts and aging programs last one to two hours.

"The duration of an activity is more important than the nature of the activity itself," reports Dr. Gene Cohen. "Long-duration or repeating activities are better for establishing new relationships and making new friends."[66] Current arts and aging programs vary dramatically, so there is no magic number. Long-tenured organizations generally run programs for a minimum of six months, and multiyear programs are common.

For frequency, if the gap between sessions is too long, participants may forget what was learned, especially if they have dementia. Anne Basting, founder of the TimeSlips storytelling project, says that "once a week seems to be the magic interval for subconscious memory—if we held sessions more than this, the activity would become stale. If we held them less, we would have to reestablish trust and understanding."[67] For older adults of all abilities, most current arts and aging programs meet once a week.

Time of day is important, as well, and the rule of thumb is to convene during daylight hours. For well elders, the evening is not ideal because many are reluctant to drive at night or leave their homes after dark. And for older adults with dementia, the twilight hours are typically a time of agitation.

If the only option because of finances or schedules is to plan fewer sessions for a shorter period, go ahead. Sometimes getting your foot in the door is a big accomplishment. Start small and grow.

Facilitating a Learning Community

A learning community is the intersection of trust, challenges, success, diversity, and participation with the purpose of continuous learning. The mutual support and mental stimulation that result from interacting with and learning from others contribute to older adults' desire to stick with arts programs. In addition, a learning community provides social engagement during art making; informal socializing at the beginning and end of the session; and motivation for everyone in the group to keep practicing.

Your role is to encourage and facilitate this interaction by

- allowing time for informal socializing;
- designing exercises to elicit personal—not private—information;
- designing the instruction so that participants have to work in pairs or teams;
- asking participants to help each other;
- modeling and encouraging respect for each other;
- celebrating and honoring accomplishments;
- emphasizing participation; and
- asking participants to assume responsibilities, such as remembering topics from one

session to the next or leading a discussion or activity.

Evaluation

Program design must include planning for evaluation, which is an ongoing process. Continually assessing effectiveness, checking in with participants, and making adjustments as necessary help ensure success. (Chapter 8 deals with evaluation in more detail.)

Build enough time for evaluation into your overall program and within specific sessions. If you plan to ask participants to complete surveys or respond to questions in a focus group, factor this into the schedule. For participants who have dementia, also consider the timing of soliciting evaluative information from family members and/or professional caregivers.

To help conceptualize evaluation, create a program logic model, which is a picture of the theory and assumptions underlying your program (fig. 6-3). It links short-term and long-term outcomes with program activities, processes, assumptions, and principles. This model also clarifies thinking, planning, and communications about

Program Logic Model

Assumptions	Inputs →	Activities →	Outputs →	Outcomes →	Impact
	You need certain resources to operate your programs.	If you have access to the necessary inputs, you can use them to accomplish your planned activities.	If you accomplish planned activities, ideally you will deliver the product or service that you intended.	If you accomplish planned activities to the intended extent, your participants will benefit in certain ways.	If these benefits to participants are achieved, certain changes in organizations, communities, or systems might occur.
Your beliefs about the program, people, environment, and the way you think the program will work	Human, financial, organizational, or community resources	Products, services, or infrastructure	Size, scope, number of services and products delivered or produced	Changes in attitude, behaviors, knowledge, skills, status, or level of functioning (expressed at an individual level)	Organizational-, community-, and/or system-level changes
	Your planned work		**Your intended results**		

fig. 6-3

a program's objectives and benefits and results in more effective programming, greater learning opportunities for participants, and better documentation of outcomes. (See Appendix 1 for a program logic model for a hypothetical program.)

Reminiscence

Reminiscence helps older adults make sense of and reconcile life experiences. Renya T. H. Larson explains that it can serve adaptive functions, including

- maintaining self-esteem;
- reinforcing personal and collective identity;
- resolving grief; and
- helping to assuage the anxiety of physical and mental decline.

It also stimulates memory function and socialization—and it can be just plain fun for older adults, as they recall pleasurable experiences and perhaps even find solace in sharing painful ones.[68]

Because older adults have accumulated a lifetime of experiences, memories, and knowledge, reminiscence is both content and a door through which you lead participants to activities at which they can succeed. "They have a lifetime of music in their heads; if you use that, the progress is so fast," explains Roy Ernst, founder of New Horizons Music. Even if teaching artists and participants elect to focus on current issues, their work together will be influenced by memories.

> *We dig behind closed memories to emotions locked away—something unhappy, but sometimes funny, sometimes in wonder, with new insight. Then we have to translate those into words that we can bear to utter, that others can bear to listen to. Our group listens, always with a constructive ear. It is this awakening, this struggle, and the listening that makes the magic.*
>
> Program participant

Reminiscence is pertinent to older adults with dementia even if they can't always connect their words or images to the past. Visual art is a communication tool with which they can tell facilitators, family, and staff about who they are and what they've experienced in life. While reminiscence works well for people in the early stages of dementia who are trying to hang on to memories, it may be too frustrating for those in the middle to late stages of the disease.

Themes that may stimulate participants' memory include: work we have loved, places these feet have walked, these hands, play, something you miss, something you wish, summertime, your favorite vacation, unexpected moment, sporting events, moments of surprise, acts of kindness, first love, first kiss, or moments of support.

Senses—sight, touch, hearing, taste, and smell—may invoke memory using fabrics, herbs, photographs, strawberries, or music. If a participant is visually or hearing impaired, appeal to his or her sense of touch or smell. Regardless of age or ability, people have some senses that are more acute than others.

Try this approach to reminiscence:

1. Ask each participant to shake hands with a partner whom they don't know well, and take the time to notice each other's hand: Are there any rings? Is the hand smooth or rough?

2. Ask questions about your partner's hand: What kind of work have these hands done? Where did that ring come from?

3. Bring the group back together and ask each person to describe how his or her hand feels and any difference in sensation before and after the exercise.

4. Ask each person to share one story about his or her partner.

5. Review the stories for familiar themes, and record them for future use — in a poem, for example.

Be aware that not all older adults want to reminisce about a particular theme or at that specific time. Cultural mores may sometimes preclude sharing personal memories as well.

Related to reminiscence is oral history. Consider employing this technique if your program is intergenerational. Plan for younger participants to interview older adults on tape to elicit subject matter for art making, transmit knowledge between generations, and give the older adults a measure of immortality as their stories live on.

Community Sharing of Art

The art-making process is where the magic happens and, for the most part, how older adult participants' lives are transformed. An important addition is the external recognition of the challenges they have overcome and their awareness that the community in which they live values who they are, as represented by what they've created.

In addition to enhancing mastery and social engagement, community sharing of the art produced in programs for older adults is intended to

- pull the group together as they focus on a common goal;
- create a public forum in which the group can express itself;
- provide a meaningful event in which the community can assert its identity or grapple with its issues; and
- create a public space to celebrate and strengthen the community.[69]

In addition, community arts activities help

- promote a program, organization, or residential facility within a community;
- educate the public about the creative potential of people with dementia;
- recruit volunteers and financial supporters;
- build connections among families of people with dementia; and

- encourage staff to feel greater pride and job satisfaction.[70]

Think about the community sharing of the art as a ceremonial conclusion to your program. In this respect, it is similar to the familiar structure of beginning, middle, and end.

Leaders in the arts and aging field, when asked about the relative value of process and "product" (an imperfect term often used to describe the art that is created), generally agree that they are equally important. John Borstel, humanities director at Liz Lerman Dance Exchange, articulates this philosophy: "The ideal is that you don't have to make a choice between the value of high-quality aesthetic experience and the value of participation. Process and product coexist and inform one another…. We can have two ideas at once; they are horizontal, not vertical."

Consider how to effect this community sharing of the art as part of planning. Participants may produce a book, sculpture, play, open workshop, visual art exhibit, note cards, or calendar, or they may do a staged reading or a choral, band, or dance performance. Don't commit to any one of these options before the program begins, however. Involve participants in the decision, and hold this discussion about halfway through the program, allowing time for participants to form a learning community.

Key Points about Program Planning

- Allow sufficient time for planning.
- Take time to inform future plans by evaluating the past.
- Assess yourself or your organization before looking at the broader community.
- Identify stakeholders who have a stake in you and your work.
- Flesh out your program with stakeholders, particularly potential participants.
- Consider forming an advisory committee.
- Articulate a purpose for your program.
- Develop specific activities that achieve the program's purpose.
- Create an instructional design utilizing the activities and supporting andragogical principles.
- Emphasize the importance of encouraging—rather than doing for—participants.
- Consider how you will evaluate the impact of your program.
- Understand the role of reminiscence and the community sharing of the art.

Finding and Working with Partners

Programs developed collaboratively among partners have a sustained impact on the older adult participants' quality of life. Staff members benefit as well from the process of developing a partnership and the support of a learning community. Keys to an effective partnership are communication among members of the partnership team, meeting each other's needs, clarifying responsibilities in writing, and educating all staff who might be involved in the program. Though there are challenges, if you and your partners commit to an ongoing dialogue and keep the needs of the participants as your touchstone, your collaboration will have a long-term, win-win-win collaboration. The adage is true: "Two heads are better than one."

Working in partnership with another organization may not be necessary if you have the expertise and resources in-house to design and implement a program that will have a positive impact on older adults. A lifelong learning institute or a community school of the arts, for example, may be effective without formal partners. Such an organization does, however, need to work in partnership with teaching artists and program participants. In community arts, all segments of the community are partners.

Much has been written about the process, benefits, successes, and challenges of partnerships. This toolkit section focuses on advice and examples that are most relevant to arts and aging work:

- Understanding partnerships
- Planning partnerships
- Identifying and securing partners
- Training partners
- Implementing the partnership

Understanding Partnerships

Writing about nonprofit arts partnerships as "an art form," Thomas E. Backer makes the following observations:

1. Systematic planning is critical to the ultimate success of partnerships, leading to a set of objectives and activities that the partnership's members can support.

2. Psychological challenges, such as power differences among the partners or resistances based upon previous bad experiences with other partnerships, can seriously jeopardize the chances for success. The partnership must focus on identifying potential challenges and then taking active steps to resolve them.

3. A strong core idea or intervention strategy lies at the heart of most successful partnerships—they're "about something" that is concrete and relatively easy for the partners to identify.

> *Stagebridge's "Storybridge" artist-in-residence program is the best language development program we have ever had in our classroom. My students are getting up in front of the room and expressing themselves, in a way that means something to them! With the current state of funding for the arts, our students don't get these opportunities.*
>
> Third-grade teacher, Fruitvale School

4. Partnerships are not cost-free. They require financial and human resources to be successful.

5. Strategies learned from other successful partnerships can be incorporated usefully into a new partnering activity, especially if these strategies are available at the critical early planning stages.

6. Partnerships that succeed over time also evolve over time, as they learn from their successes and failures and maintain responsiveness to their community environments.

7. Good partnerships begin with a due diligence process to look at the pros and cons of partnering, including an estimate of needed start-up costs, done before the initial decision to partner is made.

8. If a partnership is intended to survive over a longer period, planning for sustainability is needed at the outset, including creation of a revenue model that will provide financial support beyond initial funding (e.g., a time-limited foundation or government grant).[71]

Backer also outlines the typical life cycle of a partnership:

1. Planning
2. Setting objectives
3. Defining leadership
4. Defining membership
5. Mobilizing resources
6. Integrating with the community environment
7. Implementing the partnership
8. Evaluating the partnership
9. Promoting sustainability[72]

Planning Partnerships

Identifying and securing an organizational partner with whom you can grow (i.e., a "planning partnership") requires a systematic approach with plenty of lead time: from two months to a year. Develop as much as possible of the program with your partner or partners, with the goal of creating a win-win-win situation for each organization and for participants. This means assessing compatibility—alignment of values, mission, and philosophy of care—and capacity—what you need to do versus what can be done.

Use the following checklist when you investigate and meet with potential partners and decide collaboratively how to design, implement, and evaluate the program. This list also serves as an accountability checklist for the partnership and the foundation for the written partnership agreement:

- We have a common vision for older adults.
- We have a common vision for working together that includes flexibility, mutual respect, trust, and ongoing communication.
- We have a common philosophy about how to work with older adults.
- Our organizational missions and/or goals are complementary.
- We have a common understanding of what success looks like.
- We are prepared to deal with change or failure.
- We have a common understanding of the difference we hope to make in the lives of the older adult participants and the young people (if relevant).
- We understand the impact that the program will have on each of our organizations/facilities.
- We have developed collaboratively the objectives, activities, and instructional design for the program.
- We know who will comprise the partnership team.
- We are comfortable with the experience and qualifications of the teaching artists/facilitators.
- We know who is in charge, and we have a plan for rotating leadership of the program in future years, if relevant.
- We each understand our respective roles, responsibilities, and expectations of being a member of the partnership team.
- We commit to being agreeable and courteous.
- We agree to educate each other and other staff as relevant on topics that will contribute to the success of the program.
- We have determined by "running the numbers" that it is more cost effective to collaborate.
- We know the financial and staff resources that each organization/facility will contribute to the program.
- We know how additional resources will be allocated.
- We have a contingency plan if we don't get needed additional funding.
- If our program is intergenerational, the content corresponds with state learning standards and/or the curriculum and lesson plans of schools or out-of-school programs.
- We know the length, duration, and frequency of the program.
- We know when the program will take place (month, week, day, and time).
- We know where—in which dedicated room—the program will take place.
- We know where we will store the art supplies and works in progress so that they can be secured.
- We know the maximum number of participants that we can safely and effectively accommodate in the program.

- We know how many staff members will accompany the group of participants.
- We have a plan for problem solving.
- We have an accountability system in place for the partnership agreement.
- We agree on how to share credit for the program.
- We have considered involving additional partners.
- We agree on our respective organizational and individual roles and responsibilities in the following areas:

    Resources
    » Serving as fiscal agent
    » Writing grant proposals
    » Soliciting businesses and corporations for cash and in-kind donations
    » Obtaining art supplies

    Logistics
    » Setting up the room each time and making sure it is unlocked in advance of the scheduled start time
    » Ensuring that the layout of the room makes it accessible to all participants
    » Ensuring that the participants get to the room for the program, if it takes place in a residential facility
    » Ensuring that each participant has a nametag

    Communications
    » Recruiting participants
    » Scheduling partnership team meetings
    » Keeping team members informed of issues or emergencies
    » Reminding participants about the program
    » Reminding staff about the program
    » Marketing any event that we might have as part of the program
    » Soliciting media coverage

    Intergenerational
    » Pairing participants
    » Maintaining discipline

- On behalf of our respective organizations/facilities, we commit to honoring our roles and responsibilities.
- We commit to having backup personnel to execute our roles and responsibilities.
- We have an evaluation plan for the program that includes regular partnership team meetings.
- We commit to helping the partnership evolve over time.
- We have a written partnership agreement signed by the leaders of the collaborating organizations/facilities.

A written agreement is essential to an effective partnership. Having everything clearly stated in writing means you can focus primarily on the program, not on the mechanics. But a piece of paper doesn't always guarantee a smooth-running partnership. To mitigate challenges, be sure the signatories are leaders who convey the value of the program throughout their organizations or facilities and that you have an accountability system in place to enforce the partnership agreement.

Identifying and Securing Partners

The next step is to find a partner with whom to flesh out the details and implement the program. One source is the list compiled during your external assessment process: stakeholders. But don't rule out competitors. OASIS, for example, occasionally partners with other lifelong learning institutes. Look for organizations with enlightened self-interest. Keep in mind that self-interest may be pragmatic as well as philosophical: employing artists, increasing ticket revenue, reducing staff turnover, or attracting new residents. Indeed, for residential facilities, a professionally led, participatory arts program is a marketing tool.

The Levine School of Music found a win-win-win partnership for one of its senior choruses. When the chorus elected at the last minute to rehearse throughout the summer, the space at the school was already booked. Instead, the school initiated a partnership with a residential facility that provides independent and assisted living. The partnership helped recruit new chorus members, provide enjoyment for residents, and market the facility.

Search for partner organizations that are stable and have a track record of long-term and effective partnerships. Good indicators of stability are long-tenured staff and sustained growth in the sophistication of programs. In an arts organization, look for an aging services partner that has a person-centered approach to caring for older adults. In an aging service organization, find an arts partner that has experience in community arts education and employs teaching artists.

Ask around the community, particularly the local arts agency or area agency on aging, to gain this information.

Where to Find Partners

Though likely partner organizations will vary by community, investigate these possibilities:

If you are in the arts field:
- Senior centers
- Area agencies on aging
- Independent living facilities
- Assisted living facilities
- Nursing or skilled care facilities
- Hospitals
- Adult day programs

If you are in the aging services field:
- Community schools of the arts or community arts education organizations
- Theater groups
- Art galleries
- Local arts agencies
- Museums
- Historical societies
- Arts centers
- Dance companies and studios
- Choral groups
- Local musicians' union
- Orchestra or chamber groups

If you are in either field:
- Houses of worship
- Libraries
- Banks

- YMCAs and YWCAs
- Schools
- School boards
- Colleges, universities, and community colleges
- Lifelong learning institutes

Good information sources on potential partners are the National Guild of Community Schools of the Arts and the National Center for Creative Aging.

Each of these groups has a different entry point. While ultimately you want the buy-in of top leaders, search first for an ally with whom you can strategize on how best to get institutional support.

- In an arts organization, your primary contact should be the staff member who is responsible for education or community outreach.

- In an aging services organization, look for activities directors or coordinators. An informal route is to talk with family members and residents themselves. If you spark their interest and enlist their assistance in advocating for your program, a facility or center that has a person-centered philosophy should pay attention.

- In K–12 schools, the best bet is to excite a classroom teacher about the benefits to students.

- At the university level, if there is not a lifelong learning institute, contact the head of the art department or school of social work.

Once you know what door to open, just pick up the phone and call. One conversation topic might be results of recent research into the benefits of arts participation to older adults. Ideally, your initial dialogue will lead to a meeting where key representatives discuss some of the big-picture items on the checklist, such as vision, mission, goals, and philosophy. If the partnership looks like a good fit, start talking about timeline, number of participants, budget, and responsibilities, and confirm members of the partnership team.

At the first planning meeting, provide written information that describes your organization and outlines the proposed partnership program, including objectives, activities, instructional design, responsibilities, timetable, and projected budget. Appendix 2 describes the Center for Elders and Youth in the Arts' general program schedule and timeline.

After the partner representatives have reflected on the program and discussed any issues internally, schedule a second meeting to finalize arrangements. Keep in mind that each partner has different priorities. For example,

> a home-care agency is primarily concerned with the basic needs of the elders: food, clothing, and safety…. A youth services agency is likely to want to ensure that the program will teach the teenagers to grow up to be responsible adults…. A nursing home or hospital will be concerned about the safe use of supplies such as scissors. It will want to clarify the relationship between the arts coordinator and its own

staff, in connection with the goals of recreational therapy.[73]

Most planning occurs with the partnership team, which is also involved in training program partners and then implementing, monitoring, and evaluating the program. This group is a learning community and the locus of ongoing communication. Members include:

- The teaching artist and program "leads" from each organization
- The day-to-day program coordinator
- The activities director from the senior center, adult day program, or residential facility
- The principal and classroom teacher (for an intergenerational program with a school)
- The executive director, program director, and lead teacher (for an intergenerational program with a community organization that offers out-of-school programs)

Be careful that the team is not too small or too large; between four and eight members is a good standard. The team needs a leader and a lead organization. One plan that contributes to the growth of each partner in a multiyear partnership is for the leadership to rotate each year. A good resource to help ensure effective team discussions is *Basic Facilitation Skills* (www.iaf-world.org/files/public/FacilitatorMnl.pdf).

Training Partners

Just because the partnership agreement has been signed and everything is in place doesn't mean that all of the players have the information that they need to ensure the success of the program. Inevitably, there are differences in organizational culture and expectations that weren't discussed in the team meetings. There are staff members at all levels who aren't part of the inner circle, but will be involved in some manner—for example, professional caregivers. It is important to broaden the circle of people the partnership team educates because of turnover. And the team should be prepared to conduct periodic training sessions throughout the program and have written materials to distribute to new staff or to offer as a refresher. An effective method is to plan joint professional development opportunities among team members and other staff. This approach creates and strengthens the learning community and each person's commitment to and knowledge of the program.

Cover these topics in training:

- Community arts
  - » Stressing the value of the process
  - » Managing expectations for the art that is created
  - » Conveying the importance to participants of the process and the product
- Professionally led artistic program versus entertainment or arts and crafts
- Normal aging
- Dementia

- Mores of the facility where the program will be conducted
- Language and acronyms

Don't assume that the staff of an aging services organization understands normal aging or that the staff of an arts organization understands the nuances of community arts. In dance, for example, traditional instruction is top-down. But in creating a dance with a community, the work is bottom-up, soliciting ideas and movements from everyone.

Implementing the Partnership

The key to success as you move forward together to implement the partnership is communication among members of the partnership team. Plan regular meetings, and don't hesitate to pick up the phone. Don't let issues fester.

Whether you are new or experienced at partnerships, challenges are inevitable. According to a report from the Wallace Foundation,

> partnerships can fail for three major reasons: partners can't carry out their assignments ("capacity risk"), won't do so ("commitment risk"), or can't agree on what counts as success ("culture risk"). There is also a fourth risk—the risk of unanticipated costs.[74]

Other challenges include:

- The artistic temperament

- The activities director at a senior center, adult day program, or residential facility feeling threatened by a successful arts and aging program or by dynamic "outsiders" in the facility

- The lack of progressive thinking among some segments of the aging services network

- The difficulty in getting activities directors to pick up the phone that first time

- The lack of dedicated, experienced activities staff in some senior centers and other segments of the aging services field

- The lack of coordinators in schools because of the time and resource demands imposed on teachers and students by No Child Left Behind

If the partnership is struggling and you are facing insurmountable challenges, remember that you are not bound together for life. If you've tried hard, but the partnership isn't working, move on.

Key Points about Partnerships

- Consider funders, participants, and teaching artists, as well as organizations and institutions, as partners.
- Create a planning partnership if you don't have the necessary expertise or resources in-house.
- Allocate enough time to develop your partnership.
- Refer to the checklist in meetings with partners.
- Have a written partnership agreement.
- Use the list of organizations and facilities that you compiled during the external assessment phase—stakeholders as well as competitors—to find potential partners, and then pick up the phone.
- Enlist allies within organizations and facilities to help sell the program and get buy-in from leaders.
- Form a partnership team.
- Communicate frequently, ideally in person.
- Educate each other and other staff about topics such as organizational culture, community arts, and normal aging to ensure that everyone is clear on expectations and mores.
- Understand challenges so you can overcome or work around them.
- Find a new partner if necessary.

Securing Resources

Start by emphasizing revenue sources that make your program self-sustaining and offer a significant return on investment. You must be positioned to take advantage of opportunities, but you must also create opportunities by networking and "friend-raising." Like assembling a jigsaw puzzle, look for revenue sources of different sizes and shapes that match what you want to accomplish. Then, gather evidence of impact and make your case logically and clearly. With perseverance, flexibility, creativity, and a little bit of luck, you can put all of the pieces together to support your work in enhancing older adults' quality of life.

This section addresses:

- Exploring revenue sources
- Creating a budget
- Developing a plan
- Making the case
- Understanding challenges

Exploring Revenue Sources

The key to financial sustainability is diversity among revenue sources and types. For a larger and more established organization, having a variety of programs targeted at different populations positions you to take advantage of different funding opportunities. Whether you are a novice or an expert at generating revenue, be flexible, adaptable, and opportunistic.

Before devising a plan, consider these revenue options:

1. Charge participants or attendees by selling tickets, charging tuition, and/or assessing membership fees.

   - Pay attention to prices of comparable programs.
   - Strategize how to keep prices as low as possible.
   - Decide whether or not to develop a multitiered pricing structure.
   - Decide whether or not to charge.
   - Decide what attendees and participants receive for their money.
   - Consider whether requiring a membership fee increases members' buy-in to your organization and/or program and enhances its value in the minds of participants.
   - Decide whether to offer scholarships or financial aid to keep the program accessible to all.

   Examples of charging participants:

   - The Levine School of Music charges tuition; older adults pay 70 to 75 percent less than other students do. Prices align with nearby lifelong learning institutes and other comparable programs. The school makes up for the lower tuition with an increase in volume. Older adult classes, while still small enough to be effective, are sometimes twice as large as those with younger participants.

- New Horizons Music programs charge approximately $150 per semester depending on the location, number of weekly sessions, and charges for comparable programs in the community.

- The New Jersey Intergenerational Orchestra charges $200 for members under age 62, $85 for members over age 62, and $150 for members who also volunteer.

- Creative Aging Cincinnati offers facility memberships to all retirement communities, senior centers, adult day care centers, and nursing homes in the community. Membership entitles a facility to attend all large-group programs (20 to 25 each year) and to schedule 6 to 12 in-facility programs a year. Periodic special incentives include guaranteeing attendance at a particular large-group program or putting the facility's logo on printed materials.

2. Contract for services with an arts organization, senior center, residential facility, or department of aging services or school system.

   - Develop fees on a sliding scale based on budget.
   - Charge for-profits more than nonprofits.
   - Subsidize nonprofits in part with the higher fees paid by for-profits.
   - Be flexible in how the fees are paid.
   - Be sure to incorporate all expenses in fees unless grants are subsidizing the program.

Examples of fee structures:

- The Senseabilities program of Elders Share the Arts charges $600 for staff only (half day), $1,200 for staff only (full day), and $1,000 for staff and elders (half day).

- The Intergeneration Orchestra of Omaha charges sites $300 a performance. Sites pay in cash, through advertising in the orchestra's printed program, from taking up a collection at the door, or by a combination of these methods. If the orchestra has to travel to perform, transportation costs are added to the fee.

- The Center for Elders and Youth in the Arts charges nonprofits $4,000 to $5,000 a year and for-profits $7,000 to $8,000 a year. Fees include costs associated with high-quality exhibitions and performances.

3. Apply for grants and contributions from federal, state, and local government agencies, united arts funds, foundations, and individuals.

   - Allow for a long lead time, perhaps as many as eight months between application and notification.

   - Consider whether the time and complexity of applying to a public entity such as a local or state arts agency is worth the potential return. Instead, consider using the common application form from the Foundation Center.

   - Consult with program staff at local and state arts and aging agencies, foundations, and corporations before you write your application and during the writing. Their job is to help you succeed. Ask them to advise on which program to apply to, and encourage them to collaborate internally across program areas.

- Apply for your first grants from foundations and public agencies that fund only in your community, state, or region.

- Seek funding from family foundations.

- Attend grant panels convened by local and state agencies whether or not they are reviewing your application. If they are reviewing your application, bring an older adult participant in your program with you.

- Apply in an entry-level category such as special projects for a modest amount of money to gain experience in grant writing. After a couple of applications, submit an application for more money in a different category, such as general operating support.

- Ask participants to contribute to your program. The most effective method is a face-to-face request. Be sensitive to differences in resources; honor contributors regardless of the dollar amount that they give; use humor; and demonstrate good taste.

- Ask participants' family members and friends for support. Make it easy for them to do so through a targeted, printed appeal or in your printed materials. In addition, solicit audience members in person who attend the community sharing of the art.

- Don't be reluctant to ask for bequests or for gifts in honor of participants who have passed away.

Examples of individual solicitations:

- Kairos Dance Theatre includes a tear sheet at the bottom of its general information brochure (see Appendix 3).

- The Intergeneration Orchestra of Omaha used bequests from members to establish an endowment as a way for friends and family members to honor someone's memory. Contributors are invited to donate at six levels, from $1 to more than $1,000. The endowment awards two annual scholarships of $100, one to an older adult musician and one to a younger student who might otherwise not be able to pay the tuition. In five years, the endowment has grown to $10,000, with an ultimate goal of $25,000.

4. Seek in-kind contributions from corporations, businesses, other nonprofits, and members of the public. These contributions typically happen quickly, with just a phone call or a letter, and can include drinks and food for special events, frames, floral centerpieces at galas, items or services for auctions or prizes, printing and photocopying, and art supplies.

One very helpful gift is physical space; churches often are home to arts and aging organizations. Municipal recreation facilities are another option. Kairos Dance Theatre, for example, trades workshops for space in a community park building. Make sure you know in advance exactly how your sponsors want to be recognized for their contributions.

5. Explore other revenue sources.

- Sell advertising space in printed programs, calendars, note cards, and art created by participants. Sales raise both money and public awareness.

- Seek a line item in the municipal, county, or state budget from your elected representative. A line item is not a stable revenue source and is most appropriate for a special program or one-time event.

- Hold special events such as benefit concerts and fundraising parties. Like sales, events raise both money and public awareness. Events, however, require significant time to plan and are often expensive to produce because glitz and glamour are hard to control. You have to decide if strengthening relationships and creating visibility—rather than raising money—are a large enough return on investment.

The flip side of raising revenue is controlling expenses:

- Recycle supplies. The Center for Elders and Youth in the Arts uses the same materials: three different sizes of mats and frames for the visual art created in its programs.

- Join a community service coalition, nonprofit coalition, or chamber of commerce to get lower rates on health insurance and group purchasing privileges.

- Have a virtual office. All you need is a laptop and cell phone.

Creating a Budget

To create your budget, be as comprehensive as possible. Make sure that income projections are realistic and a plan for raising the money is in place. Research actual costs, which vary by community and artistic discipline and are informed by the activities and instructional design. For a new organization or program, include start-up costs such as computer and phone equipment. In general, be pragmatic about the program's scope, expenses, and revenue. Be "right-sized": Keep financial needs minimal and in line with what you want to accomplish.

While a budget is a budget, whether your organization is focused on arts, aging, animals, or airplanes, some budget categories are unique to the arts (see Appendix 3 for a typical budget). Condense, expand, or adjust the following categories to fit your needs:

Expenses

Personnel—Administrative: Executive, education, development, marketing, and administrative and support staff

Personnel—Artistic: Artistic director, conductor, designers, artists, and similar staff

Employee Benefits: Social security, retirement, and insurance (health, dental, short- and long-term disability, and life)

Outside Artistic Fees and Services: Contractors such as artists, set, lighting, costume or properties designers, picture framers, artistic directors, and conductors

Other Outside Fees and Services: Contractors such as graphic or Web designers; business, media, marketing, fundraising, public relations, or planning consultants; florists; and caterers.

Publications/Dues: Advertising, subscriptions, royalties, and membership fees or dues

Supplies: Office and artistic supplies; gifts and awards; and food and beverages not from a caterer

Printing: Photocopying and printing for your newsletter, marketing and promotional pieces, programs, and other materials

Postage/Shipping: Mailing marketing pieces, newsletters, and invitations; shipping artwork and sets

Transportation: Vehicle rental, gas, and mileage; local transportation; air and train tickets

Phone/Communication: Local, long-distance, wireless, and Internet provider

Equipment: Telephone system, cell phones, vehicles, copiers, postage meters, computers, server, and other depreciable equipment

Maintenance: Facility and equipment

Contingency Fund: For emergencies or unexpected opportunities

Rent: Office, rehearsal, performance, and meeting space

Insurance: General liability, workers' compensation, vehicle, and directors' and officers' liability

Depreciation

Income

Admissions

Tuition

Membership

Sales

Corporate and Business Support

Foundation Support

Individual Contributions

Government Grants

In-kind Contributions

Services

Goods and Materials

Space

Developing a Plan

Next, create a resource development plan in consultation with stakeholders, particularly partners, staff, and board members. Multiple perspectives and ideas strengthen the plan, and those who participate in its creation are more invested in success and more likely to help.

Basic Planning Principles

- Emphasize revenue sources such as fees for service or tuition, membership fees, or tickets.

- Consider the return on investment (ROI) of your resource development strategies, particularly sales and special events. Be sure that the money raised does not exceed the value of the time spent fundraising. Some strategies are more effective than others. In 2006, for example, individuals gave 83 percent of all charitable donations in the United States, according to the Giving USA Foundation.

- Align the plan with personal and organizational values. You have to decide whether to accept money from a corporation with policies or practices with which you don't agree. It is not a negative thing to base a decision on the revenue-generating potential of the program, audience, or grant. Just be thoughtful and deliberate.

Planning Strategies

Integrate a variety of strategies into your resource development plan. Consider these possibilities:

- Affiliate with a nonprofit organization that will donate administrative support.

- Raise or allocate funds to hire a business consultant to review the budget and suggest a plan for sustaining and growing the program.

- Enlist board members to help with fundraising, and look for prospective board members with this expertise. Be sure they understand this expectation before they commit to serving the organization.

- Make "friendraising" part of fundraising. Cultivate and network with trustees and staff of potential funders at social, church, community, and political events; at arts events and performances; and through stakeholders, friends, neighbors, family, colleagues, and elected officials. Most people give to people they know.

- Do joint fundraising with your partners. Funders often respond positively to a collaborative approach.

- Ask participants and their family members to help secure in-kind donations.

- Approach large nonprofits or for-profits in aging services to support special events that will attract public attention.

- Collaborate with higher education and apply together to aging-related and healthcare corporations and foundations, which tend to have an academic orientation.

- Invite current and potential funders to stop by classes or workshops and attend events. Seeing is believing.

- Acknowledge funders publicly when they attend events, in printed materials, and on your Web site.

- Devote money and time to producing high-quality promotional materials, which not only demonstrate value to funders, but also attract new participants and supporters and documents the program for evaluation and posterity (see Appendix 4 for an example).

- Invest in a grant writer or advisor.

- Enhance applications with support letters from funders, participants, experts in the field, partners, and others (see Appendix 3).

- Try out a great idea to see if it works, and then seek funding. Money often follows programming.

Foundation and Corporate Grantseeking

If your resource development plan includes grants from foundations or corporations, be sure that their giving priorities match your project. Follow these steps:

- *Do your homework.*
  Show that you respect the organization and its program officers by learning everything you can about the giving program: What are its mission and goals? Who is on the board? What kinds of gifts have they given before? What is the average donation? What kind of outcomes do they look for? Do they like to partner with other giving sources? What is the grant cycle?

- *Find a connection to someone associated with the foundation or corporation.*
  It is almost impossible to get a proposal read, let alone funded, if you do not have a relationship with someone associated with the foundation. Chances are you'll know a board member or a previous grantee who can open doors for you.

- *Follow guidelines.*
  If a foundation or corporation has published guidelines, it's important to follow them. Never simply change the name on the top of an old proposal and send it to a new organization.

- *Create a clear and realistic proposal.*
  Show that you have given thought to the program's structure and feasibility. If you propose doing a Broadway-scale production with your theater group, no one will fund you. Remember to demonstrate benefits and outcomes.

- *Teach others in the community what you have learned by doing this arts program.* Sharing knowledge with others will maximize the foundation or corporation's resources. You might suggest holding a half-day conference to show your arts program in action and teach attendees your methods.

- *Follow through.*
  Do what you say you'll do. If you find that you need to change course in the middle of a grant-supported program, let the foundation officer know right away and explain why the changes are necessary. The foundation officer is interested in learning from your experience. Write a thorough final report, and keep in touch with your foundation officer after the project is complete to let him or her know how your facility has continued the work

and still feels the positive impact of their support.[75]

Making the Case

Whether you are asking for an in-kind donation from a business, discussing an individual contribution with an older adult participant, or writing an application for a public agency, foundation, or corporation, design your proposal to follow this progression:

1. **Identify a need.** What is going on in the community or your organization that requires action?

2. **Propose a solution.** What are you going to do about this need? What actions, specifically, are you going to take?

3. **Describe the impact.** How will your actions change participants?

4. **Plan evaluation.** How will you know whether your actions have changed participants? What qualitative and quantitative evidence will you amass and how? (See chapter 8 for an in-depth discussion of evaluation.)

Appendix 3 includes an example of a successful proposal.

Each funder will respond to a different rationale. In general,

- Intergenerational programs appeal to education funders.
- Programs that build community through the arts appeal to arts funders.
- Programs that address the social, physical, and mental health of older adults appeal to healthcare funders.

As your rationale, begin with the benefits of arts participation to older adults (see chapter 2). Then consider the following tips:

- Ask for what you need.
- Have confidence in your ability to improve older adults' quality of life.
- Make sure your mission statement is clear and concise.
- Cite research and phrases from medical journals to enhance the credibility and seriousness of your work.
- Stress the importance of purposeful, creative activity to the health of older adults.
- Explain community arts to potential funders so that they have realistic expectations of your program.
- Flaunt your experience and education. Titles matter to aging services funders: if you have a Ph.D., M.S.W., or any graduate degree, mention it in your application.
- If the funder is interested in lifelong learning, discuss the results of research on the brains of older adults.
- If the funder is interested in mental health, discuss how arts participation increases social engagement.
- If the grant is for an artistic project, discuss how the participation of older adults enhances the art form.

- Use key phrases to convey what you do and why you do it:
  - With decades of experience and knowledge, older people are an underutilized resource in the community.
  - We are a participatory dance theater for traditionally underserved audiences.
  - We are accessible to well and frail older adults.
  - We have intergenerational community programs.
  - We serve X number of people.
  - Our performers span four generations.
  - We have received local and national recognition.
  - We do pioneering work in both intergenerational dance and the emerging field of creative aging.
  - We help older Americans live independently longer through high-level physical activity, community connection, and artistic development.
  - The arts sustain spirit and soul.
  - The arts help older adults remain whole people as they age.
  - You never outgrow your need for art.
  - Everybody is aging or knows somebody who is.
  - We meet the needs of the one of the fastest-growing populations in the United States.
  - If all you have is a meal, your life is fairly empty.

> *Next to my family, certainly the musical activity is the most important thing in my life.*
> New Horizons Music participant

Understanding Challenges

A major challenge in resource development for the arts and aging field is its multiple focuses. It straddles two worlds—arts and health or social services—and a third world—education—if the program is intergenerational. It is difficult to be competitive in any one world unless you confidently and effectively communicate your role in enhancing older adults' quality of life.

Arts and aging programs may also face these challenges:

- Performances in long-term care facilities are invisible to the public and funders because the care of older adults is largely hidden in our society.
- The arts are not an option in grant guidelines for health and older adults.
- Some foundations focus on the number of people served rather than on the depth of impact.
- Many funders subscribe to the traditional definition of the arts (artistic excellence) as opposed to community arts.
- Funders may want additional studies or research to prove efficacy when you already have quality information.
- Some communities and states have few foundations and corporations.

- Some funders don't respect older adults as artists.
- In a year with an election or a natural disaster, there is more competition for funds.
- Board members require significant preparation and encouragement for fundraising.
- Health and social service funders often emphasize life-and-death issues for older adults such as food, shelter, medicine, and medical equipment.

Key Points about Resource Development

- Ensure that you have a diversity of funding sources.
- Strive to be self-sustaining through program and membership fees, tuition, ticket sales, and other revenue.
- Make your budget comprehensive, carefully considering all potential expenses and allowing sufficient time to research actual costs.
- Be right-sized.
- Pitch funders by identifying the need, proposing a solution, describing impact, and planning the evaluation.
- Match your project with funders' priorities.
- Ask for what you need.
- Emphasize how your program benefits participants.
- Understand challenges so you can overcome or work around them.

Marketing to Participants

Whether your program focuses on older adults living in the community or within a residential facility, you have to attract participants. Program design should incorporate a marketing plan. Like planning, partnering, and funding, marketing doesn't stop after the first program session; confirmed participants may lose interest, become ill, or change their minds. Marketing also helps increase the demand among older adults for arts and aging programs—and that's good for your program and for the field as a whole.

Though marketing can have different purposes, this section focuses only on recruiting participants. Just as you diversify revenue sources, include a variety of strategies in your plan. Marketing strategies address where and how to market. Frequently, the "where" determines the "how." In a senior center, adult day program, or residential facility, personal communication—phone calls, conversations, and presentations—is the best technique, but it does require a significant time commitment.

This section explores:

- Getting the word out
- Motivating participants
- Using your assets
- Creating materials

Getting the Word Out

The first step in getting the word out is to activate a group of stakeholders who can help you identify and reach potential participants. These stakeholders can include:

- The advisory committee and/or board of directors—your strongest allies in the community. It is their job to make calls and presentations on behalf of the program.

- Older adults with whom you consulted during external assessment. They are not only potential participants, but also messengers. Enlist them to talk to their friends about your program. Word of mouth is one successful technique.

- Funders and partners, who have a vested interest in seeing your program succeed. Partners—particularly senior centers, adult day programs, schools, out-of-school programs, or residential facilities—may assume responsibility for the entire recruitment process.

To reach potential participants and other stakeholders, direct contact is best: a telephone call, an in-person visit, or a presentation. As an incentive, offer a "friends" discount. For ongoing programs, give a current participant a discount or gift for getting another person to register or join the group.

A word about computers: Using e-mail or Web sites to reach potential older adult participants probably is not effective. Many in this age group left the workforce before e-mailing and surfing became a way of life, and still others are not able to afford the technology. The Internet will, though, be an influential tool for marketing to baby boomers.

> ### Tips for Getting the Word Out
>
> - Speak to potential participants at a senior center, community center, or residential facility when they are assembled for lunch.
> - Be available to answer individual questions about the program.
> - Allow adequate time for potential participants to make a decision.
> - Target older adults who are opinion leaders in the community.
> - Ask for participants' phone numbers so you can issue personal invitations.
> - Enable young people to receive school credit for participating in an intergenerational program.
> - Ask the teaching artist to help identify young people who might not be suitable for an intergenerational program.

Community Organizations

After you have activated your stakeholders, turn to other organizations and individuals in the community that you might have contacted during external assessment—for example, churches, libraries, continuing care retirement communities, senior centers, literary clubs, National Urban League affiliates, hospitals, doctors, arts organizations, area agencies on aging, adult day programs, and assisted living facilities. If your program is intergenerational, add community centers, out-of-school programs, and schools to the list. (Of course, some may already be partners or funders.) Cost-effective ways of reaching your expanded list include a newsletter, press release, catalogue of programs, or a flyer and/or brochure distributed through the mail or dropped off with the director or leader. (See Appendix 4 for a sample marketing brochure.)

Media

To cast as wide a net as possible, don't overlook traditional media outlets, such as arts sections of newspapers, community-access cable stations, local television or radio public service announcements, and talk shows. Smaller community newspapers will be more receptive than larger dailies. Announcing your program is helpful; printing a longer piece is even better. Supplement your press release with information that makes it easy for reporters to write an in-depth article: Outline the story, provide anecdotes from older adults affected by the program, and send photos or other graphics. Remember to include a "hook"; for ideas, look at stories in the publication that you are targeting. You can also pay for space in newspapers and publications with an older adult or local community readership to announce informational meetings, class schedules, open rehearsals, performances, and exhibits.

Local Businesses

Ask local businesses for help in getting the word out, particularly those that provide services to older adults (such as barber shops and beauty salons, restaurants, pharmacies, and independent shoe stores and bookstores) and those that are related to the arts (such as musical instrument retailers, art supply stores, and galleries). Business owners may allow you to put up a poster or include a flyer about your program in their mailings to customers. Another method is to leave a rack with brochures next to the cash register. The Osher Lifelong Learning Institute at the University of Southern Maine asked members to "adopt-a-rack." Each volunteer was responsible for making sure his or her rack was always full of brochures.

Information Booths

Another marketing method is to pay for a booth or table at a community fair or festival, home show, or health and fitness expo. You can distribute informational materials and display art created during your program, and you can demonstrate your process (for example, a mini-performance) and invite passers-by to participate.

Motivating Participants

If you talked with potential participants during external assessment, you have a pretty good idea of what might motivate them to register or join a class or session. Appeal to what it means to age productively, stressing the opportunity to make new friends and contribute to the community. Cite specific benefits related to the outcome goals in chapter 5, such as skill development, mental and physical exercise, and having fun.

Barriers to Participation

Recalling the discussion of instructional design and building trust earlier in this chapter, it is worth noting that some older adults are reluctant to participate because they feel that they have no artistic ability or nothing of value to contribute to the process or to others in the group. If you get them in the door, you can overcome this barrier. Once you have them, involve them immediately or they will walk away. If the program is performance-based and an older adult is reluctant to perform, identify other tasks, such as turning pages for the accompanist, building sets, sewing costumes, prompting lines, or setting up the room. Chances are this person will soon be on stage.

Another barrier for older adults is transportation. Some are reluctant to venture beyond their usual haunts like home and the senior center. And many communities don't have reliable public transportation. Encourage participation among this group by taking the program to them or providing them with transportation to you.

Using Your Assets

Participants, teaching artists, caregivers, and the program itself can contribute greatly to a marketing campaign. In general, they are going to be most helpful to a program that is already up and running. Don't assume that people will automatically talk to others about the program. Ask them to do so, and make it easy for them by providing talking points and promotional materials.

Participants

Encourage them to talk about the program with friends and to make presentations with you. Having someone who can speak directly to peers is an effective technique.

Participants can also provide outreach by themselves; for example, a typical strategy of Osher Lifelong Learning Institutes is for member students to talk with community groups about their experiences and share an informational video created by the national resource center.

Program

The impact of your program on older adults' quality of life is a powerful marketing message. Promote benefits orally and in writing using clear, compelling language and illustrative photographs and images. Show draft language to participants and partners to see if you are describing your program and its impact effectively and accurately.

The program itself is an important marketing tool. Suggestions for making the most of marketing opportunities include:

- Conduct the program in a room that is visible to other older adults—ideally, one with windows (with blinds) into an often-traveled hall.

- If appropriate, encourage older adults to come in and watch.

- Schedule an open session so that older adults may attend without obligation.

- Use performances, exhibits, and other events that are open to the community as recruitment opportunities. Make sure you issue a public invitation to participate, and explain your program, its context of community arts, and the benefits.

Teaching Artists

The professionalism and experience of the teaching artist who facilitates a program are assets in marketing. Include the artist's resume and images of his or her art in your presentations and written promotional materials. Describe one or two fun exercises that the artist leads in a typical session. Better yet, invite the artist to join you at community events where you are promoting the program.

Caregivers

In a residential facility, senior center, or adult day program, staff and family members who see firsthand the effect of your program on older adults are great advocates. They can recruit additional residents or members and chat with family members or colleagues at other facilities. Remember, however, that sometimes staff and family members underestimate what older adults can accomplish. Encourage those who are supportive and have a person-centered philosophy to spread the word. Such a philosophy values each person for his or her ability, vitality, wisdom, and experience.

Creating Materials

Promotional materials must be professional and attractive. The image that you convey in writing reflects your values and the quality of your work. Good graphic design and printing don't have to be expensive or fancy to be effective. Strive for a clean look with minimal text and images. Solicit feedback on the design from participants, staff, and partners. Remember that anything in writing should be easy to read for people with low vision. This means 12-point type and high contrast between background and type color.

Ask some people with low vision to read your materials to make sure you have it right. Use disability access symbols so that everyone knows your program and facility are accessible. These symbols are available at: www.disability.uci.edu/handbook/Disability%20Access%20Symbols.pdf.

In addition to looking good and being accessible, your materials must be well written and free from typographical and other errors. You may also want to translate them into other languages. More important, they should emphasize productive aging and not perpetuate myths of aging.

The name of your program matters, too. At one facility client of EngAGE: The Art of Active Aging (formerly known as More Than Shelter For Seniors), for example, the social group of residents over age 80 is called the Wisdom Council. "Nomenclature is really important," explains Vice President Maureen Kellen-Taylor. "A Wisdom Council says so much more than if it were called the Cocoa Group: it gives purpose, that being alive matters. And that is the key."

Marketing materials include:

- Program flyers, brochures, or posters
- Organizational brochures
- Newsletters
- Press releases
- News stories in print or on radio or TV
- Photographs
- Videos, CDs, or DVDs

Photographs, videos, and DVDs are particularly effective at conveying the benefits of your program to participants. Videos and DVDs should be designed to have a long shelf life.

Key Points about Marketing to Participants

- Plan a variety of strategies for identifying and attracting participants.
- Get the word out through your advisory committee, stakeholders, and other individuals and organizations identified during the external assessment.
- Recruit in person whenever possible.
- Understand what motivates older adults to participate and prepare for resistance.
- Use your assets as marketing tools: participants, teaching artists, caregivers, and the program.
- Emphasize benefits and demonstrate impact in writing and imagery.
- Produce high-quality, cost-effective materials.
- Ensure that your materials are well written and respectful of older adults.

Summary

We have covered a large quantity of information in this chapter on program design. Our in-depth discussion of concepts and considerations, illustrated with advice and examples, demonstrates the importance of planning for success and designing an effective program that will enhance older adults' quality of life. Even if you have already implemented a program, you might find some of the tips and examples useful or inspirational. Or you may discover that revisiting some steps in planning or marketing, for example, solves a problem.

As you review the key points at the end of each section, reflect on the common characteristics across topics: you and your program or organization should be adaptable, opportunistic, strategic, evolving, principled and embedded in the community that you serve. These traits allow you to attract a broad base of support, from participants and partners to funders. Supporters or stakeholders, in turn, can help you to plan a more successful program. Partners, in particular, should be involved as early as possible in the design. Creating a learning community of participants does not just happen by chance; it requires careful planning with plenty of lead time and an understanding of andragogy and instructional design. In order to experience mastery and benefit from social engagement, older adults need to be challenged, to learn from and be inspired by others, and to succeed regardless of their abilities. They should also be respected and honored for their lifetime of experiences.

> *Last year my mother was afraid of her shadow. And now look at her! In this play, she's dyeing her hair red and living it up. My mother's a different person now.*
>
> Daughter of Generating Community (ESTA) participant

Thank you for all your patience and understanding, which allowed Dick to continue to do what he loved most— right up to the end. Thank you all for the years of care and concern, for the rides to and from, for the open door, the offered chair, the smile, the watching lest he fall, all the things you did.

Widow of a member of
The Golden Tones

7

Program Implementation

As you move from program design to implementation, your work intensifies. Like a juggler with many balls in the air, you must attend not only to the ongoing elements of program design, but also to program implementation: the details that contribute to an environment of trust; the challenges that arise and decisions that have to be made during programs; and the training and ongoing support of teaching artists. Fortunately, staff members, partners, and teaching artists can help.

This team pays attention to detail and monitors quality throughout implementation. Arts and aging programs are community arts, and so the process of creation is highly valued. What is created also is important to the older adults' journey toward mastery and social engagement; the community sharing of the art has many benefits, as well.

As you move forward, pay attention to even the smallest detail. From the size of the type on written instructions and the spacing between chairs, to the frame around a watercolor and the tone of the teaching artist's voice, every aspect counts—and contributes to program effectiveness.

This chapter looks at program implementation in three segments:

- Setting the stage
- Keeping on track
- Supporting teaching artists

Setting the Stage

In chapter 6, we stressed the importance of establishing trust through the instructional design of the program. This section examines how ensuring physical and programmatic accessibility and setting group expectations contribute to creating an environment of trust in which participants can learn and succeed.

Ensuring Physical and Programmatic Accessibility

Accessibility means that everyone, regardless of age or ability, is included in all physical structures, programs, and means of communication (for example, Web sites, e-mail, telephone). The Americans with Disabilities Act (ADA) prohibits discrimination based on disability in employment, state, and local government services, public accommodations, commercial facilities, transportation, and telecommunications.

Whether older adults have disabilities or not, they benefit from accessibility features and customer service practices in stores, museums, performing arts venues, restaurants, and printed publications. Older adults are most likely to use accessible features when they are integrated into the overall design (universal design) because they are reluctant to request special consideration or fear ageism.

For arts and aging programs, consider in particular the accessibility of the space in which participants meet or rehearse, how you communicate, and how participants travel to the program.

Accessible Space

The facility used for an arts and aging program must have better-than-average accessibility.

An accessible facility or space helps keep older adult participants safe. If there are no physical barriers or significant visual or aural distractions, they are more likely to concentrate and less likely to trip or fall. Here are some tips to consider when planning for accessibility:

- Look for a building without steps to the entrance and doors that are easy to open, are automatic, or have a power-assist. Fortunately, steps and doors are not an issue in most residential facilities or senior centers.

- Look for a room that is designated solely for your use during the session. Other activities in the same space are distracting to participants, and vice versa. "Outside" people also disrupt the environment of trust in your learning community.

- Ensure that you have clear, wide paths of travel throughout the facility to allow for people who are unsteady on their feet or use wheelchairs, canes, or walkers to maneuver easily.

- Make sure corridors and the designated program space are free of clutter or other hazards.

- Adjust the lighting in the room to reduce glare.

- Make your designated space special. Play music, change the lighting, bring in plants or objects, or drape tables with colorful cloths. The entrance to the space also contributes to the mood:

  > [Have] a designated threshold created to be crossed, in order to enter into ritual space. The threshold can take various forms. It can be as concrete as creating an arch to walk under, providing a rug to walk on, or an entryway to walk through, or there could simply be a white board on which participants sign their names.[76]

- Minimize distractions, especially if the participants have dementia.

- Allow for ample spacing between chairs. Ensure that participants feel connected to the group and not cramped. Make metal folding chairs more comfortable by supplying inexpensive foam cushions.

- Monitor the room temperature, watch for signs of discomfort, and learn how to control the thermostat. If participants are too hot or cold, they won't focus.

- Monitor the acoustics and minimize unnecessary noise, but don't limit conversation. Participants, particularly those with hearing aids that often amplify background noise, are distracted by sounds that echo around a space without any fabric, padding, or carpet.

- Position participants who have difficulty hearing and seeing at the front of the group or in a place with a good sight line to the conductor, director, or teaching artist.

Communication

Whether or not participants have hearing or vision losses, take special care in your communications:

- Use a portable PA system.
- Use as many printed instructions as you can to minimize misunderstanding due to hearing problems.
- Practice your best projection and diction when speaking to a group.
- Repeat directions. Verbal repetition not only helps with memory, but also can make the words clearer.
- Enlarge music and scripts.

Because some older adults have disabilities, these language tips are applicable:

- Never use the word *handicapped*; the word is *disability*.

- Never use a disability as an adjective: a *writer who is blind*, not a *blind writer*. Focus on the person, not the disability.

- Never use *special*, because this term separates the individual from the group. For example, information is not required regarding the *special needs of the group*, but *needs of the group*.

- Never use euphemisms, such as *physically challenged* or *handicapable*. These terms are condescending.

- Never use labels: *the disabled, the blind, the deaf, A.B.s* (able-bodied), *T.A.B.s* (temporarily able-bodied), or *normal*. Labeling people is never acceptable.[77]

When communicating with frail older adults or those with dementia:

- Face the person when you speak.
- Establish eye contact.
- Use hand gestures (point).
- Speak distinctly, calmly, and softly.
- Use simple sentences.
- Allow ample time for answers.
- Minimize background noises.
- Touch only when acceptable.
- Do not over use the word *no*; *yes* or *maybe* might be adequate.
- Sudden, quick, unexpected movements can be frightening.
- Let the person know the time of day and where they are, and reiterate what is going on every now and then.[78]

Transportation

While transportation is not directly related to creating an environment of trust, it is an issue of physical accessibility and a major concern for older adults living in the community. Some have given up driving at night or at all times. Many of those with cars are anxious about traffic and parking. The lack of public transportation and accommodations to enhance the safety of older adults who are still driving is a challenge.

Accessible transportation means:

- A range of affordable travel modes within the community, including services for people with disabilities
- Age-friendly public environments, signage, and infrastructure
- Street infrastructure such as curb cuts, ramps, sidewalk surfaces, and signs for older adults with motor and/or sensory problems in public spaces, businesses, and community institutions
- Mobility amenities for walkers
- Trails, walking paths, and sidewalks
- Monitoring and feedback mechanisms to ensure adherence to speed limits and stop signs.[79]

To assist older adult participants, partner with the municipal senior transportation service; facilitate car pools; and investigate models such as volunteer drivers for cancer patients through the American Cancer Society or organizations that focus solely on older adults, like Senior Connection in Montgomery County, Maryland.

Most states have online guides to senior or retirement living with community transportation resources. Search for "retirement living guide" and the name of your state.

Setting Group Expectations

Clearly communicating expectations contributes to an environment of trust. Participants need to know the basic ground rules, such as dates, times, performances, rehearsals, and locations. Deliver these details verbally and in writing (in large type) on a one- or two-page information sheet. (See Appendix 5 for a sample policies and procedures handout.)

The intangible expectations are more important than the tangible. Participants have to understand the programmatic parameters or rules, such as

- maintaining confidentiality within the group, particularly if the topics are personal;
- listening actively to each other without interrupting;
- respecting different points of view;
- valuing all artistic contributions; and
- making constructive — not judgmental — comments.

One effective technique is for the program leader or teaching artist to facilitate a discussion in which participants develop their own group expectations or norms. They can revisit their decisions at any time or when a member needs a refresher. For participants with more advanced dementia, group norms are likely too abstract to be relevant.

Related to group expectations is honoring the work created by older adult artists. They determine what happens to their art, and they need to trust that you will respect their decisions. Just as with any other artist, ask each one to complete a written consent form if you select his or her work for a publication, exhibition, performance, or presentation.

Key Points about Setting the Stage

- Pay attention to detail.
- Strive for universal design or at least seamless accessibility.
- Ensure physical and programmatic accessibility:
  » No stairs
  » Easily opened doors
  » Bright, glare-free lighting
  » Designated room
  » "Special" décor
  » Minimal background noise
  » Comfortable temperature
  » Space between tables and chairs to accommodate a person who uses a wheelchair
  » Comfortable chairs
  » Transportation options
- Ensure that communications are accessible:
  » Large type
  » High contrast
  » Written and verbal instructions
  » Distinct enunciation
  » Respectful language
  » Attention to needs of frail older adults or those with dementia
- Communicate logistical expectations
- Facilitate the establishment of group norms

Keeping on Track

Once your program is up and running, don't rest on your laurels. In addition to the various aspects of program design that require ongoing attention, assess the progress of participants and the effectiveness of the process and revisit the initial plan for sharing the art created with the community.

This section looks at:

- Assessing progress and process
- Planning the community sharing of the art

Assessing Progress and Process

At routine intervals, sit down with staff, teaching artists, and organizational partners (if you have them) to assess participants' progress in achieving outcome goals and evaluate the instructional design. Committing to these meetings should be in the partnership agreement and the overall program evaluation plan. This step enables the team to address challenges and make corrections in enough time to ensure success. It can also support your ongoing marketing, fundraising, and public awareness campaigns with anecdotes and observations about how participants are benefiting.

This assessment process is often referred to as *formative evaluation*. Formative evaluation typically is "conducted during the development or improvement of a program or product (or person, and so on) and it is conducted, often more than once, for the in-house staff of the program with the intent to improve."[80]

There is nothing particularly complicated or intimidating about discussing your participants' journey: where they have been, where they are today, and where they are heading. Review the original goals, objectives, activities, and instructional design, and compare each to reality. If they don't correlate, make adjustments. It is important that all team members are present at these meetings, particularly the teaching artist who has hands-on experience with participants.

What can go wrong in a program? Some examples:

- Members of the group don't feel that they are in an environment of trust or part of a learning community.

- Program leadership or staff may be ineffective.

- Challenges are either too easy or too difficult, or not appropriate to participants' abilities.

- The session is too long or too short, or not scheduled often enough to establish continuity.

- The physical environment might be uncomfortable, or the space may make it difficult for people with disabilities to participate because of temperature, distractions, accessible entrance, or arrangement of chairs and tables.

Other issues might relate to the roles and responsibilities of each partner organization or facility—for example, professional caregivers are not helping participants get to the program; the teaching artist doesn't understand normal aging; or the activities staff schedules conflicting activities or events.

Regular meetings with the team provide a good opportunity not only to assess the progress of participants, but—in a program with organizational partners—to evaluate the operation of the partnership. Review your partnership agreement or the checklist provided in chapter 6 to reinforce and clarify responsibilities. If the team understands that the team meeting is the time and place to discuss challenges, then raising awkward issues is a little easier.

It can be helpful to involve your advisory committee in program evaluation. Ask members for their insight on challenging issues. They are part of your learning community, and they serve as a sounding board for your ideas as you think through potential program changes.

Last but not least, don't ignore the ability of cognitively fit participants to be self-reflective and solve problems. Older adults who have a lifetime of experience and are invested the program's outcomes are a great resource. They, too, can be involved in evaluation.

> **Program Example:**
> **Involving Participants in Assessing Progress**
>
> Generating Community (ESTA) uses the last five minutes of every workshop session as a quick assessment period. The participants—young people and seniors together—share their thoughts about how the program is going, what worked that day, what needs to be clarified, and what needs improvement. In this way, the participants determine the direction of the group. This discussion session also allows the teacher and artist to evaluate the development of critical thinking and cooperative interaction among participants.[81]

Planning Community Sharing of the Art

As you assess the progress of participants and the effectiveness of the process, focus as well on how to share the art created with the community. This section looks at:

- Making the decision
- Developing content
- Communicating context
- Planning the event
- Marketing the event

Making the Decision

As we explained in chapter 6, it is advisable to consider the decision to share the art in advance but not finalize it until later. About halfway through the program is the appropriate time to review the initial plan and revise it as necessary. It is important to involve staff members, partners, the teaching artist, and the participants in these discussions; however, older adults with more advanced dementia are unlikely to be able to contribute.

Cognitively fit participants may be uncomfortable with any kind of performance or celebration. While you always respect their choices, there are a number of benefits associated with sharing the art that accrue to older adults, the partners, the program, and the arts and aging field in general (see chapter 6). Explain these reasons and encourage them to share their work.

Program Example: Sharing the Art with the Community

With six months left in the program, the women in the Penn South Living History Theatre group—a program of Elders Share the Arts—realized that a presentation of some kind would give them a way to celebrate the culmination of their time together and share their pride of the group with others. The teaching artist suggested a montage format that would accommodate different artistic skills and comfort levels with performing. *The Heart of the Matter: Our Lives—A Work in Progress* included songs, jokes, poems, and an original work of art. The participants had created two group poems over the two years, as well as an original finale song. A third group poem was created live during the presentation. Roughly 60 people came to the event, including family members, friends, and residents and staff from Penn South.

Developing Content

Content for community sharing of the art can take many forms, including:

- Visual art exhibition
- Chorale or instrumental performance
- Reader's theater
- Live radio play
- Conflict resolution theater
- Pageantry/spectacle
- Group dance
- Multimedia with performed text
- Open workshop
- Festival
- Mural
- Word/image booklets
- Video
- Theatrical collage (i.e., presentation-style pieces such as introductions, group poems, movement work, and dramatic scenes)

Regardless of the form, consider incorporating gestures, movements, or songs of group members who have died as a way to keep their memories alive.

How participants shape the content and structure of the culminating event corresponds with the program's original instructional design. One effective technique is to divide the group into several smaller groups or committees to work on sections of the final piece and then bring them back together to critique, refine, and assemble the parts into a whole.

Sitting in the wings waiting to go on, it was hard to believe that it had been only six weeks ago that our patient creative writing instructor guided us through the proper steps of penning a stage play. He would let us try anything, except quitting. "There's Always Tomorrow" was the result, and now there were only three minutes until we went on stage to perform it. A man gently tapped his microphone three or four times, and for the first time I realized how full the theater at the Duarte Community Center had become. Our stage director was tremendously professional, her training and talent evident in every example she set forth for us. And she was very patient with her fledgling cast. The lights dimmed. We started up the three steps to the stage. The three minutes were up. Show time.

From an article by Thyda, a resident of Pacific Villas in Pomona, California, written for *The SAGE*. Pacific Villas is a client community of EngAGE: The Art of Active Aging (formerly known as More than Shelter For Seniors).

If your program is multiyear, consider how the scope and complexity of the community sharing increases over time. The broader arc of your sessions needs to demonstrate effective instructional design, specifically setting challenges and ensuring success for older adult participants.

Communicating Context

Explain the context of community arts to participants, partners, and the public:

- *Participants*—The experience of performing or exhibiting visual art will be more stressful and less beneficial to older adults if they are striving for artistic excellence. As you talk about community arts with the group, keep in mind that what each participant creates is respected and honored.

- *Partners*—Make community arts a topic for ongoing training with the partnership team and other staff. Be sure they know what the concept means, and reinforce their learning by explaining the application of community arts to exhibits, concerts, and performances and any accompanying celebrations and printed materials.

- *Public*—Manage the expectations of a residential facility's residents and staff, a senior center or adult day program's attendees, and family members and the broader community so that they appreciate the participants' accomplishments and support the program. Try these methods:

    » Before a performance, the teaching artist, facility director, or program designer explains the program and its goals and then introduces the piece and the performers.

    » In the printed program, include a page describing the program and its goals.

    » If you create a book, include a page describing the process.

» If you create a gallery exhibit, include a poster that talks about the process.

Planning the Event
Whether the event is a visual art exhibition, calendar, book, theater piece, or concert, it must reflect your value of respecting and honoring what participants create. This commitment plays out in the venue, the materials, and the celebratory activities.

Selecting the Venue
The venue that you select for a performance or exhibit should be appropriate to the size and experience of the group. Participants in a new program may be more comfortable in an intimate space. Those who have performed or exhibited before may prefer something larger. For performances, look at senior centers, houses of worship, schools, colleges and universities, movie theaters, and performance venues. Call performing arts groups in your community to ask where they perform. You have more options for finding appropriate space if you are creating a visual art exhibit. In addition to approaching for-profit, nonprofit, and collegiate art galleries and museums, look at banks, libraries, and community centers, long-term care facilities, senior centers, hospitals, and performing arts centers.

Particularly if the venue is not arts related, the recommendations shared in *Legacy Works: Transforming Memory into Visual Art* are helpful:

> It's important to understand that adequate exhibition space has certain minimal requirements: security from theft and vandalism, good light, and prepared walls. Preparing the walls means clearing off whatever may be on them and providing picture hooks or a picture rail. Attaching hooks requires that the wall be made of plaster. An excellent alternative is a rail on which picture hooks can be hung. Such a rail can be attached to the concrete-block walls common in institutions; it allows for considerable versatility. You can also hang the work with pushpins on room dividers covered with fabric or on bulletin boards.[82]

The best way to contact prospective venues is in person or by phone. When you stop by to check out a venue, find out who you need to talk to if you decide to move forward. Ask board members, partners, participants, family members, and friends to help secure the venue. They may know the right person who can say "yes" and perhaps donate the space or offer a discount on the rental fee.

Creating Materials
Materials refer not only to how visual art is presented, but also to printed invitations, programs, and catalogues. Ensure that all materials are as professional as possible to convey your values and respect for the participants:

- Use high-quality frames for works of visual art.

- Produce a book — either professionally or in-house — of participants' writings and images to distribute to caregivers, family members, and participants.

- If the exhibition includes freestanding works such as sculptures or small objects such as jewelry, display them on fine pieces of fabric to highlight their special qualities. Raise them on bricks or pieces of wood to create dimension. Shine a light on them to bring out their surfaces and form.[83]

- If the artwork will be turned into note cards, put each artist's bio and photo on the back of the card featuring his or her creation.

- For a calendar, include a section in the back for "emerging artists," so more than 12 older adult artists can be featured.

- If relevant, make sure the older adult artists sign their works of art, and be sure that they do so as close as possible to the image so that it will be visible when framed. Each person should decide on a title or appropriate quote and/or statement.

Cost-effective options for obtaining high-quality presentation materials include soliciting in-kind contributions from a frame shop and a printer; buying frames and mats on sale from a crafts store; incorporating the cost of materials into fees for service; and recycling mats and frames from year to year.

Printed programs in the performing arts are important not only for the participants, but also for the audience members, particularly if they are in long-term care facilities. A program makes residents feel that they are at a real performance.

Celebrating Success

Like the venue and materials, the quality of the celebration around the community sharing of the art helps to reinforce the benefits to older adults—especially for those with dementia and those who live in a residential facility. Their celebrations are too rare. Ask for in-kind donations of good food and drink, festive decorations, and fresh flowers from local businesses. Ask a nonprofit or for-profit music school in the community if top students are willing to perform as practice, but ensure that their sound level is low to facilitate conversation.

Marketing the Event

Program staff, volunteers, or members of the partnership team, advisory committee, or board need to follow these basic marketing steps:

- Assemble a mailing list. A good source is the list you compiled as part of the external assessment process. Include staff, family members, funders, community leaders, policy makers, elected officials, and media. Ask participants to contribute names.
- Create and mail an invitation.
- Write and mail a press release.
- Create, post, and distribute one-page flyers.
- Receive and tally RSVPs.

The best way to market your event is to enlist the help of program participants. Prepare them to spread the word through informal conversations with friends and targeted phone calls. Write out talking points and specifics—who, what, where, when, and how. Participants can also customize printed invitations with short notes. If your program involves residents of a long-term care facility, mailing an official invitation to other residents demonstrates your respect for them as individuals.

Don't forget to offer transportation for older adults who live in the community who no longer drive. At the event, remember to acknowledge funders, community leaders, and elected officials, and give them a chance to speak briefly. This recognition is vital to public awareness efforts (see chapter 9).

There are a great many resources on marketing. For guidance that pertains to the arts, read chapter 6 of *Seasoned Theatre: A Guide to Creating and Maintaining a Senior Adult Theatre* or chapter 9 of the *Fundamentals of Arts Management*.[84]

Key Points about Keeping on Track

- With program staff, teaching artists, and/or the partnership team, compare the original goals, objectives, activities, and instructional design with what is actually happening. Discuss problems and their causes, and make necessary corrections.

- Evaluate the operations of the partnership team by reviewing your written agreement.

- Seek advice from advisory committee members and participants.

- Encourage participants to share the work that they have created with the larger community.

- Consider instructional design in creating the content for the event.

- Ensure that participants, partners, and the public understand community arts.

- Demonstrate the value of honoring the art as high quality and the older adult artists as professionals through your selection of venue, preparation of presentational and promotional materials, and celebration of the event.

- Market the event.

Supporting Teaching Artists

The number one key to the success of your program is a professional teaching artist. But that person can only be effective with your help, which begins with training and continues throughout the life of the program. As in any job search, first ensure that the candidate has the skills, motivation, and "fit." Then focus on training. Providing compensation and support in a learning community are also important. As always, attention to detail is necessary: "It is a challenge to get good teachers," notes Lisa Shaw, former director of adult programs at the Levine School of Music, "but the biggest challenge is dealing with the ones that turn out not to be good."

This section looks at:

- Assessing qualifications
- Making the hire
- Conducting training
- Providing support
- Train the trainer programs

Assessing Qualifications

A good place to start is with the definition of a teaching artist. According to Eric Booth, teaching artist and founding editor of *Teaching Artists Journal*:

> The term is usually applied to those artists who draw people into arts experiences, without the intent to make them skilled practitioners. (Although they certainly may hope their involvement will inspire participants to investigate the art form further.)

For a New Horizons Band, the absolute home run is the retired music teacher who is legendary in the community.

Roy Ernst, Founder, New Horizons Music

> These TAs work with students in schools, with prisoners, seniors, businesspeople, and teachers. Their work serves many purposes (not just development of skills in the art form), which include boosting learning, preparing people to see performances, awakening individual expressiveness and creativity, transforming a group's interpersonal dynamics, enhancing appreciation of art and life.
>
> The teaching artist's expertise is the capacity to engage almost anyone in arts experiences… Their gift is to draw people into arts experientially, and not through the traditional routes of giving information first or direct instruction. They create a safe and exciting atmosphere that leads people into authentic work in the art form before they get insecure, judgmental, or doubtful that they are skilled enough to be engaging artistically. TAs are masters at tapping people's artistic competence.[85]

Because this expertise corresponds with outcome goals for participants, a professional teaching artist enhances a program's effectiveness and success.

In the search for the best candidate, look for a practicing artist with these skills:

1. Understanding of your art form
   - Knowledge of basic formal language
   - Knowledge of trends, history, and styles of the discipline
   - Knowledge of key practitioners of the discipline, both historical and contemporary
   - Understanding of the creative process (e.g., inspiration, planning, developing an idea, using materials and techniques, expression)

2. Understanding of the classroom environment, andragogy, and human development
   - Process and product, the continuum in experiencing the arts
   - Planning a lesson, including modeling, demonstration, and differentiated instruction
   - Time management
   - Hallmarks of normal aging
   - Curriculum unit and residency planning
   - Classroom management
   - Evaluation and assessment, strategies and practices

3. Understanding of the collaborative process; working in a facility
   - The residency planning process
   - Working with others[86]

Leaders in the arts and aging field emphasize the importance of these skills and competencies for the teaching artist:

- Must be able to orchestrate group dynamics, which builds trust, makes participants comfortable with expressing what they think and feel, and sparks spontaneity. He or she must have experience teaching groups and teaching sequentially.

- Should commit to the entire program, which could be multiyear.

- Should be a practicing professional artist. The quality of the artist supports your value of honoring and respecting older adults.

- Should be committed to community arts and understand the value of the process of making art

- Must be organized, a problem solver, and a talented communicator

- Must commit to being part of the team and be willing to prepare financial reports or any other bureaucratic documentation with minimum fuss

In addition, some skills are linked to specific artistic disciplines and types of programs. Those who direct New Horizons bands, for example, ideally should be music educators because they are experienced in group instruction at different levels and with different instruments. For intergenerational programs, regardless of discipline, the teaching artist or facilitator must be able to communicate and work with both young people and older adults.

Most of these skills are tangible. Perhaps greater determining factors of the effectiveness of a teaching artist are intangible qualities:

- Willing to go the extra mile
- Flexible
- Sociable
- Able to figure out what people want
- On the side of older adults
- Able to deal with people
- Compassionate
- Patient

Finally, artists who are successful in working with older adults usually have had or want a connection to older adults.

Making the Hire

The most effective way to find a teaching artist is by word of mouth. Talk to

- school or out-of-school art, music, and chorus teachers;
- educators who work at arts organizations or institutions such as museums, symphonies, chamber music groups, choruses, and opera, dance, and theater companies;
- those associated with community schools of the arts; and
- artists whom you see at arts events or festivals in the community.

Look for community arts organizations and institutions that use professional teaching artists. Arts education organizations such as community schools of the arts are good places to start. Identify resources in your community through the member directory of the National Guild of Community Schools of the Arts (www.nationalguild.org/non_member_search.cfm). Identify other arts education organizations through the Americans for the Arts field directory (ww2.americansforthearts.org/vango/custom/directory.aspx). Arts programs at colleges, community colleges, and universities are also likely to be helpful.

In addition, almost all local, state, and regional arts agencies have adjudicated rosters of artists. In New England, for example, MatchBook.org features a free searchable directory of artists, performance spaces, and presenting organizations designed to match artists with presenters. In the *audiences served* search category, selecting *elders* is an option. Locate regional and state arts agencies through the National Assembly of State Arts Agencies (www.nasaa-arts.org) and local arts agencies through Americans for the Arts (www.americansforthearts.org).

Don't overlook older teaching artists who add value to arts and aging programs. Writing in *Vital Involvement in Old Age*, the authors explain:

> Observing and reacting to the aging of their contemporaries seems to help [older adults] to integrate aspects of their own aging, to view their individual experiences in a reassuring social perspective. For all of its frightening concomitants—recognized and unrecognized—growing old, in these terms, is a powerful confirmation of membership in a human race that is more expansive and more enduring than any one lifetime.[87]

Janine Tursini, executive director of Arts for the Aging adds: "For many of our older adult teaching artists, they now recognize the importance of their work. They are enriched in new ways by participants, and vice versa."

Aside from conducting a job interview to ascertain whether a candidate has the necessary skills and qualities, ask him or her to do a teaching audition. Go see and hear the artist perform, or view his or her work.

Conducting Training

Creating a plan and allowing sufficient time for training helps ensure the success of a teaching artist. Chances are great that you are not going to find the perfect person who has all of the necessary skills and qualities. Do the best that you can, and rely on training to address any deficiencies. Remember to pay the teaching artist for time spent in professional development.

One common deficiency is experience in working with older adults. Most professional teaching artists work with students in schools or in community arts facilities and other settings. Likely training topics are:

- Normal aging
- Special considerations for working with frail elders or older adults with dementia
- How to work in a senior center, adult day program, or long-term care facility
- The relative importance of the process of making art compared with the art that is created
- Administrative requirements, such as attending partnership team meetings and maintaining records

While most professional teaching artists are experienced at group facilitation, consider providing a refresher. The International Association of Facilitators has an online publication, *Basic Facilitation Skills* (www.iaf-world.org/files/public/FacilitatorMnl.pdf), and other resources on its Web site, www.iaf-world.org. Another option is the Technology of Participation facilitation method created by the Institute of Cultural Affairs. Check out www.ica-usa.org/index.html.

As noted in chapter 6, an effective method is to plan joint professional development opportunities among team members and other staff. This approach creates and strengthens the learning community and each person's commitment to and knowledge of the program.

Anne Basting and John Killick have a good description of considerations for training teaching artists who work with older adults with dementia:

> [The artist] may never have worked with people with dementia before and may suffer a kind of culture shock in coming into contact with unusual behaviors and unexpected communication problems. To let the artist sink or swim in these circumstances would not be a recipe for getting the best out of the situation. In a spirit of goodwill, staff could adopt a process of induction which might include a preliminary information session about

what to expect (not necessarily full of medical explanations, though these could be supplied if requested), followed by a gentle taking of the hand in the early sessions especially, until they have settled in. It is a good idea to have one member of staff with a special responsibility for helping the artist out with practical problems and acting as confidante.[88]

Basting and Killick also provide advice about working in a facility with older adults of various abilities:

> Working in your organization may be a new experience for the artist. This doesn't just apply to the large parameters within which it operates but small customs, even quirks, which make it individual and distinguishable from other organizations of a similar kind. A visiting artist can easily fall foul of the rules and procedural niceties that the regular staff take for granted. They can be helped to come to terms with these. For example, some facilities have rules about knocking before entering a room. Artists might need to learn a code to turn off an alarm, or what your facility sets as bathroom protocol.[89]

Train teaching artists by giving them direct instruction and reading material, and facilitating their experiential learning. The latter is typically the most effective

Program Example: Training Teaching Artists

Arts for the Aging contracts with approximately 18 teaching artists. There are one or two openings a year for new artists, who are identified mostly by word of mouth and faculty recommendations. Interested candidates submit resumes, interview with the program director, and visit programs in three different disciplines. The artist's training is guided by an Instructor Observation Sheet (Appendix 6), which also includes questions to answer specific to each observation, so that the learning is sequential. The trainee meets with each of the three teaching artists and completes a Program Proposal Form (Appendix 6). At the same time, the program director gives the trainee reading materials on creativity and aging and dementia and Alzheimer's disease.

Once the proposal is reviewed and revised, the trainee receives a stipend to lead the program at five different senior centers under the program director's supervision. Experienced teaching artists continue to provide mentoring. Finally, following a post-mortem discussion with the prospective artist and with senior center staff, Arts for the Aging offers the teaching artist a one-year, renewable contract.

Executive Director Janine Tursini notes that this experiential training is an effective way for potential teaching artists to learn the importance of process and understand that little movements such as toe tapping signify success. It also familiarizes them with diverse classroom settings in day care centers, nursing homes, and community centers. Observation, supervision, and mentorship ensure that the teaching artist is prepared to effect positive change in participants and to cope with challenges.

technique. Regardless of the amount or quality of the training, teaching artists are likely to be overwhelmed at first. They will also encounter challenges. But with a clear understanding of goals and expectations, and the ongoing support of you and the entire partnership team or staff, they—and your participants—will succeed.

Providing Support

Teaching artists require two kinds of support: adequate compensation for their services and a learning community in which they share advice and methods with peers and supervisors.

Compensation

Teaching artists are professionals who are providing a service. An important principle is to pay them adequately for teaching, professional development, and administration (e.g., planning and evaluation meetings). Remember to reimburse them for transportation expenses. Few organizations are financially able to provide full-time employment to teaching artists—especially in the aging services field, where facilities typically devote only a small percentage of their budgets to activities.

How much to pay artists depends on the geographic region and what you ask them to do. One information source is the National Guild of Community Schools of the Arts' *Survey of Member Schools Report*, which includes teaching artist salaries, faculty pay rates, and more (www.nationalguild.org/publications.htm).

Teaching Artists' Fees

Music for All Seasons (New Jersey): $120 to $140 each for a 50- to 60-minute performance plus transportation expenses.

Center for Elders and Youth in the Arts (California): $64 for each 90-minute session. Some programs are 12 sessions, but most are 24 to 46 sessions. Artists also receive $20 per hour to attend an average of 12 training and planning meetings a year.

Organization on the East Coast: $55 to $95 for each hour-long workshop based on experience, quality of programs, and tenure. It also reimburses for mileage incurred traveling to programs.

You may encounter the perception among some funders and aging service organizations that teaching artists should volunteer their time and talents. Educate these people about the skills and qualities of professional teaching artists, connecting who they are and what they do with outcome goals for older adults. Remember, it always circles back to programmatic impact and benefits to participants.

Learning Community

A learning community is a group of people who have common values and beliefs and who are actively engaged in learning together and from each other. In a learning community, teaching artists, supervisors, staff, the partnership team, other teaching artists, and participants problem solve, celebrate triumphs, learn new skills and information, and share ideas and techniques. They renew themselves mentally and emotionally, combating burnout, reconnecting with the value of their work, and moving forward together.

> **Program Example: A Learning Community**
>
> EngAGE: The Art of Active Aging (formerly known as More Than Shelter For Seniors) has in-service training in which teaching artists are encouraged to examine their own assumptions about aging and about art while sharing communication tools, strategies, and experiences and engaging in "group thinks" about future programming and classes. EngAGE staff are a learning community in which they all continue to learn and grow from and with each other. Collectively and individually, they learn with and from the older adults in their client facilities; for example, a performance teacher collaborated with the teacher of a writing group, using hats as props and improvisation to stimulate imaginative storytelling. The ways in which the senior participants in the writing group used the props, the stories they told, and the experiences they shared provided great learning opportunities for everyone involved.

The counseling function of a learning community is particularly important for teaching artists who work with older adults who have dementia. Anne Basting and John Killick explain that staff who work with people with dementia experience stress that can lead to burnout. Because an arts project, which "provides opportunities for the access of buried memories and the release of hitherto unacknowledged emotions," can cause distress in participants, they need an appropriate support system in place. Staff, too, can experience anxiety, especially if they are not used to working with people with dementia. "One of the problems of accompanying people with dementia on their respective journeys," Basting and Killick say, "is that the grief they may express is often unresolvable and therefore has to be carried by others."[90]

To create a learning community, schedule a regular time for everyone to come together, ideally in a comfortable space with sofas and easy chairs. Have snacks and soft drinks available. One person facilitates the free-form discussion, and this role rotates among members of the group. Ask people to share problems or successes, and encourage others to chime in with advice.

Train the Trainer Programs

"Train the trainer" is a method of training a nonartist to facilitate a program. It is most appropriate for programs targeted at people with dementia. Since the primary outcome goal for this population is social engagement and not mastery, the artistic expertise and skill level of a professional teaching artist are less important. Consider, however, using a teaching artist to conduct the training.

If you plan to train others to lead a program, focus on staff of residential facilities, senior centers, and adult day programs. The key qualifications are compassion and knowledge of how to work with people with dementia. Other tips for planning the training include:

- Encourage administrators to attend, thus gaining the necessary buy-in from the top and freeing up other staff to be trained.

- Train staff members, including activities directors and others, who *aren't* responsible for day-to-day care. This makes the arts program special for residents.

- Train staff or others who have self-selected to be trained. Those who are assigned will lead the programs, but fewer benefits will accrue to participants.

Two programs in the arts and aging field are Memories in the Making and TimeSlips. Their training topics include:

- **Memories in the Making**
  - » How to conduct an art class
  - » How to motivate individuals with Alzheimer's dementia to paint using techniques developed in the Memories in the Making Art Training Program method
  - » How to be to be sensitive to physical impairments
  - » How to listen to and validate the participants
  - » How to create a social setting that encourages a safe place to be
  - » How to process feelings

- **TimeSlips**
  - » The meaning and value of creative expression
  - » An introduction to dementia and dementia care
  - » The basics of person-centered care
  - » The TimeSlips storytelling process in detail
  - » Models for sharing the stories with your community

As in the familiar game of "Telephone," a challenge for train the trainer programs is ensuring quality all the way down the line and ensuring that your philosophy is transmitted accurately. A related challenge occurs when a trained staff member — for example, an activities director — leaves his or her facility and attempts to train others, further diluting the philosophy and affecting the quality. Knowing how to facilitate a Memories in the Making or TimeSlips program could be a selling point for a staff member seeking a new job. While this is also true for professional teaching artists and arts organization staff, turnover is generally higher among the professional caregivers and activities staff who are the primary cadre of trainers. Other challenges include:

- Staff members who are facilitators underestimate the abilities of their older adult participants.
- One facility requires repeated trainings because of high staff turnover.

Mish Mash in America

A man is reading in an o.k. room in New York City.

He is silently analyzing.
He is quietly happy.

He's putting something together.

He'll be at it for 2 hours.

The room is messy.

A woman gave him that hat.

He has no family of his own.
His family is his books.

He is squinting and closing his eyes so he can concentrate.

He is accepting the responsibility to organize all this into something.

He is looking for something, but he hasn't found it yet.

He is orchestrating an orchestra in his mind.

There is a desk beneath all those books.

He has a very smart finger.

He is very bright.

He is singing a song of sixpence,

and then a song of Daisy.

—*TimeSlips story*

Program Examples:
Train the Trainer Programs

Memories in the Making has one trainer who conducts three-hour classes for anyone interested in learning how to use visual art as a communication tool for individuals with dementia and related disorders. The ideal facilitator for the program is a person familiar with Alzheimer's disease who has an interest in art.

The *TimeSlips* program trains trainers who train facilitators. It has one national and eight regional training bases, which include an Osher Lifelong Learning Institute, an Alzheimer's Association, a university, several long-term care facilities, and Elders Share the Arts.

The TimeSlips method is taught in a daylong intensive workshop that can accommodate as many as 50 trainees and is ideal for all levels of professional and informal caregivers. Certification lasts for three years, and continuing education credits are available. Those who train the hands-on facilitators offer ongoing support through phone and e-mail counseling. Facilitators are also asked to keep a journal, which the trainers review. For larger facilities whose staff has been trained, trainers sometimes return to conduct a refresher class, and they usually return for the culminating celebration.

Key Points about Supporting Teaching Artists

- Understand the definition of a teaching artist and what tangible skills and knowledge he or she should possess, particularly group facilitation, community arts, and high artistic quality.

- Seek out those with the intangible qualities such as people skills, motivation, compassion, and flexibility.

- Find likely candidates through a variety of community arts organizations, and encourage artists and educators to get the word out for you.

- Create a plan and allow sufficient time for training, which should emphasize experiential learning.

- Ensure that teaching artists are prepared to work with older adults regardless of their abilities and whether they live in the community or in a residential facility.

- Foster a learning community to provide ongoing support to teaching artists and program and partner staff.

- Demonstrate how much you value teaching artists by providing sufficient compensation.

- Understand that train the trainer programs empower others—often staff of long-term care facilities—to use the arts to facilitate social engagement of older adults who have dementia.

The Golden Tones gives me a purpose in life. Learning new songs has improved my mind and memory. Performing has improved my posture, health, and appearance. Making others happy makes me happy.

Edith, member of the Golden Tones

Evaluation

If your reaction to the word *evaluation* is anxiety, you are not alone. In all fields, not just arts and aging, many leaders confess that evaluation plays second fiddle to programming because there is not enough time or money to do both. They may solicit reactions and ideas from participants and teaching artists after sessions, and they may collect data on participants or audience members. Otherwise, they rely on informal observation and anecdotes. This tactic is perfectly valid and a good way to begin.

Ideally, however, you should aim for something more sophisticated: evaluating impact. You want to be able to prove that what you are doing is making a difference to participants and respond with more than attendance statistics and heartwarming stories, though these measures play a role. With the right kind of information on the impact of your program, you can gain access to more resources, garner greater public visibility, improve instructional design, and ultimately affect the lives of more older adults.

Like so many other aspects of arts and aging programs, effective evaluation requires planning. Figuring out what you want to learn, what you can afford to learn, who can help, and how to communicate results to various audiences takes time and creativity. Start modestly by tracking quantitative data such as attendance and administering satisfaction surveys to participants and partners. Or conduct a more sophisticated evaluation as a small pilot project. Supplement this data with anecdotes that you've heard, and you are ready to write an evaluation report. Remember that many funders have requirements for or strong preferences about evaluation.

This chapter looks at:

- Defining terms
- Understanding benefits
- Planning the evaluation
- Implementing the evaluation
- Evaluating people with dementia

Defining Terms

Just as you can be tangled up in the differences among mission, goals, objectives, and activities, so too can the various types of evaluation be confusing. It is a science that often seems mysterious, understandable only by highly paid experts. But you are really just exploring what happens to participants during program sessions. This exploration is usually defined as either *process* or *outcome* evaluation:

- **Process evaluation** examines the effectiveness of a program in progress so you can make adjustments.

- **Outcome evaluation** assesses how the results of a program affected the community and whether the program met its stated goals.

Two concepts nearly identical to process and outcome are *formative* and *summative* evaluation:

- **Formative evaluation** helps *form* the program, from the initial development through its ongoing improvement. Its primary audience is internal—the partnership team.

- **Summative evaluation** *sums up* the entire program, figuring out whether the program did what it was designed to do. Its primary audience is external—the stakeholders, particularly funders.

Evaluation expert Robert Stakes explains the difference this way: "When the cook tastes the soup, that's formative; when the guests taste the soup, that's summative."[91]

Qualitative and *quantitative* are perhaps the most common terms in evaluation. They describe the type of information collected, the method of collection, and the analysis (fig. 8-1). The qualitative method is further characterized as "deep" and the quantitative method as objective.

In reality, the distinction between methods is not absolute. Surveys, in particular, often include questions that elicit qualitative information—for example, those that assess satisfaction or quality—and interviews can collect demographic data.

Not surprisingly, evaluation experts sometimes disagree over definitions. Craig Dreeszen's advice is helpful: "Don't panic about variations in evaluation jargon. Just be sure that folks within your organization know what you are talking about."[92]

Qualitative vs. Quantitative

	Type	Method	Analysis
Qualitative	Anecdotes Reactions Impressions Feelings	Interviews Observations Focus groups Journals	Words Pictures Objects
Quantitative	Numbers Statistics	Surveys Questionnaires	Numerical data

fig. 8-1

Understanding Benefits

Outcome evaluation is important. Conducted with forethought, credibility, and purpose, the results can benefit an organization or program by

- building shared meaning and understanding;
- supporting and enhancing the program;
- supporting human and organizational development; and
- generating new knowledge about effective practice.

According to the American Society on Aging,

1. *Evaluations affect funding.*
   One of the greatest challenges community organizations face is finding funding for important programs. Your organization's capability to systematically demonstrate past successes will give funding sources confidence in your ability to effectively carry out the programs they are asked to finance.

2. *Evaluations document achievement.*
   If the approach and strategies you developed successfully increased physical activity among older adults or changed dietary habits, the evaluation will document the program's effectiveness. The maxim, "If it isn't documented, it didn't happen," holds true for future program development and justification.

3. *Evaluations can help you correct mistakes and maintain program flexibility.*
   Success fuels success. Evaluation lets you build on the strengths of past programs and learn from their problems to develop stronger future efforts. Continued evaluation keeps programs fresh and adaptable

to changes in the environment or community.

4. *Good evaluations motivate staff.* Knowing that the program met its goals will motivate staff to continue the long hours of community-building work.[93]

Additional benefits from evaluation include

- setting standards and accountability for future performance;
- informing decisions on what programs to cut if hard choices need to be made; and
- providing the rationales for advocacy.

Because funding is a key issue, it is worth emphasizing that many public agencies and private foundations require information about the impact of their dollars on the targeted populations. They need to be accountable to the public or their boards of directors. Funders want this topic addressed not only in final reports, but also in grant applications.

Planning the Evaluation

Assessing impact on participants takes place throughout a program, not just at the end. Indeed, some measures such as attendance or enrollment and methods such as experimental design have to be in place *before* the program begins. Plan an evaluation by following these steps:

- Determining what you want to learn
- Assessing costs
- Identifying audiences
- Devising communications tools
- Seeking help

Determining What You Want to Learn

This decision drives the evaluation. What you want to know is whether participants achieved any of the outcome goals listed in chapter 5. Review these goals as you plan and implement your evaluation so you can maintain focus on the bottom line: participants' physical, mental, and social health. Craig Dreeszen lists these key questions:

- What did you intend to achieve with your program?
- Were program activities consistent with your intentions?
- If so, did you observe the intended outcomes? What unintended outcomes did you also observe?
- How do you account for the variations (observed outcomes from intended objectives)?
- What changes should you make in your program based on evaluation?

- How likely is it that observed outcomes were caused by the program activities?
- How close were your actual outcomes? You may achieve some positive results or negative consequences that were not part of your plan.
- What did you learn from your evaluation that will improve your program or plan new ones?[94]

Assessing outcomes also informs evaluation of how the program affected personnel, budget, and partnerships. If the program is a success for the participants, it softens the blow of higher-than-anticipated expenses or mitigates the impact of grumpier-than-usual staff members or partners. Questions include:

- What were the costs of each activity (include direct costs such as staff time, supplies, honoraria, advertising fees, and room rental)?
- How many participants, media contacts, distribution sites, or phone calls did that activity generate?
- Based on the desired results of these activities, how do these costs compare?
- Did some activities appear to work as well as others but cost less?
- What assumptions did you make in determining which approaches worked better than others?
- Did any conflicts occur among the program partners' organizational agendas or operating styles?
- How did the timing of the program coordinate with the different organizations involved?
- Did the collaboration strengthen the program?
- Would the program have functioned as well without the partnership?[95]

To delve deeper into the partnership dynamics at the conclusion of your program, revisit the checklist in chapter 6.

Another answer to the question "What do you want to learn?" is the impact of the community sharing of the art created during the program. If external validation of accomplishment is beneficial to older adults' experience of mastery, then the audience's reaction to a performance or exhibit is important to measure. Questions should explore basic reactions to the art, perhaps by asking respondents to circle descriptive adjectives. More important, assess the change in audience members' perceptions about the capabilities of older adults.

If you are working with other organizations, determine the specific questions in collaboration with the partnership team. Remember to raise this topic with the major funders. Many of them have a particular interest in evaluation and a penchant for certain kinds of information.

A common pitfall in figuring out what you want to learn is focusing solely on the outcomes that pertain directly to your field. Aging services organizations need to evaluate older adults' skill development and learning in the arts; arts organizations need to evaluate older adults' physical, mental, and social development.

Program Example: How to Measure an Objective

Objective	Outputs	Outcomes		
Initiate a partnership between our organization—the local community music school—and the nearby senior center to form an older adult chorus with a target membership of 40 older adults at the beginning of the first year and 50 at the beginning of the second year.	Number of people recruited to serve on the advisory committee Number of people who attended an informational session Number of members at the beginning of the first year Number of members at the beginning of the second year Attendance at each rehearsal Number of performances in the community Attendance at each performance	Members socialize before and after rehearsals. Members help each other during rehearsals. Members carpool to rehearsals and performances. Members socialize outside of rehearsals and performances. Senior center staff and community music school students, faculty, and staff recognize and greet chorus members.	Social Engagement	Improved mental and physical health for participants
		Members are better singers. Members learn about music. Members enroll in private or group vocal instruction at the community music school.	Mastery	
		Friends or family members enroll in private or group vocal instruction at the community music school. Data generated make the case for continuing the program.	Organizational Outcomes	

Assessing Costs

Don't devote more time, energy, and money to evaluation than you did to implementation. Reflect on these issues:

> Be clear about the purpose of the evaluation. Ask where does information already exist. Consider how easy is it to get and use the information. Do you have to reorganize the data? Would less-straightforward measures work as well? Is there some information that we can get at easily enough, well enough to make competent decisions about the program?[96]

With respect to cost, some experts suggest devoting 5 to 7 percent of the total program budget to evaluation. Others say 10 to 15 percent. Expenses include:

- Evaluation staff salary and benefits
- Consultants
- Travel
- Communications
- Printing and duplication
- Printed materials
- Supplies and equipment

Obviously, spending this amount of money isn't always possible. Fortunately, there are options. Start modestly with some basic quantitative measures and a few qualitative questions on a survey form. Or conduct a pilot evaluation that utilizes a variety of more sophisticated measures to assess the impact on a small number of participants. In subsequent years, increase the scope of your evaluation as you gain experience (and funds).

Program Example: Pilot Evaluation

Music for All Seasons conducted a pilot project in collaboration with the New Jersey Neuroscience Institute at JFK Medical Center to measure the quality of life among 23 nursing home residents with dementia. Staff tracked the number of falls, number of times sedating medication was given, and quality of life using the Quality of Life in Dementia scale. Using a repeated measures design, the participants were tested before and after two live music performances given six weeks apart. Each set of measures was taken at two-week intervals. The principal result was a measured increase in quality of life. Scores increased significantly following each performance and maintained this increase for as long as six weeks.

Identifying Audiences

Typical audiences are:

- Your board of directors or other key advisors
- Partners, including participants and staff
- Funders
- Community leaders, including policy makers and elected officials
- Colleagues in your field
- Media

Not every one will be interested in the same type of information. Indeed, each group has different responsibilities and interests. Focusing on the needs of partners, Stephanie Golden notes:

> Hospitals and nursing homes… need process notes documenting whether a patient's ability to interact improved and whether the workshop stimulated [his or] her creative imagination. Schools require a portfolio of each student's work, including both art projects and their journals. The teacher uses the portfolio to assess the students' learning in the program. Senior and community centers may only want a report based on the survey information, or they may request a record of attendance, skills learned, and works produced.[97]

Participants are most likely to be interested in qualitative information—the anecdotes and images that provide tangible evidence of a productive and happy experience. Members of the media, too, will want photos and stories with a human interest "hook." Funders and your board of directors, who are more interested in the program's success, may prefer quantitative data. Community leaders will probably want both to provide content for speeches and show constituents that they support older adults. Catering to all of these audiences doesn't mean conducting different evaluations or distorting the results. It simply means emphasizing different information in each report.

Don't overlook the importance of broadening the circle of those who receive the results of your evaluation. Sharing information and knowledge with each other contributes to the growth of the arts and aging field. In addition, evaluation results provide the content for public awareness efforts and the ammunition you sometimes need within your own organization.

Creating Communication Tools

The basic document is a comprehensive, written, final report that includes all of the evaluation results and an executive summary. Adapt this report to produce:

- One- or two-page "briefs," each summarizing a key finding, included in the general information package
- Press releases
- Stories with images for the community newspaper
- Presentations of different lengths and focuses to deliver at:
  » Community meetings: Invite local leaders to a brown-bag lunch to announce the evaluation results and lead a discussion of implications.
  » State-level meetings: Call the state arts agency or aging services office and offer to provide content at their meetings.
  » National meetings of organizations in the arts and aging services fields
- A "low-tech" book for program participants that includes images and anecdotes
- A Web site section devoted to the evaluation results. Include a PDF version of the entire report and each brief; links to media stories about the program; key findings arranged in bullet points; and images.

Optimize your time by writing some of these pieces shortly after completing the final report so that you can respond quickly to requests for details or just follow up on any expressed interest.

Seeking Help

You don't have to wrestle with evaluation on your own. In addition to assistance from the partnership team or staff members, identify an evaluation partner such as a university, or hire a consultant. You are more likely to need external help if your evaluation is sophisticated. Sometimes an outside expert enhances the credibility of your results. It is important to decide early in the planning process whether to use an external evaluator because the evaluation may include surveying or interviewing participants before the program begins. Moreover, making arrangements with an external partner takes time.

Good resources for finding an evaluator are local and state arts agencies, large state and local universities, and large foundations.

Universities

Look for a university with a research center or an academic program in psychology, sociology, arts administration, aging services, or social work to be your evaluation partner. While you will probably pay for services, aim to establish a mutually beneficial partnership in which you exchange free evaluation advice and/or services for real-life experience for the university's students. Designing an evaluation might be a good class project. If you intend to find an academic partner, invite a representative of the institution to serve on your advisory committee.

Consultants

Many consultants specialize in planning and conducting evaluations of all shapes and sizes for varying fees. You may be able to contract with a consultant for a short period to give you specific advice, but chances are that he or she will want to be involved for the entire program. This arrangement can be the best investment. Like a partner in higher education, a consultant not only designs the evaluation, but also helps ensure that your objectives are measurable; you are clear about what you want to learn; and you know — and know how — to communicate with various audiences.

Look for a consultant who

- has experience in evaluating arts or humanities education programs and writing results for nonacademic audiences;
- wants to give you the knowledge and tools to evaluate programs yourself;
- understands that evaluation is a means to an end; and
- is interested enough in the topic to negotiate a reasonable price.

Partnership Team

Each partner has a unique perspective and valuable skills to contribute to the evaluation process. Staff members of senior centers, adult day programs, and long-term care facilities are well positioned to assess the impact of arts and aging programs on participants. Not only do they observe older adults on a routine basis, but they also can administer surveys. Teachers and coordinators at a school or in an out-of-school program are similarly equipped and able to evaluate students who participate in an intergenerational program. A challenge in schools, out-of-school programs, and aging services facilities is lack of time. Activities directors, certified nursing assistants, and teachers are underpaid, overworked, and underbudgeted. This argues for involving them in designing the evaluation: if they are invested early, they are more likely to follow through, and their input will strengthen the process.

Implementing the Evaluation

Most evaluators use a combination of tools to assess the efficacy of their programs and the satisfaction of partners and participants.

As you consider which tools best match what you need to learn about impact and whom you want to measure, consider these questions:

- Is the instrument valid? Does it measure what it claims to measure?
- How reliable is the measuring instrument? Will it provide the same answers even if it is administered at different times or in different places?
- Are the methods and instruments suitable for the population being studied and the problems being assessed?
- Can the methods and instruments detect salient issues, meaningful changes, and various outcomes of the project?[98]

According to the American Society on Aging, quantitative methods are best to

- gather data that are representative of a large group of people;
- get large amounts of data from many different people; and
- validate findings of qualitative data.

Use qualitative methods to:

- gain insight into the opinions, perceptions, and experiences of program participants;
- get a better understanding of the context that informs responses; and
- illustrate relationships found in quantitative data.[99]

Regardless of the method, remember to collect only the information that you are going to use and use all of the information that you collect.

You may encounter concerns about confidentiality when assessing older adults. Promising discretion and anonymity and aggregating results are logical solutions. In addition, the privacy regulations mandated by the Health Insurance Portability and Accountability Act (HIPPA) are a barrier in long-term care facilities to collecting medical data such as blood pressure or medication usage. Residents need to sign waivers allowing you access to this information.

Leaders of arts and aging programs universally comment that older adults vote with their feet. And they are rarely shy about sharing their opinions with you. While this is useful feedback, include a variety of evaluation tools to get an objective and credible picture of the program's impact. In order of complexity, these tools are:

- Attendance, enrollment, and membership data
- Informal feedback
- Observation
- Program surveys
- Interviews
- Focus groups
- Portfolio review
- Experimental design

Attendance, Enrollment, and Membership Data

Use these three measures to obtain answers to basic quantitative questions, such as:

- How many participants paid for or signed up to take the series of classes?
- How many paid a membership fee to join or committed to participating in the orchestra or chorus?
- How many actually attended each session? Was there an increase or decrease in attendance rate as the program progressed?
- What are the demographics of these participants or members—age, race, ethnicity, and education level—and where do they live?
- How many friends, other residents, staff, family members, and others attended the community sharing of the art?

Informal Feedback

Informal feedback is information you receive from participants, caregivers, family members, partners, and anyone involved with the program, plus what you overhear at the celebration of the community sharing of the art—or in the hallway. Often, these anecdotes will enliven an evaluation report or presentation. To be effective, ask leading questions and listen.

Observation

Informal or formal observation includes what you see with your own eyes and through the lens of a camera. Observation is often used with people with dementia. Evaluation of this population is discussed later in this chapter.

Informally, observe participants as they perform or exhibit and audience members who join you in honoring the art created by the older adults. In a session or rehearsal, note

- who has become more talkative, outgoing, and engaged;
- who remembers the sequence of movement; and
- who is now, after many weeks, participating in the program.

For a more formal observation, use specific questions to ensure consistency among observers and across multiple sessions.

> **Program Example:**
> Formal Observation
>
> The Visual Analog Recreational Music-Making (RMM) Assessment (VARMMA), developed by Dr. Barry Bittman, is designed to rate six parameters:
>
> 1. Attentiveness (appearing connected to and observant of the RMM activity)
> 2. Active participation (the state of actually performing the designated RMM activity)
> 3. Socialization (positive interaction with others in the group)
> 4. Positive mood/affect (a cooperative favorable disposition)
> 5. Happiness/contentment/joy (signifies a pleasurable or satisfying experience)
> 6. Meaningful self-expression (appropriateness of one's contribution and actions to the program content)
>
> *The assessment uses a five-point rating scale:*
>
> 0 = none;
> 1 = minimal;
> 2 = at times;
> 3 = often; and
> 4 = frequent.[100]

In addition to providing invaluable documentation that contributes to marketing, public relations, and advocacy efforts, videography is an effective evaluation tool. Instead of attending sessions and recording observations on the spot, videotape the session and conduct analysis later. A researcher at the University of Oklahoma is reviewing videos of three different sessions of the Alzheimer's Poetry Project and cataloguing the responses of participants. She will compare these findings with reactions to other types of intervention, such as pet therapy and volunteers reading aloud from the newspaper.

Program Surveys

These surveys assess participants' satisfaction with a program. They can also gauge motivations and expectations for participating and collect quantitative data and anecdotes through open-ended questions. Program surveys are the best way to get audience members' reactions to community sharing of the art, using a short response card rather than a longer survey. Traditionally, responses are anonymous, though you can include an optional name field.

The W. K. Kellogg Foundation has the following tips for making written evaluation surveys as effective as possible:

1. Make the questions short and clear, ideally no more than 20 words. Be sure to give the respondents all the information they will need to answer the questions.

2. Avoid questions that have more than one central idea or theme.

3. Keep questions relevant to the problem.

4. Do not use jargon. Your target population must be able to answer the questions you are asking. If they are not familiar with professional jargon, do not use it.

5. Avoid words that are not exact (e.g., generally, usually, average, typically, often, and rarely). If you do use these words, you may get information that is unreliable or not useful.

6. Avoid stating questions in the negative.

7. Avoid introducing bias. Slanted questions will produce slanted results.

8. Make sure the answer to one question relates smoothly to the next. For example, if necessary add "if yes… did you?" or "if no… did you?"

9. Give exact instructions to the respondent on how to record answers. For example, explain exactly where to write the answers: check a box, circle a number, etc.

10. Provide response alternatives. For example, include the response "other" for answers that don't fit elsewhere.

11. Make the questionnaire attractive. Plan its format carefully using subheadings, spaces, etc. Make the survey look easy for a respondent to complete. An unusually long questionnaire may alarm respondents.

12. Decide beforehand how the answers will be recorded and analyzed.[101]

Biased Question

Don't you agree that professional teaching artists should earn more money than they currently earn?

Unbiased Question

Do you believe professional teaching artist salaries are a little lower than they should be, a little higher than they should be, or about right?

Program Example: Program Survey Questions

The Legacy Works program of Elders Share the Arts asks participants:

- What was the highlight of this program for you?
- What, if anything, did you find that surprised you?
- How did you like working with your partner?
- If you were to do this program again, what would you do differently?[102]

To administer a program survey, encourage participants to complete it at the last session. You will net a higher return rate than with a mail-in survey. When conducting audience surveys or response cards, include them in performance and exhibit programs, and have a staff member or volunteer hand them out to attendees. Set up several visible boxes to collect the completed forms. Don't forget to provide pencils or pens.

Appendix 7 includes two examples of evaluation surveys: the New Horizons Music Evaluation Form and the Empowerment Group Care Partner Survey, which is targeted to family caregivers.

Interviews

Interviews enable you to explore issues in depth and follow up on answers provided in written surveys. Follow these steps when planning and conducting interviews:

1. Determine a sample of participants to interview.

2. Schedule interviews.

3. Develop an interview guide of evaluation questions.

4. Conduct the interview.

    - Explain why you are asking questions and what will be done with the information.

    - Promise anonymity (and keep that trust!).

    - Ask permission to take notes or record the conversation.

    - Ask and/or observe and record demographic questions (i.e., age, gender, race).

    - Ask program evaluation questions starting with simple descriptive inquiries (What did you make?) and move toward more subtle questions (How did you feel?).

    - Thank the interviewee.

5. Listen well.

6. Probe as needed to clarify answers or elicit more details.

7. Take notes.

8. Summarize on a form.[103]

Select interviewees that represent the diversity of participants in terms of age, gender, ethnicity, education, experience in the art form, and other factors.

Focus Groups

Focus groups are more efficient than interviews because one person's comments often stimulate others to contribute related ideas. Sometimes people are less candid and more cautious in a group, however, because they feel intimidated by the perceived or actual social status of others. When you use this method, ask the same questions as you would in a one-on-one interview, and assemble the group using similar criteria.

Portfolio Review

For visual or literary arts, you can use the art created by older adults—and students—to assess change over the course of a program. Review their respective portfolios at the beginning and end of the program to measure skill development. In the performing arts, you can assess skill development over time through participants' performances. Of course, we have made the point repeatedly that older adults benefit equally from the process of making art; nevertheless, portfolio assessment is an option.

Experimental Design

Even though *experimental design* sounds intimidating and may be time and labor intensive, it is an effective means of capturing how participants change because of your program. Both written surveys and guided observation that test knowledge, beliefs, attitudes, behaviors, skills, condition, or status fit in this category when they are administered *before* and *after* the sessions. This method is also known as a pre-test/post-test design. The obvious challenge is that older adults—and young people in an intergenerational program—may be affected by other variables as diverse as pet therapy, church, or another class.

Adding a control group to your experimental design further enhances the evaluation because it helps eliminate alternate explanations of experimental results. Members of a control group who do not participate in the program must be comparable in terms of numbers and demographics to the experimental group—the participants. Once you identify control group members, administer the same pre- and post-test at roughly the same time.

If you have not planned adequately for evaluation or have a limited budget and want to use a modified experimental design, ask respondents at the end of the program to reflect on how they have changed.

Surveys or tests that are appropriate for use in an experimental design evaluation include:

- The Mini-Mental State Examination (MMSE), a brief, quantitative measure of cognitive status in adults. It can be used to screen for cognitive impairment, estimate the severity of cognitive impairment at a given point in time, follow the course of cognitive changes in an individual over time, and document an individual's response to treatment.[104]

- The Cornell-Brown Scale for Quality of Life measures the quality of life in people with dementia by assessing their mood-related signs (anxiety—comfort, sadness—happiness, lack of reactivity to pleasant events—enjoyment of life's pleasant events, irritability—tolerance) and ideational disturbance (suicide—value of life, self-deprecation—self-esteem, pessimism—optimism, mood-congruent delusions—secure feelings).

Be aware that you may require special expertise or a specific "key" to scoring to analyze some established measurement tools. Research these types of tools on the Internet, or consult with your evaluation partner. Your area agency on aging or local or state arts agency may have a staff member knowledgeable about evaluation or be able to point you to someone who can help.

Appendix 7 includes an example of a survey used in experimental design evaluation: the Empowerment Group Survey: Initial and Six Months.

Evaluating People with Dementia

Guided observation is a method often used to evaluate people with dementia. Tools like surveys and interviews may work as well, depending on each participant's level of cognition. While you want to honor older adults' ability to make choices and be self-reflective, consider designing an evaluation for professional caregivers or family members to complete.

Program Example: Guided Observation

The Greater Cincinnati chapter of the Alzheimer's Association conducted an evaluation of Memories in the Making using an observational instrument. One staff member observed and evaluated one participant for one 60-minute session, measuring objective and subjective indicators of each person's affect (feeling or emotion) state and self-esteem. Observations were completed when six staff persons observed and evaluated 41 artist participants at the six sites. (See Appendix 7 for the survey instrument.)[105]

Anne Basting and John Killick explore evaluation-related issues in *The Arts and Dementia Care*:[106]

> Measuring the success of arts projects is always difficult because the responses to art are of such a personal nature. With people with dementia, it is especially problematic because of the communication difficulties frequently encountered. We favor a multisided approach, involving all those concerned with the project, and even those whom it may only have touched indirectly. Evaluation could include any or all of the following:
>
> 1. Interviews with participants.
>
> 2. Questionnaires filled in by staff and relatives.
>
> 3. Journals kept by the artist(s).
>
> 4. Videos of sessions (these don't have to be of professional quality, just for the record: to remind you of what occurred).
>
> 5. Sound recordings of sessions (again, very basic, but hopefully with sufficient clarity for you to be able to hear contributions).
>
> 6. Photographs of sessions (not for publicity purposes but to catch the moments as they fly).
>
> In finding out from people with dementia themselves their reactions to an arts program, we need to bear in mind both the difficulties they may experience

in accessing their memories of what has been provided, and those involving language and the formulation of answers to questions.

In order to stimulate recall, some or all of the following methods can be used:

1. Showing extracts from videos.

2. Playing sound recordings of sessions.

3. Showing photographs of sessions.

4. Showing props/tools/artifacts used or made in the sessions.

5. Showing evaluation cards with words that describe emotional states such as "silly" or "funny."

Key Points about Evaluation

- Learn the difference among types and methods of evaluation.

- Understand the various and multiple benefits of evaluating the impact of your program on participants.

- Start small, but set your sights on outcome evaluation.

- Determine what kind of evaluation your funders would like you to conduct.

- Decide with your partnership team or staff what you want to learn from the evaluation and what questions to ask to address outcomes.

- Balance the outcomes achieved with the program's impact on personnel, budget, and partners.

- Evaluate how audiences respond to the community sharing of the art.

- Make sure that your evaluation plan is feasible, and understand the costs and cost-effective options.

- Emphasize different aspects of your evaluation results for different audiences.

- Publicize your results to benefit the broader arts and aging field.

- Be creative—and professional— in how you communicate evaluation results, using different types of printed pieces and several presentations of varying lengths and focuses.

- Seek help in evaluation from your partnership team, higher education, and/or consultants.

- Ensure that the evaluation tools measure what you want to measure and are appropriate for the participants, particularly those with dementia.

- Aim to use experimental design.

Your dedication and enthusiasm shine through the music and bring so much enjoyment to all your listeners. For many who had not heard the group before, it was both a surprise and a treat! Thank you, thank you, thank you!

Member, Board of Selectmen,
Wayland, Massachusetts

Public Awareness

Shifts in attitude and changes in policy have stimulated a growing awareness in the United States that older adults are vital assets to our communities—and that the arts are part of the process and part of the solution. Keeping the public awareness momentum moving is important not only to you and your program, but also to the arts and aging field as a whole, because "a rising tide lifts all boats." Unlike marketing, which is geared toward finding participants, and unlike developing resources, raising public awareness ultimately improves the environment for *all* of our programs.

There is no one best way to build public awareness. Different methods work with different audiences, messages, and messengers. It's important for each program and each organization to find the right fit, be creative and persistent, and push its message year-round. This responsibility is not just another task on your to-do list. It is an ongoing activity, accomplished in large measure through relationships and interactions with funders, elected officials, policy makers, and community leaders.

This section looks at:

- Defining terms
- Identifying audiences
- Developing messages
- Selecting messengers
- Developing methods

Defining Terms

Public relations and advocacy both contribute to increasing public awareness. According to the *Fundamentals of Arts Management*, public relations consists of activities

> that build goodwill within a community or audience. Public relations concerns how the public perceives and regards your work. Aims of public relations efforts might be to enhance visibility or credibility for your organization, to build trust with a particular market segment (often a new one), to develop a particular image for your organization (defining your niche or character), to inform your audiences of recent accomplishments, or to counteract general misperceptions, such as the effects of a particular controversy.[107]

The word *advocacy* intimidates some nonprofit leaders who believe that getting involved in advocacy will jeopardize their tax-exempt status or who think that they don't know how to do it. Both of these assumptions are false. Their concern results, in part, from a conflation of the terms *advocacy* and *lobbying*. Thomas L. Birch, legislative counsel to the National Assembly of State Arts Agencies, explains the difference:

> The words advocacy and lobbying are often confused. Advocacy encompasses a wide range of activities. Lobbying is a small part of advocacy; advocacy does not always involve lobbying.

> *There are red states and blue states, but aging is purple.*
>
> Dorcas Hardy, Chairman, Policy Committee, 2005 White House Conference on Aging

> Lobbying is about making positive change to laws that affect us and the causes we serve. Lobbying is trying to influence the voting of legislators; it is urging the passage (or defeat) of a bill in the legislature. Lobbying is citizen action at any level of government. It is part of the democratic process.

> Advocacy is something all of us should do if we believe in the value of public support for the arts; it is democracy in action. Advocacy is building familiarity and trust between you and your elected officials. It is providing reliable information to legislators. Advocacy is offering a personal perspective where public policy decisions are made. Arts advocacy means speaking up for what we believe is important and talking about the arts with the people whose support and influence can help our cause.[108]

Advocacy, in other words, is increasing awareness and appreciation among elected officials, public and private funders, and policy makers of how arts programs enhance older adults' quality of life and benefit the community. It is telling the story.

Identifying Audiences

In communicating the benefits of your arts and aging program, be strategic. What you say and how you say it—and to whom—are important. Key audiences are:

- Arts leaders—who need to understand that older adults are vital members of the community

- Aging services leaders—who need to understand that the arts can enhance older adults' quality of life

- Elected officials—who can set policies favorable to arts and aging programs and allocate funding for them

- Policy makers—who run departments such as parks and recreation, arts, aging services, and public works and can set policies and open doors that support your work

- Businesses and corporations—that can fund your programs through sponsorships

- Foundations—that can fund your programs and drive policy changes through their funding priorities

- Family members—who can
  » use the "power of the purse" to encourage senior centers, adult day programs, and long-term care facilities to offer professionally led, participatory arts programs
  » influence older adults' decisions
  » enable older adults to achieve their outcome goals

- Staff members—who can
  » elect to work in an arts-friendly facility
  » influence older adults' decisions
  » influence policies within their organizations
  » enable older adults to achieve their goals

- Older adults—who are the raison d'être of our work and need to understand its value in their lives

- Media—who can influence public opinion

While implementing a comprehensive public awareness campaign is an option, time and dollars are precious commodities. As you look at these audiences and begin to think about priorities and strategies, consider what audience gives you the "biggest bang for the buck" and can best benefit you and your program.

Developing Messages

As a first step, consider why you want to increase public awareness. The answer is:

- You want all segments of the public to understand that older adults are vital assets to your community.

- The arts can help older adults accomplish the outcome goals described in chapter 5.

- Your programs strengthen community.

> **Program Example:**
> **Public Awareness Goals**
>
> The goals of the Arts and Inspiration Center developed by the Alzheimer's Association's Heart of America and Great Plains chapters are:
>
> 1. To increase understanding about what happens in the Arts and Inspiration Center, therefore decreasing the unknown for the potential participant and his/her family
> 2. To give an opportunity to talk about the importance of addressing Alzheimer's disease in the early stages
> 3. To inform the public about the various supportive services of the Alzheimer's Association, the area agency on aging, and other community resources
> 4. To give a different face to Alzheimer's disease
> 5. To give participants an opportunity to assume an advocacy role
> 6. To allow community members to share their stories about experiences with Alzheimer's disease
> 7. To reduce stigma related to the disease and support a community role in helping those families that are facing this disease[109]

Next, focus on the specific rationales that demonstrate these benefits. You don't have to invent anything new; you already have the content in your grant applications and other funding requests; the overarching benefits (detailed in chapter 2); and the evaluation results that demonstrate your impact.

Ensure that your messages are compelling:

- Be specific, clear, and concise.
- Use active verbs and vivid language.
- Avoid jargon.
- Motivate and stimulate. Emphasize the benefits of the program—don't over-promise.
- Emphasize unique aspects of your program—what sets it apart from similar programs.
- Be consistent in editorial style.
- Edit more than once.
- Get feedback before finalizing copy.[110]

Program Example: Public Awareness Message

EngAGE: The Art of Active Aging (formerly known as More Than Shelter For Seniors) sponsors a weekly one-hour radio show on the local Pacifica Network station. The organization describes the program this way:

> Beamed from Santa Barbara to the Mexican border, *Experience Talks* is a live radio program that shares the experience of dynamic baby boomers and beyond in a way that communicates across generations.
>
> Our program has changed over the two years we've been on the air, and so has our name. You may know us as *Good for Life*. Our tag line has also changed—from *The Voice of Southern California's Seniors*, to *The Voice of the 2nd 50 Years*, to *Experience Talks*.
>
> We've come to learn that it's not so much the age of our guests that unites them, but their ability to learn from and pass on experience. Experience in the hands of people like Patagonia founder, Yvonne Chouinard, actor Ed Asner, State Senator Sheil Kuehl, and playwright John Patrick Shanley leads to reflection, perspective, and—dare we say—wisdom.
>
> In a time when there is so much emphasis on the ephemeral—on passing trends, youth, and novelty—we feel inclined to give a voice to those who've seen a few things, to discuss the subjects that make a difference to how we view ourselves and our world, and perhaps to discover the things that endure.
>
> We know that age isn't necessarily an indicator of wisdom, but it's the baby boomers and those beyond who—like it or not—are now our village elders. In seeking out what the best of them have to say, we hope to give you, the listener, something to reflect on, to smile about, to ponder, and to share with the people in your lives.
>
> Sometimes the tag line says it all. So, we're no longer *Good for Life*—we're now simply *Experience Talks*.[111]

Selecting Messengers

A rule of thumb in public awareness is that the people your program affects are the best messengers. Obviously, in the arts and aging field, this means the program participants. Family members, too, can speak eloquently about benefits. Community leaders—elected officials or business, foundation, or corporate executives—are also effective messengers. If you enlist their help, they can talk about your program to a variety of audiences in different settings. Indeed, your message—the combination of personal stories and the type of hard evidence that you've amassed from outcome evaluations—gives them the content they need to demonstrate their community involvement.

Developing Methods

Public awareness efforts must be ongoing. The success of advocacy, in particular, is directly related to your ability to cultivate policy makers and elected officials throughout the year and over time. Every opportunity that you have to talk or write about the benefits of your arts and aging program is an opportunity to increase public awareness.

In addition to the marketing strategies listed in chapter 6, try these methods:

- **Conduct your program**. Just the act of conducting a program increases public awareness among participants and their friends, family members, and caregivers. Performances and exhibits, in particular, inform these groups and the public in general about the capabilities of older adults, helping to dispel myths of aging. Intergenerational performances reinforce the values of collaboration and community.

- **Create synergy among program components**. In designing the program, consider how to maximize the public awareness potential of each activity. Ensure that participants, partners, funders, and facility and organization staff get something that they want—the classic "win-win"—but don't compromise your principles or lose sight of your goals. A performance of an older adult choir can be a recruitment tool for the senior center where rehearsals are held. Poetry created by participants in a writing program at the library can be featured in the quarterly newsletter from a member of Congress to demonstrate his or her connection to this constituency and support of library funding. Publishing an anthology of this same poetry would be a good opportunity for a reception in honor of program participants; a public presentation of the book to elected officials; and a showcase of library services to the broader community.

Program Example: Creating Synergy

The Foundation for Quality Care's Art from the Heart program is a visual arts competition among residents of long-term care facilities. The winners' works illustrate a calendar, and additional top selections are framed for exhibition. These pieces are loaned to state-level elected officials to be displayed prominently in their offices. Each politician who participates has to pick up the work of art from the facility in which the older adult artist resides. The facility creates a celebratory event around this visit and invites members of the media to attend.

Meanwhile, the calendars are distributed widely to all elected officials and within all relevant state departments, such as health and human services. This practice personalizes residents not only to policy makers, but also to lobbyists and department staff, thus raising awareness.

- **Document your program and related events**. Useful in marketing and evaluation, photographs and videos of participants provide a permanent visual record with many different uses. Images are powerful. Focus on capturing how your program benefits participants. Invest in quality by hiring a professional photographer or videographer. Remember that digital images should be 300 DPI (dots per inch) to be clear and crisp when printed or 72 DPI for your Web site. Be sure to obtain written permission from participants before visually documenting the program.

> **Program Example:** Using a Program to Increase Public Awareness
>
> The creators of the Arts and Inspiration Center set up one-time groups in various settings such as retirement communities, senior housing, churches and physicians' offices. By participating in these groups, individuals learned about the actual programs at the centers. At the senior high-rise, for example, interested residents joined a sample Memories in the Making group, which they found enjoyable and meaningful, dispelling misconceptions of suitable activities for individuals with Alzheimer's disease. The residents' experience also catalyzed conversation about the importance of early diagnosis. In the physician's office, staff and nurses participated and subsequently referred patients to the centers.[112]

- **Ask participants and partners to speak on your behalf or write letters of support.** Prepare a draft of the letter for the signer to edit. Similarly, write talking points for people to use in their presentations. (See Appendix 3 for sample letters of support.)

- **Provide visibility to elected officials and other funders.** You don't want your only interaction with funders to be as a supplicant. In addition to scheduling meetings just to share good news or to thank them for their community activism on behalf of older adults and the arts, invite them to the community sharing of the art created by program participants and the related celebration. Be sure to ask them to say a few words. If you have a newsletter, ask them to write a column.

- **Leave something behind.** Permanent visual art exhibits and CDs or DVDs of performances are good ways to display tangible evidence of your arts and aging program. Another option is for participants to create art that becomes part of a building. In a program of SPIRAL Arts, Inc., for example, older adults designed and made mosaic floor numbers to be installed next to the elevators in their independent living building in Portland, Maine. Their functional artwork is a permanent reminder to all residents of the value of the arts.

- **Talk with the media.** "Friend-raising" applies to journalists as well as funders. Cultivate journalists year-round and push your message. There is much good news to share about the benefits of arts and aging programs. Journalists respond to human-interest stories. In general, they are more likely to pay attention if major media outlets have already published pieces on arts and aging.

No matter what methods you choose, be persistent. If you want a funder or community leader to speak on your behalf or attend an event, don't assume that a "no" means that he or she is not interested; perhaps there is just a schedule conflict. Keep extending the invitation, and explore other options for his or her involvement with your program.

Remember that the quality of your materials and presentations matters. Not only do the print pieces transmit your values and professionalism, but they also attract attention. Audiences will want to read something that looks good and listen to a message that is delivered effectively.

Key Points about Public Awareness

- Push your message about the benefits of arts and aging programs to improve the environment for the field.
- Understand that everyone can and should advocate.
- Develop public awareness goals.
- Ensure that the audience, message, messenger, and method all fit together.
- Identify and think strategically about audiences.
- Turn existing rationales and arguments into messages.
- Enlist participants whenever possible to be your messengers.
- Anticipate that your public awareness efforts will be ongoing and that you must be persistent.
- Be imaginative and strategic in developing methods.
- Cultivate the media.

When I become a grandmother, I would really like to become a part of the Seasoned Performers.

Fifth-grade audience member

Looking to the Future

Erik H. Erikson, Joan M. Erikson, and Helen Q. Kivnick wrote this about older adults:

> By relegating this growing segment of the population to the onlooker bleachers of our society, we have classified them as unproductive, inadequate, and inferior. Offering them, on occasions, status honors, and honorary memberships shows respect and may be gratifying to them. Taking care of them in innumerable ways is being responsible. Entertaining them with bingo games and concerts is, however, patronizing. Surely, the search for some way of including what they can still contribute to the social order in a way befitting their capacities is appropriate and in order.[113]

One way is the arts. And a growing number of older adults and people of all ages are coming to this realization. Thanks in part to the baby boomers who have driven so many changes in the United States, the concept of aging productively is in vogue. Research has proliferated, and some of it points toward the arts. There is also a renewed emphasis on community in all senses of the word, with a strong desire among many to reconnect with each other.

Leaders in both the arts and aging services fields are working hard to respond to individuals' needs. Their common goal is to be embedded in the communities that they serve. Their common value is to honor and respect the experiences of and choices made by all community members. These commonalities make our field of arts and aging a logical, effective, and mutually beneficial partnership. We are a movement. We are making a difference. And the movement is inextricably linked to community arts, in which the process of making art is as important as the art that is created and shared.

While we learn from the past and work hard in the present, we also plan for the future. The issues that we face are not unique to the arts and aging field. Increasing capacity to meet demand, determining how best to share strategies and models in a learning community, and training a new generation of leaders preoccupy many organizations and institutions. What is unique to the arts and aging field is the creativity and passion that has kept us optimistic and energized about moving forward.

In large measure, our optimism and passion are derived from the learning community that we have formed with the participants in our arts and aging programs. Connecting with the older adults—and young people— who benefit from our programs, whose lives are profoundly affected by our work, keeps us going.

We also learn and grow from each other's successes and failures. Indeed, there is a hunger in the arts and aging field for models and advice. One resource is this toolkit. Another is the existing body of work that codifies what we do: the publications of Elders Share the Arts, National Center for Creative Aging, National Guild of Community Schools of the Arts, Liz Lerman Dance Exchange, and Transitional Keys, and those by Anne Basting and John Killick, Martha Haarbauer, and La Doris "Sam" Heinly. The leadership of organizations like the New Jersey Performing Arts Center, National Guild of Community Schools of the Arts, and National Center for Creative Aging also contributes to our progress. And conferences like the National Conference on Arts and Aging: Creativity Matters and the membership meetings of the National Guild of Community Schools of the Arts are effective networking and celebratory opportunities. Honoring our accomplishments strengthens our identity as a field with common hopes and dreams.

As the art and aging field moves forward, we need to nurture a new—and larger— generation of leaders. The demand for our work will only increase. One method is to offer academic training—like the Certificate in Creative Aging program that the Brookdale Center on Aging of Hunter College in New York City launched in 2005 in partnership with Elders Share the Arts. We also need to support and train the professional teaching artists who are so vital to the success of our programs.

Experiencing firsthand the impact of arts and aging programs on participants makes believers out of skeptics. So, too, do quantitative and qualitative assessment data that answer the question, "How do you know that what you are doing is making a difference?" Outcome evaluation is important to our future growth and success. While *we* know the benefits, we have to know how to communicate them to others with persistence, professionalism, and quality.

Older adults, regardless of ability, gain many benefits by participating in professionally led arts programs that are effectively and purposefully designed and implemented. By engendering mastery, facilitating social engagement, and igniting a zest for life, the arts are transformational. The arts sustain spirit and soul. The arts enhance older adults' quality of life. The arts are part of the process, part of the solution.

"The Heart of the Matter: Our Lives—A Work in Progress"

(To the tune of "There's No Business Like Show Business")

There's no age like our age like no age we've known.

Everything about it is revealing.

Grey hair, countless candles on your cake.

Yet, many things about it are appealing.

To know that we've still got just what it takes!

Oh, there's no bunch like this bunch.

Two great years we have known.

Secrets shared, with smiles and tears that were concealed.

We've shed our guard and we've shed those shields.

With love and trust and strength we say with heartfelt zeal:

Let's go on with our show! Let's go on with the show!

Finale song in the final presentation by the Penn South Program for Seniors Living History Theatre Group, a program of Elders Share the Arts, New York City, May 2003

NOTES

Chapter 1

1. Susan Perlstein, "Arts and Aging Across America," *Community Arts Network*, October 2002, www.communityarts.net/readingroom/archivefiles/2002/10/arts_and_creati.php.

2. 2005 White House Conference on Aging, Index of Resolutions, www.whcoa.gov/about/resolutions/Resolutions.pdf.

3. "Alzheimer's Disease Fact and Figures 2007" (Chicago, IL: Alzheimer's Association, March 2007), www.alz.org/national/documents/Report_2007FactsAndFigures.pdf.

4. Ibid.

5. Adapted from "Module Two: Understanding Normal Aging," *Care for the Caregiver: A Manual for Implementing Workshops* (Veterans Affairs Canada), www.vac-acc.gc.ca/providers/sub.cfm?source=caregivrmanual/sect4/module2/workshop2#agingprocess.

6. Administration on Aging, *A Profile of Older Americans: 2004*, www.aoa.gov/prof/Statistics/profile/2004/2.asp; Federal Interagency Forum on Aging-Related Statistics, *Older Americans 2004: Key Indicators of Well-Being*, www.aoa.gov/prof/statistics/keyindicators.asp; U.S. Census Bureau, 2000 Census; Wan He and others, *65+ in the United States: 2005, Current Population Reports, Special Studies* (Washington, DC: U.S. Department of Health and Human Services, National Institutes of Health, National Institute on Aging; U.S. Department of Commerce, Economics and Statistics Administration, U.S. Census Bureau, December 2005), www.census.gov/prod/2006pubs/p23-209.pdf; "Facts About Senior Citizens Packaged by Census Bureau," *Seniorjournal.com*, April 26, 2006.

7. Maria C. Norton and others, "Senior Citizens Enjoying Health, Life Much Longer than Expected," *Seniorjournal.com*, December 28, 2005.

8. "Expanding Your Market: Accessibility Benefits Older Adult Customers" (Washington, DC: U.S. Department of Justice, Civil Rights Division, Disability Rights Section, December 2006).

9. "Demographic Profile of American Baby Boomers" (Metlife Mature Market Institute), www.metlife.com/WPSAssets/34442486101113318029V1FBoomer%20Profile%202005.pdf, based mainly on 2000 U.S. Census Bureau data; and also includes information from the U.S. Department of Labor's Bureau of Labor Statistics, Centers for Disease Control and Prevention, and other Census Bureau reporting.

10. "Projections of the Labor Force" (Washington, DC: Congressional Budget Office, September 2004), www.cbo.gov/ftpdocs/58xx/doc5803/09-15-laborforce.pdf.

11. "The New Retirement Survey" (Merrill Lynch, February 22, 2005), www.ml.com/?id=7695_7696_8149_46028_46503_46635.

12. Lori P. Montross and others, "Correlates of Self-Rated Successful Aging Among Community Dwelling Older Adults," *American Journal of Geriatric Psychiatry* 14 (January 2006): 43–51, quoted in "How Do Seniors Define Aging?" *Seniorjournal.com*, January 18, 2006.

13. Erik H. Erikson, Joan M. Erikson, and Helen Q. Kivnick, *Vital Involvement in Old Age* (New York: W.W. Norton, 1986), 301.

14. Ibid.

15. "MetLife Foundation Alzheimer's Survey: What America Thinks" (Rochester, NY: Harris Interactive for MetLife Foundation,May 2006), www.metlife.com/WPSAssets/20538296421147208330V1FAlzheimersSurvey.pdf.

16. "Study: U.S. Unprepared for Aging," "Maturing of America—Getting Communities on Track for an Aging Population" funded by MetLife Foundation, in partnership with Partners for Livable Communities, NACO, National League of Cities, and ICMA—International City/County Management Association, as reported in *Aging Today*, November–December 2006.

17. Kerry Tremain, "Where Will All the Boomers Go?" (San Francisco: Civic Ventures), www.civicventures.org/publications/articles/where_will_all_the_boomers_go.cfm.

Chapter 2

18. The AdvantAge Initiative, Center for Home Care Policy and Research, Visiting Nurse Service of New York, www.vnsny.org/advantage.

19. See www.secondjourney.org.

20. Don Adams and Arlene Goldbard, *Creative Community: The Art of Cultural Development* (New York: Rockefeller Foundation, 2001), 107.

21. Ibid.,14.

22. Arlene Goldbard, keynote address, Conference for Community Arts Education, National Guild of Community Schools of the Arts, November 2006.

23. Adams and Goldbard, *Creative Community*, 65.

24. Executive summary, "Out of the Shadows, Envisioning a Brighter Future for Long-Term Care in America" (Providence, RI: Brown University Center for Gerontology and Health Care Research, 2006), 6, www.chcr.brown.edu/pdfs/brown_university_LTC_report_final.pdf.

25. Anne Davis Basting and John Killick, *The Arts and Dementia Care: A Resource Guide* (Brooklyn: National Center for Creative Aging, 2003), 8–9.

26. Susan Perlstein, *Generating Community: Intergenerational Partnerships Through the Expressive Arts* (New York: Elders Share the Arts, 1994), 8.

27. Joe Verghese and others, "Leisure Activities and the Risk of Dementia in the Elderly," *New England Journal of Medicine*, June 19, 2003.

28. Carla E. S. Tabourne and Yongho Lee, "Study of Kairos Dance Theatre's Dancing Heart Program," University of Minnesota, Department of Kinesiology, 2005–2006.

29. Joe Verghese, "Cognitive and Mobility Profile of Older Social Dancers," *Journal of the American Geriatrics Society* 54, no. 8 (August 2006): 1241.

30. www.healthfinder.gov/news/newsstory.asp?docID=536042.

31. www.amc-music.com/musicmaking/wellness/hormone.htm.

32. www.mind-body.org/rmm.html.

33. "Creating Art Inspires Wellness Among North Dakota Seniors," *State Spotlight* (Washington, DC: National Assembly of State Arts Agencies, 2005), www.nasaa-arts.org/spotlight/stspot_0805.shtml.

34. Clarissa A. Rentz, "Memories in the Making: Outcome-Based Evaluation of an Art Program for Individuals with Dementing Illnesses," *American Journal of Alzheimer's Disease and Other Dementias* 17, no. 3 (2002): 175–81.

35. Martin Gizzi, with Brian Dallow, "Music and Quality of Life Among Nursing Home Residents with Dementia" (Edison, NJ and Scotch Plains, NJ: New Jersey Neuroscience Institute at JFK Medical Center and Music for All Seasons, n.d.), www.musicforallseasons.org/SadlerApplication.pdf.

36. Cynthia Kincaid and James R. Peacock, "The Effect of a Wall Mural on Decreasing Four Types of Door-Testing Behaviors," *Journal of Applied Gerontology* 22, no. 1 (2003): 76–88.

37. www.timeslips.org/faq.html.

38. Eva Götell, Steven Brown, and Sirkka-Liisa Ekman, "Caregiver Singing and Background Music in Dementia Care," *Western Journal of Nursing Research* 24, no. 2 (2002): 195–216.

39. Sherry L. Willis and others, for the ACTIVE Study Group, "Long-term Effects of Cognitive Training on Everyday Functional Outcomes in Older Adults," quoted in Shankar Vedantam, "Short Mental Workouts May Slow Decline of Aging Minds, Study Finds," *Washington Post*, December 20, 2006.

40. Arthur F. Kramer and others, "Fitness Training and the Brain: From Molecules to Minds," presentation, University of Illinois at Urbana-Champaign, August 11, 2006.

41. Robert S. Wilson and others, "Loneliness and Risk of Alzheimer Disease," *Archives of General Psychiatry* 64 (2007): 234–40.

Chapter 3

42. Matt Salo, Choices for Independence 2006: A National Leadership Conference (Washington, DC: U.S. Administration on Aging, December 2006).

43. "Fact Sheet: President Bush Signs the Deficit Reduction Act" (Washington, DC: February 8, 2006).

44. Executive summary, "Out of the Shadows."

Chapter 4

45. Raquel Chapin Stephenson, "Promoting Self-Expression Through Art Therapy," *Generations XXX*, no. 1 (Spring 2006).

46. Ibid.

Chapter 5

47. Eric Booth, "Seeking a Definition: What Is a Teaching Artist?" *Teaching Artists Journal* 1, no. 1 (2003): 11.

48. John W. Rowe and Robert L. Kahn, *Successful Aging* (New York: Dell Publishing, 1993), 161.

49. www.alz.org/oc/in_my_community_10849.asp.

50. Adapted from Stephen Lieb, "Principles of Adult Learning," *Vision*, Fall 1991, http://honolulu.hawaii.edu/intranet/committees/FacDevCom/guidebk/teachtip/adults-2.htm.

51. Ibid.

52. Adapted from "The Flow of Life," in Linda Winston, with Matthew Kaplan, Susan Perlstein, and Robert Tietze, *Grandpartners* (Portsmouth, NH: Heinemann, 2001), 62–79.

Chapter 6

53. Craig Dreeszen, "Strategic Planning: Helping Arts Organizations Find Their Way," in *Fundamentals of Arts Management*, ed. Craig Dreeszen, (Amherst, MA: Arts Extension Service, University of Massachusetts, 2003), 49.

54. Pam Korza, with Denise Boston-Moore, "Program Development: Connecting Art with Audiences," in *Fundamentals of Arts Management*, ed. Dreeszen, 118.

55. *W. K. Kellogg Foundation Evaluation Handbook* (Battle Creek, MI: W. K. Kellogg Foundation, 1998), 21.

56. Martha Haarbauer, *Seasoned Theatre: A Guide to Creating and Maintaining a Senior Adult Theatre* (Portsmouth, NH: Heinemann, 2000), 6.

57. *Wikipedia*, s.v. "SWOT Analysis," en.wikipedia.org/wiki/SWOT_analysis.

58. Dreeszen, "Strategic Planning," 53.

59. Ibid., 49.

60. Rowe and Kahn, *Successful Aging*, 138.

61. Ibid., 137–38.

62. Renya T. H. Larson, *A Stage for Memory: A Guide to the Living History Theater Program of Elders Share the Arts* (Brooklyn, NY: National Center for Creative Aging, 2004), 32.

63. Andrea Sherman and Marsha B. Weiner, *Transitional Keys—A Guidebook: Rituals to Improve Quality of Live for Older Adults* (Dobbs Ferry, NY: Transitional Keys, 2004), 18.

64. Barry B. Bittman and others, "Testing the Power of Music-Making," *Provider*, November 2004.

65. Perlstein and Bliss, *Generating Community*, 25.

66. Gene D. Cohen, *The Mature Mind: The Positive Power of the Aging Brain* (New York: Basic Books, 2005), 48.

67. Basting and Killick, *Arts and Dementia Care*, 20.

68. Larson, *Stage for Memory*, 9.

69. Perlstein and Bliss, *Generating Community*, 43.

70. Basting and Killick, *Arts and Dementia Care*, 30.

71. Thomas E. Backer, *Partnership as an Art Form: What Works and What Doesn't in Nonprofit Arts Partnerships*, report on a study conducted for the John S. and James L. Knight Foundation (Encino, CA: Human Interaction Research Institute, November 2002), 4–5.

72. Ibid., 12.

73. Stephanie Golden, with Susan Perlstein, *Legacy Works: Transforming Memory into Visual Art—A Program for Older Adults* (Brooklyn, NY: National Center for Creative Aging and Elders Share the Arts, 2002), 9.

74. Chris Walker, *Arts and Non-Arts Partnerships: Opportunities, Challenges, and Strategies* (Washington, DC and New York: Urban Institute and Wallace Foundation, 2004), 10; www.wallacefoundation.org/KnowledgeCenter/KnowledgeTopics/ArtsParticipation/ArtsandNonArtsPartnerships.htm?byrb=1.

75. Adapted from Basting and Killick, *The Arts and Dementia Care*, 21–22.

Chapter 7

76. Sherman and Weiner, *Transitional Keys*, 18.

77. *Design for Accessibility: A Cultural Administrators Guide* (Washington, DC: National Assembly of State Arts Agencies, 2003), 158.

78. http://caregiverpa.psu.edu/careinfo/selfhelp/personal.htm#toppage.

79. *Guide to Elder-Friendly Community Building* (Cleveland: Cuyahoga County Planning Commission and Cleveland Foundation, June 2004), 9.

80. Michael Scriven, *Evaluation Thesaurus*, 4th ed. (Newbury Park, CA: Sage Publications, 1991), 169.

81. Perlstein and Bliss, *Generating Community*, 57.

82. Golden, with Perlstein, *Legacy Works*, 42.

83. Ibid.

84. Haarbauer, *Seasoned Theatre* (see n. 56); Craig Dreeszen, ed., *Fundamentals of Arts Management* (Amherst, MA: Arts Extension Service, University of Massachusetts, 2003).

85. Eric Booth, "The Emergence of the Teaching Artist," *Art Times Journal*, May 2003, www.arttimesjournal.com/speakout/may03speakout.htm.

86. Adapted from www.teachingartists.com/gettingstartedTA.htm.

87. Erikson, Erikson, and Kivnick, *Vital Involvement in Old Age*, 61–62.

88. Basting and Killick, *Arts and Dementia Care*, 22.

89. Ibid., 22–23.

90. Ibid., 23–24.

Chapter 8

91. Quoted in Scriven, *Evaluation Thesaurus*, n.p.

92. Craig Dreeszen, "Program Evaluation: Measuring Results," in *Fundamentals of Arts Management*, 254.

93. www.asaging.org/cdc/module1/phase5/index.cfm.

94. Dreeszen, "Program Evaluation," 258.

95. www.asaging.org/cdc/module1/phase5/index.cfm.

96. Dreeszen, "Program Evaluation," 260.

97. Golden, with Perlstein, *Legacy Works*, 47.

98. *Kellogg Foundation Evaluation Handbook*, 71.

99. Betsy M. Dorsett, "Program Evaluation: How to Focus Your Evaluation Using Quantitative and Qualitative Methods," Issue Brief 2, *Live Well, Live Long: Health Promotion and Disease Prevention for Older Adults* (San Francisco: American Society on Aging, 2006), www.asaging.org/CDC.

100. Bittman and others, "Testing the Power of Music-Making."

101. *Kellogg Foundation Evaluation Handbook*, 80–81.

102. Golden, with Perlstein, *Legacy Works*, 47.

103. Dreeszen, "Program Evaluation," 278–9.

104. www.minimental.com.

105. Jennifer M. Kinney and Clarissa A. Rentz, "Observed Well-Being among Individuals with Dementia: Memories in the Making©, An Art Program, versus Other Structured Activity," *American Journal of Alzheimer's Disease and Other Dementias* 20, no. 4 (2005): 220–27.

106. Basting and Killick, *Arts and Dementia Care*, 26–28.

Chapter 9

107. Shirley K. Sneve, with Dorothy Chen-Courtin and Barbara Schaffer Bacon, "Marketing: Tools for the Arts," in Dreeszen, ed., *Fundamentals of Arts Management*, 306–7.

108. Thomas L. Birch, "Advocacy and Lobbying: Speaking Up for the Arts," *NASAA Advocate* 10, no. 1 (2006): 1.

109. *Creating an Arts & Inspiration Center* (Kansas: Alzheimer's Association, Heart of America and Great Plains Chapters, n.d.), 22.

110. Sneve, with Chen-Courtin and Bacon, "Marketing," 311.

111. www.experiencetalks.org.

112. *Creating an Arts & Inspiration Center*, 22.

Chapter 10

113. Erikson, Erikson, and Kivnick, *Vital Involvement in Old Age*, 298.

GLOSSARY

accessibility. The capacity of everyone regardless of age or ability to be included in all physical structures, programs, and means of communication (e.g., Web sites, e-mail, telephone).

activities of daily living (ADLs). The functional ability of a person. The primary ADLs are bathing, eating, grooming, dressing, toileting, and medicating. Others include shopping, housekeeping, and driving.

adult daycare center. Structured programs with stimulating social activities and health-related and rehabilitation services for older adults who are physically or emotionally disabled and need a protective environment. The participant is usually brought to the care facility in the morning and leaves in the evening. Also called *adult day program*.

adult learning. An educational philosophy based on the understanding that adults are autonomous and self-directed; have accumulated a foundation of life experiences and knowledge; are goal-oriented; are relevancy-oriented; are practical; and need to be shown respect.

advisory committee. A group of key stakeholders and experts who provide advice and guidance on program design and implementation.

advocacy. Increasing awareness and appreciation among elected officials and public and private funders.

ageism. Stereotyping and prejudice against individuals or groups because of their age.

Aging and Disability Resource Center (ADRC). A one-stop shop that provides information and assistance to people who need public or private resources, professionals seeking assistance on behalf of their clients, and people planning for their future long-term care needs. Resource center programs are the entry point to publicly administered long-term supports, including those funded under Medicaid, the Older Americans Act, and state revenue programs.

aging in place. Remaining in the community—ideally in one's own home—as one grows older.

aging services field. Organizations, corporations, institutions, and individuals such as the Administration on Aging, state units on aging, local-level area agencies on aging, senior centers, continuing care retirement communities, corporations or foundations that own these communities, healthcare-focused community organizations (such as the Alzheimer's Association and the Visiting Nurse Association), family and professional caregivers, adult day programs, and hospitals.

Americans with Disabilities Act (ADA). Signed into law in 1990, this act prohibits discrimination based on disability in employment, state and local government services, public accommodations, commercial facilities, transportation, and telecommunications.

andragogy. An approach to learner-focused education that describes the art and science of helping adults learn.

assisted living. A facility that bridges the gap between independent living and living in a nursing home or skilled care facility. The staff provides assistance with activities of daily living in a small group home or a larger facility, both of which are licensed by the state.

arts and aging field. Organizations and individuals in the arts and aging services fields who are focused full-time or part-time on providing sustained, high-quality, professionally led, participatory, community arts programs to older adults.

arts education. Sequential, curriculum-based, arts instruction and projects that provide young people with the opportunity to learn the arts by actual experience. Arts education can occur in school or out-of-school. Also called *arts learning*.

arts field. Public, nonprofit, and for-profit arts organizations and institutions such as the National Endowment for the Arts, state and local arts agencies, performing arts organizations, visual and literary arts organizations, arts presenting organizations, and individual artists.

assessment. The process of documenting, knowledge, skills, attitudes, and beliefs in measurable terms. One can assess, for example, educational progress, health status, and community assets.

asset-based model. A model of care in communities that acknowledges the vitality, wisdom, experience, and value of all residents regardless of ability. Residents are respected and their desire to remain independent and make their own choices is encouraged. Also called *strength-based model*.

baby boomer. A person born between 1946 and 1964 during the unusual spike in birth rates that occurred in the United States after World War II.

baseline. A specific value or values that can serve as a comparison or control. Evaluating participants at the beginning of a program, for example, provides a baseline for comparison when evaluating participants again at the program's conclusion.

Boston Matrix. A grid that charts benefit to participants versus impact on organizational or individual resources. Typically used to prioritize among several programmatic options.

caregiver. An individual who helps a person with his or her activities of daily living. Caregivers can be professional staff, family members, or both.

certified nursing assistant (CNA). The primary professional caregiver of residents in assisted living and long-term care facilities.

charge nurse. An registered nurse or licensed practical nurse who is responsible for supervision of a unit in a long-term care facility. The charge nurse schedules and supervises the nursing staff and provides care to facility residents.

civic engagement. Individual and collective actions designed to identify and address issues of public concern. Civic engagement can involve individual volunteerism, organizational involvement, and electoral participation and include efforts to address an issue directly, work with others in a community to solve a problem, or interact with institutions of representative democracy.

community. A physical and social construct that include cities, neighborhoods, apartment buildings, condominiums, residential facilities (for example, independent living, assisted living, skilled care/long-term care), and a group of people who interact and share certain things such as values or proximity.

community arts. A concept based on the premise that cultural meaning, expression, and creativity reside within a community. The artist's task is to collaborate with community members so they can free their imaginations and give form to their creativity.

community cultural development. A range of initiatives undertaken by artists in collaboration with other community members to express identity, concerns, and aspirations through the arts and communications media, while building cultural capacity and contributing to social change.

community schools of the arts. Nonprofit, nondegree-granting, community-based institutions offering open access to quality arts instruction by professional faculty.

community sharing of the art. A celebration at the conclusion of an arts and aging program during which the art that is created is shared with other residents, staff, family members, friends, and members of the public.

continuing-care retirement community (CCRC). A community that offers a continuum of housing, services, and healthcare—independent living, assisted living, nursing care—on one campus or site.

continuum of care. Care services available to assist older adults over their lives and during varying abilities and disabilities, from well to frail. It may include independent living, assisted living, nursing care, home health, home care, and home- and community-based services.

control group. Often part of an evaluation that uses experimental design, a group of people with the same demographics and abilities as the group that participates in the program. The control group—the nonparticipants—helps eliminate alternate explanations of the results of the experiment.

creative arts activity. In the arts and aging field, an arts activity led by a professional teaching artist trained to work with older adults that emphasizes participatory, sequential learning and the process of making art.

creative arts therapies. Art, dance and movement, drama, music, poetry, and psychodrama used during intentional intervention in therapeutic, rehabilitative, community, or educational settings to foster health, communication, and expression; promote the integration of physical, emotional, cognitive, and social functioning; enhance self-awareness; and facilitate change.

culture change. Creating an asset-based model in long-term care facilities so that the environment is one of community rather than of medicine.

curriculum. A complete program of learning that includes identified, desired results; a design for activities and a suggested sequence; and suggested assessment methods.

deficit-based model. A model of care in communities that focuses on old age as a disease and older adults as patients. Also called *medical model*.

dementia. A condition in which there is a gradual loss of brain function. The main symptoms are usually loss of memory, confusion, problems with speech and understanding, changes in personality and behavior, and an increased reliance on others for activities of daily living. There are a number of types of dementia; Alzheimer's disease is the most common.

director of nursing (DON). The staff member who oversees all nursing staff in assisted living and long-term care facilities. The DON is responsible for formulating nursing policies and monitoring the quality of care delivered, as well as for monitoring the facility's compliance with federal and state regulations pertaining to nursing care. Also called *wellness director*.

effective practice. In the arts and aging field, a program that is sustained over the long term; produces the intended results; meets needs; demonstrates participatory, sequential learning; includes professional teaching artists; evaluates impact; demonstrates high quality and excellence; and engenders learning communities.

elder-friendly community. A community that facilitates aging in place by addressing basic needs; promoting social and civic engagement; optimizing physical and mental health and well being; and maximizing independence for those who are frail or have disabilities.

environmental scan. A common technique to determine external opportunities and concerns affecting an organization and to assess the competition for a program or service. See also *external assessment*.

experimental design. Design of an evaluation method to capture how participants change as a result of a program. The evaluation instrument is administered before and after the program. Also called *pre-test/ post-test design*.

external assessment. Scanning the organization's environment to discover strengths, weaknesses, opportunities, and threats and assess the needs of community members and stakeholders. See also *environmental scan*.

formative evaluation. Evaluation conducted during the course of a program that helps shape the program, from the initial development through ongoing improvement. Its primary audience is internal (the partnership team). See also *summative evaluation*.

goals. Future- and results-oriented statements that explain what you want to accomplish in the long term; what difference you are trying to make in the lives of those served; and what you want the program to look like in a specified number of years.

group expectations. Logistical and programmatic ground rules that help ensure harmony among participants (for example, maintain confidentiality, respect different points of view). Often established by group members with a facilitator's guidance.

Health Insurance Portability and Accountability Act (HIPAA). Federal law that gives an individual rights over his or her health information and sets rules and limits on who can look at and receive this information.

icebreaker. Exercises at the beginning of a session designed to warm-up participants by focusing their attention, awakening senses, unlocking memories, and preparing the group for creative expression.

independent living. A residential living facility for older adults that may or may not provide supportive services. Generally referred to as elder or senior housing in the government-subsidized environment, independent living also includes rental-assisted or market-rate apartments or cottages where residents usually have complete choice in whether to participate in a facility's services or programs. Also called *retirement community*, *congregate living*, or *senior apartment*.

instructional design. A task-oriented lesson plan or activity sequence that implies strategic solutions to specific situations.

intergenerational. A program, initiative, or activity in which older adults and children and/or youth explore their commonalities and differences, creating mutual understanding and strengthening community.

internal assessment. Looking at an organization's own strengths, weaknesses, resources, values, and vision.

learning community. A group of people who have common values and beliefs and are actively engaged in learning together and from each other.

lifelong learning. A process of accomplishing personal, social, and professional development throughout the lifespan of individuals in order to enhance the quality of life of individuals and their communities. Lifelong learning also refers to educational classes, usually affiliated with a college, community college, or university, designed by or for older adults, and often taught by older adults.

lobbying. Citizen activities that attempt to changing laws and influence the decisions of federal, state, and local legislators.

long-term care facility. A residence that provides a variety of services to residents 24 hours a day, such as a room, meals, recreational activities, assistance with activities of daily living, and protection or supervision. Some nursing homes specialize in areas such as Alzheimer's disease, pain management, and cardiac rehabilitation. Also called *skilled care facility, nursing facility*, or *nursing home*.

mastery. Skill or knowledge of a technique or topic. In the arts and aging field, a primary programmatic goal is for older adult participants to gain mastery.

Medicaid. The largest source of funding for medical and health-related services for individuals and families with limited income. It is jointly funded by the states and federal government and managed by the states. Among those served are eligible low-income parents, children, seniors, and people with disabilities.

medical model. See *deficit-based model*.

Medicare. A health insurance program administered by the U.S. government covering people who are either age 65 and over or who meet other special criteria. It can cover hospital, medical, and prescription drug expenses.

mission statement. A clear, concise explanation of why an organization exists and what it seeks to accomplish.

naturally occurring retirement community (NORC). A geographic area in which a significant proportion of older adults reside in housing that was not designed or planned with seniors in mind.

No Child Left Behind Act (NCLB). Federal law that authorizes education programs, mechanisms, and spending.

normal aging. A progressive and cumulative process of change occurring throughout one's life and over time. It is affected by many factors, including environment and genetics.

objectives. Statements that describe how to achieve programmatic goals. Objectives are specific, measurable, and short-term.

Older Americans Act. Federal law that authorizes policies, spending, and mechanisms such as the Administration on Aging that serve older adults. It is reviewed and reauthorized approximately every 10 years, most recently in 2006.

oral history. A field of study and a method of gathering, preserving, and interpreting the voices and memories of people, communities, and participants in past events.

out-of-school programs. Community-based education programs for young people that occur after school, on weekends, or in the summer.

outcome evaluation. Evaluation that assesses how the results of a program affected individuals and/or the community and whether the program met its stated goals.

outcome goals. Big-picture goals that describe the effects a program should have on participants.

Program of All-Inclusive Care for the Elderly (PACE). A program model centered on the belief that it is best for the well-being of seniors with chronic care needs and their families to be served in the community whenever possible. PACE serves individuals who are age 55 and older, certified by their state to need nursing home care, able to live safely in the community at the time of enrollment, and live in a PACE service area.

participatory, sequential learning. Instruction is sequential, with each activity building on the one before it. Each step is challenging yet achievable, and the content emphasizes participation.

partnership team. A learning community and the locus of ongoing, routine communication for a project. Important for planning, training, implementing, monitoring, and evaluating the partnership program.

pedagogy. Teacher-focused education; typically used to describe the art or science of educating children.

pre-test/post-test. Evaluation instruments administered before and after a program.

process evaluation. See *formative evaluation*.

productive aging. A concept that celebrates older adults' capabilities, potential, and social and economic contributions.

program logic model. An illustration of the theory and assumptions underlying a program. It links short- and long-term outcomes with program activities, processes, assumptions, and principles. The model also clarifies thinking, planning, and communicating about program objectives and benefits.

qualitative evaluation. Evaluation typically conducted through interviews, observation, focus groups, and journals that elicit anecdotes, reactions, impressions, and feelings.

quantitative evaluation. Evaluation typically conducted through surveys and questionnaires that elicit statistics.

recreational therapist. The activities director or staff in hospitals and long-term care facilities. He or she assists patients in leisure activities such as cooking, arts and crafts, and music therapy that can provide a cognitive component to the "work" of physical rehabilitation.

reminiscence. The process or practice of thinking or telling about past experiences.

residents' council. A group of residents in an independent living, assisted living, or skilled care facility who represent the interests of all residents in planning, developing programs, resolving differences, and communicating with the facility's leadership.

return on investment (ROI). The ratio of money gained or lost on an investment relative to the amount of money invested. In common usage, the term applies to the relative value of a variety of inputs and outputs in different situations.

senior center. A place where older adults gather for services and activities that reflect their experience and skills, respond to their diverse needs and interests, enhance their dignity, support their independence, and encourage their involvement in and with the center and the community. Senior centers often serve the entire community with information on aging; support for family caregivers, training professionals, lay leaders, and students; and development of innovative approaches to aging issues.

social capital. The collective value of all social networks and the inclinations that arise from these networks to do things for each other.

social engagement. Active involvement in the community and with other people, not for the sake of being involved, but to accomplish something of meaning and value for the community. Also refers to a strong social support network of friends and family.

stakeholders. Individuals and groups who care about an organization's work. Typically, they are funders, partners, participants, and participants' family members.

strength-based model. See *asset-based model*.

summative evaluation. An evaluation method that determines whether a program did what it was designed to do. The primary audience is external (stakeholders, particularly funders). See also *formative evaluation*.

Strengths, Weaknesses, Opportunities, Threats (SWOT). A method of analyzing internal and external assessment results that helps clarify whether the proposed program can work.

teaching artist. An artist with the complementary skills and sensibilities of an educator who engages people in learning experiences in, through, or about the arts.

train the trainer. A method in which a nonartist is trained to facilitate programs. It is most appropriate for programs targeted at people with dementia since the primary outcome goal is social engagement and not mastery.

universal design. An orientation to any design process that starts with a responsibility to the experience of the user. It is a framework for the design of places, things, information, communication, and policy to be usable by the widest range of people operating in the widest range of situations without special or separate design.

values statement. Communicates the values or principles of an organization.

vision statement. Communicates what an organization believes its future could be.

CONTACT INFORMATION

Alzheimer's Poetry Project
12 Highview Lane
Santa Fe, NM 87508
gary@alzpoetry.org
www.alzpoetry.com

Arts and Inspiration Center
Alzheimer's Association—
Heart of America Chapter
3846 W. 75th Street
Prairie Village, KS 66208
Phone: 913-831-3888
Fax: 913-831-1916
michelle.niedens@alz.org
www.alz-heartofamerica.org

Arts for the Aging
6917 Arlington Road, Suite 352
Bethesda, MD 20814
Phone: 301-718-4990
FAX: 301-718-4992
info@aftaarts.org
www.aftaarts.org

ArtAge Publications
The Senior Theatre Resource Center
PO Box 19955
Portland OR 97280
Phone: 503-246-3000 or 800-858-4998
Fax: 503-246-3006
bonniev@seniortheatre.com
www.seniortheatre.com

Baldwin-Wallace College Conservatory of Music
275 Eastland Road
Berea, OH 44017-2088
Phone: 440-826-2366
Fax: 440-826-8069
info@bw.edu
www.bw.edu

Center for Elders and Youth in the Arts/Institute on Aging
3330 Geary Boulevard
San Francisco, CA 94118-3347
Phone: 415-447-1989, ext. 535
Fax: 415-447-1250
jchapline@ioaging.org
www.ioaging.org

Creative Aging Cincinnati
7970 Beechmont Avenue
Cincinnati, OH 45255
Phone: 513-561-7500
Fax: 513-232-2631
www.creativeagingcincinnati.org

Drum Circle Facilitators Guild
Nelli Hill, Secretary
(Founder, Playful Spirit Adventures)
301-776-2382
playfulspirit@mac.com

Elder Craftsmen, Inc.
307 Seventh Avenue, Suite 1401
New York, NY 10001
Phone: 212-319-8128
Fax: 212-319-8141
info@eldercraftsmen.org
www.eldercraftsmen.org

Elders Share the Arts
138 S. Oxford Street
Brooklyn, NY 11217
Phone: 718-398-3870
czablotny@estanyc.org
www.elderssharethearts.org

EngAGE: The Art of Active Aging
240 East Verdugo Avenue, Suite 100
Burbank, CA 91502
Phone: 818-563-9882
Fax: 818-563-9315
maureen@engagedaging.org
www.engagedaging.org

Evergreens Senior HealthCare System
4007 W. Wendover Avenue
Greensboro, NC 27407
Phone: 336-218-7587, ext. 151
jjohnson@eshc.org
www.evergreenseniorcare.com/renaissance.mgi

The Golden Tones
41 Cochituate Road
Wayland, MA 01778
Phone: 508-358-7091
Fax: 508-358-1684
msifantus@aol.com
www.maddiesifantus.com
www.goldentones.org

Foundation for Quality Care
33 Elk Street, Suite 300
Albany NY 12207-1010
Phone: 518-462-4800
Fax: 518-426-4051
rpatterson@nyshfa.org
www.foundationforqualitycare.org

Intergeneration Orchestra of Omaha
4223 Center Street
Omaha, NE 68105
Phone: 402-444-6536, ext. 221
Chris.Gillette@hhss.state.ne.us
www.igoomaha.homestead.com

Kairos Dance Theatre
4524 Beard Avenue South
Minneapolis, MN 55410
Phone: 612-927-7864
info@kairosdance.org
www.kairosdance.org

Levine School of Music
Sallie Mae Hall
2801 Upton Street, NW
Washington, DC 20008
Phone: 202-686-8000
Fax: 202-686-9733
info@levineschool.org
www.levineschool.org

Liz Lerman Dance Exchange
7117 Maple Avenue
Takoma Park, MD 20912
Phone: 301-270-6700, ext. 15
Fax: 301-270-2626
borstelj@danceexchange.org
www.danceexchange.org

Luella Hannan Memorial Foundation
4750 Woodward Avenue
Detroit, MI 48201
Phone: 313-833-1300, ext. 23
phalladay@hannan.org
www.hannan.org

Memories in the Making
PO Box 3419
Via Lido, #354
Newport Beach, CA 92663-3908
Phone: 949-673-8231
sheinly@sbcglobal.net
www.alzheimersartspeaks.com

Music for All Seasons, Inc.
336 Park Avenue, Suite 2R
Scotch Plains, NJ 07076-1100
Phone: 908-322-6300
or 866-524-MFAS (6327)
Fax: 908-322-0161
ruth@musicforallseasons.org
www.musicforallseasons.org

National Center for Creative Aging
4125 Albemarle Street, NW
Washington, DC 20016-2105
Phone: 202-895-9456
Fax: 202-895-9483
ghanna@creativeaging.org
www.creativeaging.org

National Coalition of Creative Arts Therapies Associations
c/o American Music Therapy Association
8455 Colesville Road, Suite 1000
Silver Spring MD 20910
Phone: 732-787-6503
lauragreenstone@gmail.com
www.nccata.org

National Endowment for the Arts
1100 Pennsylvania Avenue, NW
Washington, DC 20506
Phone: 202-682-5726
bergeyb@arts.endow.gov
www.arts.gov

National Institute of Senior Centers
National Council on Aging
1901 L Street, NW, 4th floor
Washington, DC 20036
Phone: 202-479-6683
Fax: 202-479-0735
info@ncoa.org
www.ncoa.org/content.cfm?sectionid=342

New Horizons Music
201 Pine Street
Corning, NY 14830
Phone/Fax: 607-962-1125
royernst@aol.com
www.newhorizonsmusic.org/nhima.htm

New Jersey Department of Health and Senior Services
PO Box 360
Trenton, NJ 08625-0360
Phone: 609-292-7837
Toll-free in NJ: 1-800-367-6543
Patricia.Polansky@doh.state.nj.us
www.state.nj.us/health/senior

New Jersey Intergenerational Orchestra
PO Box 432
Cranford, NJ 07016
Phone: 908-522-0100
Fax: 908-665-0929
speterson@njio.org or info@njio.org
www.njio.org

New Jersey Office of Area Agency on Aging Administration
Department of Health and Senior Services
PO Box 360
Trenton, NJ 08625-0360
Phone: 609-292-7837
Toll-free in NJ: 1-800-367-6543
Tina.wolverton@doh.state.nj.us
www.state.nj.us/health/senior

The OASIS Institute
7710 Carondelet, Suite 125
St. Louis, MO 63105
Phone: 3140862-2933, ext. 269
Fax: 314-862-2149
mkerz@oasisnet.org
www.oasisnet.org

Osher Lifelong Learning Institute National Resource Center
University of Southern Maine
96 Falmouth St.
Portland, ME 04104
Phone: 207-780-4076
kalil@usm.maine.edu
www.osher.net

Roland Corporation U.S.
5100 S. Eastern Ave.
Los Angeles, CA 90040-2938
Phone: 323-890-3700
lsmith@rolandus.com
or musicforlife@rolandus.com
www.rolandus.com/community/musicforlife

The Seasoned Performers
701 Montgomery Highway, Suite 204
Birmingham, AL 35216
Phone/Fax: 205-978-5095
martha@seasonedperformers.org
or mail@seasonedperformers.org
www.seasonedperformers.org

SPIRAL Arts, Inc.
156 High Street
Portland, ME 04101
Phone: 207-775-1474
Fax: 207-842-6317
jbadran@yahoo.com
or community@spiralarts.org
www.spiralarts.org

Stagebridge Senior Theatre Company
2501 Harrison Street
Oakland, CA 94612
Phone: 510-444-4755
Fax: 510-444-4821
director@stagebridge.org
www.stagebridge.org

TimeSlips
Center on Age & Community
University of Wisconsin—Milwaukee
PO Box 413
Milwaukee, WI 53201
Phone: 414-229-2740
Fax: 414-229-2713
Basting@uwm.edu
www.timeslips.org

Transitional Keys, Inc.
PO Box 465
Dobbs Ferry, NY 10522
Phone: 914-980-9801
andreasherman@optonline.net
www.transitionalkeys.org

**Wabash County Council
on Aging, Inc.**
PO Box 447
239 Bond Street
Wabash, IN 46992
Phone: 260-563-4475
Fax: 260-569-1535
bpferry@yahoo.com
www.wabashcountrytransit.com

Yamaha Corporation of America
6600 Orangethorpe Avenue
Buena Park, CA 90620
Phone: 714-522-9210
mbates@yamaha.com
www.clavinovaconnection.com

APPENDIXES

Appendix 1: Sample Program Logic Model

Resident-Staff Chorus in an Assisted Living Facility

Assumptions →	Inputs →	Activities →
- Residents and staff with different skills, abilities, and temperaments will sing together. - Residents and staff have time to attend rehearsals.	- Chorus director - Rehearsal space - Choral music - Residents - Coordinator - Activities schedule - Accompanist - Piano - Facility staff at all levels and with all types of jobs - Funding	- Produce and distribute marketing flyer. - Chorus director and accompanist do short performance as recruiting tool. - Informational meeting and signups. Music selections discussed with potential participants. - Arrange singers so that staff are next to residents. - Try to pair up staff and residents for mentoring between rehearsals. - Rehearsals: warm-ups and skill-building exercises. - Performance for residents, staff, and families. - Pre-test/post-test evaluation.

Outputs →	Outcomes →	Impact
- Number of residents who joined chorus. - Number of staff who joined chorus. - Attendance at each rehearsal. - List of songs learned. - Numbers of residents, staff, and family members who attended informational meeting.	- Staff members talk more with residents. - Residents attend more activities. - Family members visit residents more frequently. - Residents interact more with each other. - Residents are better singers. - Residents have learned about music. - Staff members have a longer tenure. - Staff members and residents spend more time with each other. - Staff members suggest new activities for residents and for them to do together. - Data are generated to support the case for programs.	- Staff members see residents as interesting people who can still contribute to the community. - Residents feel that they have accomplished something of value. - Residents feel that they are assets to the community. - Residents are mentally and physically healthier. - Staff and residents feel that they are part of the same community. - Staff members feel that they are valued.

Appendix 2: Project Timeline Formula and Curriculum Planning Format

Institute on Aging, Center for Elders & Youth in the Arts
General Project Timeline Formula and Format for Curriculum Planning
Jeff Chapline, Director, Artistic Director

July/Aug	Sept/Oct	Nov/Dec	Jan/Feb	Mar/Apr	May/June
Initial planning and preparation, all sites. Train artists. Begin elder site component	Train artists and teachers Youth orientations, if there is a youth component. Begin youth site component & joint elder/youth component, <u>if crossgenerational</u>	Weekly, 1.5 hr Arts Programming at sites, including a minimum of two joint elder/youth classes each month, <u>if crossgenerational</u>	Weekly, 1.5 hr Arts Programming at both sites, including a minimum of two joint elder/youth classes each month, <u>if crossgenerational</u>	Weekly, 1.5 hr Arts Programming at both sites, including a minimum of two joint elder/youth classes each month, <u>if crossgenerational</u>. Exhibition or Presentation Design, preparation & promotion	Arts Programming Execution of exhibits, Final presentation. 2 Reflection Sessions. Post-project evaluations
*	Quarterly planning and assessment meeting. Evaluations		Quarterly planning and assessment meeting *	Evaluations	Quarterly planning and assessment meeting

- Visual Art projects begin with basic skill building exercises in drawing, painting and collage. The exercises focus on line, shading, volume, composition, layering, negative space and vanishing point perspective. At the 12 week mark, a theme is decided upon based on the evolution of the groups work and skills, and a longer term project is developed using that theme. Final works are curated and everyone is represented in the exhibition which culminates the classes.

- Writing and poetry projects begin with basic wordplay that, over the weeks and through various exercises develops into structured poetry, narrative, haiku, and various approaches to structured and unstructured creative writing. Samples of the writing become a part of the exhibitions and are also presented as spoken-word at openings.

- Movement Performances are a kind of dance developed by the artist in collaboration with older participants who are frail and may have limited movement capability. They can involve music, spoken word and a variety of objects to assist in creating layers of movement and sound which could be of interest to a performing audience.

Appendix 3: Fundraising Tools
Kairos Dance Theatre Brochure

Kairos Dance Theatre
4524 Beard Avenue South
Minneapolis, MN 55410

For more infromation:
(612) 927.7864
info@kairosdance.org
www.kairosdance.org

(outside)

APPENDIX 3   205

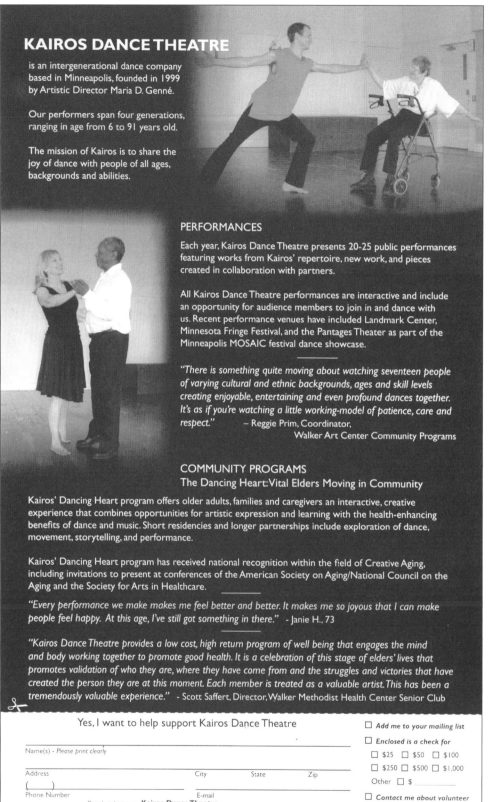

KAIROS DANCE THEATRE

is an intergenerational dance company based in Minneapolis, founded in 1999 by Artistic Director Maria D. Genné.

Our performers span four generations, ranging in age from 6 to 91 years old.

The mission of Kairos is to share the joy of dance with people of all ages, backgrounds and abilities.

PERFORMANCES

Each year, Kairos Dance Theatre presents 20-25 public performances featuring works from Kairos' repertoire, new work, and pieces created in collaboration with partners.

All Kairos Dance Theatre performances are interactive and include an opportunity for audience members to join in and dance with us. Recent performance venues have included Landmark Center, Minnesota Fringe Festival, and the Pantages Theater as part of the Minneapolis MOSAIC festival dance showcase.

"There is something quite moving about watching seventeen people of varying cultural and ethnic backgrounds, ages and skill levels creating enjoyable, entertaining and even profound dances together. It's as if you're watching a little working-model of patience, care and respect." — Reggie Prim, Coordinator, Walker Art Center Community Programs

COMMUNITY PROGRAMS
The Dancing Heart: Vital Elders Moving in Community

Kairos' Dancing Heart program offers older adults, families and caregivers an interactive, creative experience that combines opportunities for artistic expression and learning with the health-enhancing benefits of dance and music. Short residencies and longer partnerships include exploration of dance, movement, storytelling, and performance.

Kairos' Dancing Heart program has received national recognition within the field of Creative Aging, including invitations to present at conferences of the American Society on Aging/National Council on the Aging and the Society for Arts in Healthcare.

"Every performance we make makes me feel better and better. It makes me so joyous that I can make people feel happy. At this age, I've still got something in there." - Janie H., 73

"Kairos Dance Theatre provides a low cost, high return program of well being that engages the mind and body working together to promote good health. It is a celebration of this stage of elders' lives that promotes validation of who they are, where they have come from and the struggles and victories that have created the person they are at this moment. Each member is treated as a valuable artist. This has been a tremendously valuable experience." - Scott Saffert, Director, Walker Methodist Health Center Senior Club

---

Yes, I want to help support Kairos Dance Theatre

Name(s) - *Please print clearly*

Address   City   State   Zip

(   )
Phone Number   E-mail

Detach and return to: **Kairos Dance Theatre**
4524 Beard Ave S, Minneapolis, MN 55410
(612) 927.7864 • www.kairosdance.org • info@kairosdance.org

☐ *Add me to your mailing list*
☐ *Enclosed is a check for*
☐ $25 ☐ $50 ☐ $100
☐ $250 ☐ $500 ☐ $1,000
Other ☐ $ _____

☐ *Contact me about volunteer opportunities*

Thank you.

(inside)

New Horizons Budget

FALL 2005 OPERATING COSTS

	Number	Number of Services	Length of Service	Amount per Hour	
Director-Conductor					
Rehearsals	1	12	3 hours	$65.00	$2,340.00
Assistant Director					
Rehearsals	1	12	2 hours	$30.00	$720.00
Certified Teachers					
1 hour	—	12	1 hour	$20.00	—
2 hours	1	12	2 hours	$20.00	$480.00
3 hours	—	12	3 hours	$20.00	—
Student Teachers					
1/2 hour	1	12	0.5 hour	$14.00	$168.00
1 hour	3	12	1 hour	$14.00	$504.00
2 hours	3	12	2 hours	$14.00	$1,008.00
Manager	1	12	5 hours	$6.00	$360.00
Assistant Manager	1	12	5 hours	$6.00	$360.00
Office Assistant	1	12	6 hours	$6.00	$432.00
Subtotal Personnel					**$6,372.00**
Full-Time Benefits		subtotal	$2,340.00	$0.415	$971.10
Part-Time Benefits		subtotal	$4,032.00	$0.083	$334.66
Subtotal benefits					**$1,305.76**
Facilities Rental		12		$120.00	$1,440.00
Music Purchase/Rental**					—
Marketing					$500.00
Copying					$300.00
Coffee Hour		12		$15.00	$180.00
Subtotal Operations					**$2,420.00**
TOTAL					**$10,097.76**

	Number of Participants	Amount per Participant	
Tuition/Enrollment Fees			
High	100	$100.98	
Low	80	$126.22	
Average	90	$112.20	
Actual	89	$125.00	$11,125.00

**Many New Horizons Music programs will have music purchase/rental expenses.
NOTE: Many Horizons Music programs will have a budget line for instrument rental.

Adapted from Baldwin-Wallace College Conservatory of Music

Kairos Dance Theatre Support Letters

The Kairos Dance Company

It was about one year ago that the Kairos Dance Company came to the Senior Club at Walker Health Care.

Headed up by Maria Genné, along with other members- Catherine, Peter and Carla-they came to Scott Saffert, the Director of the Senior Club to see if they could work with us Seniors.

So the fun began. Each Tuesday from 10:30 to 12:00 noon we gather together with Kairos and do motion exercises and dance routines.

Now for someone like me who has had two knee replacements, plus a rod implanted beside each femur above my new knees, I enjoy working out the exercise and dance routines. This has helped all of the Seniors to become more limber and be able to move with more agility then we ever could do if we did not work out to the music and dance Kairos helps us do.

I have found that performing with Kairos has given me more support in moving about and becoming more flexible then if I just sat still and observed. Kairos does put you through the paces of the dance and music exercises.

I feel Kairos is a very needed Company. They not only work with our Senior Club but also do work with other Senior groups throughout the Twin Cities area. Kairos has put on dance productions within the Twin Cities and other states in the United States.

Kairos is a very needed group, and by the way, they help us exercise through the dance, it enhances our lives and keeps us on our toes.

Thank you,
Myrna Landrum
Senior Club member
At the Walker Health Care Adult Services

Volunteers of America
Minnesota

Volunteers of America
Southwest Center
3612 Bryant Avenue South
Minneapolis, Minnesota 55409
Tel: 612-822-3194
Fax: 612-822-0627

To whom it may concern:

This is a letter of support regarding the dance project that we have completed with Kairos Dance Theatre. We have seen transformation in the DayElders throughout the course of our dance project with Kairos. Alphia is relaxed when we dance. Grady can participate without needing to remember details. Dorothy only shares her feelings about the recent death of her husband when we dance. Ocie is awake, alert, and energized. Melvin, his left side paralyzed following a stroke three years ago, dances with a smile on his face. "Dance is good communication," he says.

"I like it," said Alphia. "I enjoy it. It gets me exercising. It helps me a whole lot. I'm relaxed. I don't feel too nervous or excited. It's good for me. The other thing I like about it is she (Maria Genne) asks us questions. It helps me remember. It helps me relax."

Grady added, "I like dancing. I would like to see more of it – an hour or two hours everyday. It looks like everyone seems to be happy."

As Dorothy spoke, she moved her hands and fingers out in front of her. "You're doing something with your hands. I like to see people – I do. And dancing is really good for you."

"It keeps your blood running and gives you energy and something good to think about," said Ocie Mae. "Looking at one another dancing is a lot of fun."

Jack especially liked the intergenerational component of the dance project. "I think they're a very energetic mixture of ages. I love the kids – such exuberance! It's good for the old heart. There's no part of it I don't like. I'd highly recommend that this project continue."

The DayElders are eager to share their love for dancing with others. The elders have told stories about their youth, the struggles and joys of raising children, the heartache of losing loved ones, and the challenges and frustrations of the body growing old. "When I was young, I didn't think I would ever get old," said Grace. "I didn't know that I could still dance. I guess I can." Janie would like to dance for other seniors, to show others that people can dance regardless of age or physical ability. "It would make them feel better – especially about themselves," she commented. Dancing with Kairos Dance Theatre has been a wonderful experience. We hope this is only the beginning.

Sincerely,

Maria Ricke & Amy Petersen
DayElders staff at Southwest Senior Center

Funding Proposal

"Acting is giving and I still have a lot to give."
Cecil Pierce, 87, Stagebridge actress/student

"Our clients are on a fixed income and cannot afford to go to movies or plays. Stagebridge offers an alternative, not just for entertainment, but to bring joy and laughter to many seniors."
Linda Diamond, Director, St. Mary's Senior Center

"…definitely an important part of our nursing education."
Nursing student, Samuel Merritt College

Date

Name
Title
Org
Address
City, State, Zip

Dear _____:

I am writing to introduce _____ to Healthy Aging, an innovative program that helps seniors stay healthier through participation in the arts and educates healthcare professionals about older people, resulting in better communication and patient treatment. We understand that _____ has an interest in supporting programs that benefit the geriatric population, and hope that you will consider a $10,000 grant to fund our program for older adults.

Organizational Description:
Since its founding in 1978, Stagebridge has pioneered ways of giving older adults a creative voice in a culture that denies aging and makes older people socially invisible. Our work with older adults is helping change the limiting stereotypes and negative attitudes that many people associate with growing old. We have developed life-enhancing programs to engage seniors in performing arts, brought together grandparents and youngsters to share life experiences through stories, and imagined how theatre can assist healthcare workers better relate to their elderly patients.

Stagebridge is the oldest senior theatre in the nation and the only professional theatre training company for older adults on the West Coast. Managed by a small group of professional staff, the company is composed of approximately 150 actors and storytellers who average 70 years of age. Recently cited as a "Model Program" by the National Endowment for the Arts, Stagebridge is committed to dispelling the notion of older adults as obsolete, non-contributing members of society, and to demonstrating the many ways in which seniors improve and enrich our culture.

Stagebridge currently has five overlapping program areas. They are: Theatre Training, which offers classes to older adults in the areas of beginning through advanced acting, improvisation, scene study, storytelling, and singing; Public Performance Season, which presents one or two new plays a year for public audiences that are mostly comprised of families, seniors, and children; Storybridge Schools Program, which brings intergenerational theatre, oral history, and storytelling by older adults to elementary school children in the San Francisco Bay Area. Healthy Aging (detailed in this proposal); and the Center for Creative Aging – West, a network of artists and organizations working with older adults that trains, produces, and advocates for creative aging programs.

Stagebridge has created and produced more than 30 plays about aging and toured them to over 250,000 individuals in senior centers, schools, nursing homes, libraries and theatres throughout the Bay Area. Last year, we presented 68 performances and 391 workshops for 27,450 people.

Project Description:
Stagebridge's "Healthy Aging" Program is designed to help seniors stay healthier by participating in the arts, and employ the arts to educate healthcare professionals about older people resulting in better treatment. Our premise is: a) health is improved through active involvement with others, creative stimulation, and opportunities to flex the muscles of imagination b) the more that older adults are "seen" as human beings who still have much to offer, the better treatment they will receive by healthcare professionals, who routinely see them in their most vulnerable state, as dependent and ineffective. However, when they are able to reveal their experience and knowledge by participating in the arts, they not only alter their self perceptions, but also change the way others see them. This "shift of awareness" results in greater insight and sensitivity for both older adults and healthcare professionals.

To accomplish these aims, our program includes:

1. "See Me!" Training
"See Me!" provides training for nursing students, nurses, doctors, paraprofessionals and aides to improve their attitudes and be more understanding in their treatment of older patients—the most rapidly growing medical population.

In 2005, a grant from Johnson & Johnson and the Society for Arts in Healthcare enabled Stagebridge to inaugurate "See Me!"

training with student nurses at Samuel Merritt College School of Nursing. Results of evaluations from the pilot program indicated that the program strongly impacted students' attitudes and knowledge. The response was unanimously positive. Merritt College nursing professor Jennifer Winters commented, "I had never seen a group of students react in such a positive way to a classroom activity… This is learning that cannot be achieved from traditional models such as textbooks, films or lectures." Subsequent evaluations showed that the nurses became far more aware of their patients as people, and thus more caring and sensitive in their treatment.

Word of "See Me!" Training spread among health educators locally, leading to invitations to expand the program to the University of San Francisco, UCSF and San Francisco State. This positions the San Francisco Bay Area at the leading edge of this promising new approach to geriatric practice. Now in its third year, the program has earned honors from the Blair L. Sadler International Healing Arts Competition, which cited Stagebridge for "one of the most innovative integrations of arts into healthcare that improves the quality of the health care experience for patients, their families and caregivers." Stagebridge also was recently selected for an expansion grant from Johnson & Johnson/Society for Arts in Healthcare program. The company was one of 26 grantees nationally (out of more than 200 applicants). Dr. Gay Hanna of the Society of Arts in Healthcare called Stagebridge "pioneers in this emerging field." Dr. Gene Cohen of George Washington University has described it as "groundbreaking important work."

In See Me! Training, Stagebridge staff and actors work with nursing school staff to create learning modules that address specific issues that nurses face in working with older patients. These include: finding effective/affective ways to communicate, death and dying, sexuality, loneliness, among others. Stagebridge then creates a workshop around a particular issue that utilizes improvisation, storytelling, role-playing and other performance techniques. The workshop is then presented and discussed. Our approach has several advantages over traditional lectures. We offer a senior "voice" and point-of-view, which is communicated with humor in performances and reinforced through small group interactive discussion.

Our long term goal is to produce replicable training modules that will include a DVD, program guide and resource guide. We believe that this project will be a model for a variety of training programs for nurses and doctors, as well as for paraprofessionals and aides employed by nursing and convalescent homes and long-term care facilities. It may also have value as part of the continuing education programs for health care professionals.

2. Seniors Reaching Out (SRO)
This program is designed to bring performances of plays and workshops in music, singing and storytelling to approximately 10,000 seniors annually. Stagebridge primarily serves seniors in East Bay retirement communities/homes, convalescent hospitals, senior centers and community organizations.

These seniors are often unable to enjoy the benefits and creative stimulation offered by workshops or performances due to ill health, impaired mobility, or lack of financial resources. Audiences range from inner city to suburbs, from poor to wealthy, and typify the cultural diversity of the Bay Area. Many of these people are forgotten audiences, who rarely see anything more lively than television. Activity directors often remark that Stagebridge brings "light to their lives." Older audiences connect deeply when they see their peers performing, especially when the stories or plays relate to their lives.

SRO was initiated as a pilot project in 2000. It was founded on an assessment of the senior facilities in Alameda and Contra Costa Counties made by staff at Stagebridge. To date, the company has presented 600 workshops and performances for over 32,000 people. The response of senior audiences and staff has been overwhelmingly positive. Staff and participants agree the quality of life, especially for senior adults with limited means and few resources, is greatly enhanced. Stagebridge provides life-affirming opportunities that offer inspiration, humor, entertainment and the opportunity to participate, interact and learn.

Each year the company creates an all-new version of its popular variety show "Never Too Late." The musical variety show brings old age up to date and features a dozen talented senior actors and singers. The company also commissions/creates other original plays designed to tour senior audiences. Our productions are always uplifting and carry positive messages that help many seniors recall happier times in their lives, which encourage an improved, healthier emotional outlook.

Stagebridge raises funds to provide these services free or at very low cost to facilities, so that there is no financial barrier. As the result of free introductory workshops, a number of facilities are now partnering with Stagebridge to have on-going workshops. Excell Health Care in San Leandro, Aegis of Pleasant Hill, Coventry Retirement Center in San Francisco and Center for Elders Independence in Oakland are all co-sponsoring workshops at their facilities. They pay a small fee to offset our costs. Our goal is to establish new partnerships with other facilities to increase the number of workshops we offer and reach a wider senior audience.

Currently, Stagebridge has a very limited number of professional teachers trained in working in these community settings. We will address this issue in 2006-2007 by creating a Training Institute, as described in the next section.

3. Performing Arts Training Institute

Stagebridge will expand its theatre arts training program at Arts First Oakland in 2007–08 by inaugurating a new Training Institute. The purpose of the Training Institute is twofold: to expand learning opportunities for our constituency, and to develop a core of trained teachers to meet the growing demand for creative opportunities for Bay Area seniors.

Every 30 seconds a Baby Boomer is turning 60. In the Bay Area, the 60+ population ranges from 13% to 20% (in communities like Walnut Creek). The old model of senior centers providing arts and crafts and slide shows is of limited interest to the "new elderly." These people are often still working part time and looking for meaningful, engaging activity. Unfortunately, in the Bay Area, there are few opportunities for participating in the performing/creative arts geared to this population. Stagebridge is the only organization in the Bay Area that provides performing arts training for older adults. By expanding our course offerings the Company will better be able to serve this population.

Many of those who are 65+ or disabled, are limited in their ability to attend classes due to lack of transportation or limited/fixed income. (In fact, the fastest growing segment of the population is 85+). These seniors often live in retirement homes or attend local senior centers. There is a growing need to serve this population with programs that stimulate and engage the imagination and creativity. Stagebridge receives many requests from facilities and organizations around the Bay Area to provide training and classes. However, the Company has been unable to adequately serve this population because it has a limited number of available teachers, who mostly reside in the East Bay. By recruiting trainees from around the Bay Area, Stagebridge will have the potential to serve a much wider audience.

The Training Institute will expand and organize our current class offerings by providing comprehensive, sequential courses that include: acting (basic, advanced, scene study); improvisation (basic, advanced); storytelling (basic, advanced, storytelling for performance); dance, voice, writing for theatre (comedy, playwriting). Taught by a staff of experienced professional artists, most classes will be ongoing and also include short term, weekend, and special single workshops taught by guest artists. The Training Institute will provide students a certificate for completing a specific curriculum of courses in acting, storytelling, dance, etc.

In order to significantly extend theatre arts training to older adults throughout the San Francisco Bay Area, the Training Institute also will develop a certification program to train more professional teachers. This program will be geared to people with significant performing arts skills and background, primarily older adults (60+), but also some middle age adults (45+). A professional staff will train people to teach performing arts to older adults, including course work and practical internship. Students will observe teachers working in community settings, co-teach classes, and then teach classes with staff members observing. Finally, they will be assigned a class to teach on their own with periodic monitoring by the staff. On the successful completion of their work, they will be offered paid teaching jobs.

How the "Healthy Aging" Program Benefits the Target Population:

In the next 25 years, the number of people over the age of 60 will double—worldwide. Yet our culture has not caught up with the coming "age wave." Attitudes towards older adults and the aging process are still stereotypic, largely negative and most often, laughable. The images we see in the media are crafted by a youth-oriented culture. And there are few opportunities for older adults to be determinants of popular culture, to be seen in realistic portraits of what it means to grow old, or to be included in the performing arts. The need for realistic and positive images of older adults is paramount, as evidenced in a recent study profiled in the NY Times October 5, 2006. Seniors who held positive images of aging actually lived an average of 8 years longer than others whose self images were more negative.

Groundbreaking new research carried out by the National Institute of Mental Health is also substantiating what those of us in the field have known for years—that creativity with older adults is not just a pleasant pastime, but actually helps people stay healthier. Older adults who participated in arts activities were more involved with others, less reliant on medication, experienced fewer falls, less depressed and maintained greater overall morale.

If nursing students can begin to perceive their geriatric patients as vital individuals who deserve care and respect, versus the more common perception of people at the end of their lives, we will have achieved our goal. We believe that there is no better way to bring this notion to health care professionals than through live theatre and storytelling with older adults.

Evaluation
For the "See Me" project, the main evaluation tool is a written evaluation (that we have been using for two years) soliciting responses from the students immediately after the Stagebridge class and then again six months to a year after they've been working as health care professionals. Each session is also videotaped and the tape used to help evaluate the project. We hope to develop our training module based on feedback garnered during the evaluation process. For "Seniors Reaching Out" we get informal feedback from the activity directors and client response to our workshops/ performances. We evaluate the "theatre training" program by videotaping student's work and self evaluation/discussion with students.

Healthy Aging is a core program at Stagebridge which has a demonstrated positive impact in addressing the special creative needs of our burgeoning senior population. Funding from _____ would help us to sustain the program and begin developing a specific training module for "healthy aging" curriculums for eventual distribution to other training programs. We hope that our clear vision and demonstrated track record will give confidence to _____ that we merit your support for this important and timely program.

If you have any questions or would like to arrange a site visit to observe a Healthy Aging workshop with nursing students, please feel free to contact me (510) 444-4755 or at director@stagebridge.org. Thank you for your consideration of our request.

Sincerely,

Stuart Kandell, Ph.D.
Executive Director

Appendix 4: Marketing Tools
New Horizons Music Brochure

It's Easy and Fun!

As an adult, you have advantages that will help you learn music. If you played an instrument in school years ago, you will be amazed at how much you remember and how quickly you will be able to play again. Even if you've never played music, you are already familiar with the sound of a lot of the music that will be included in your early instruction.

"This is a life after retirement. You can take the boy out of the band, but you can't take the band out of the boy."
—A New Horizons Music® member

Most adults are more motivated, self-disciplined, and have more time to practice than their younger counterparts. If you attend lessons and practice, you'll be playing music before you know it! From then on, it's even more fun to play with others in classes, chamber music groups, bands and orchestras.

In one study, nearly everyone who participated in a New Horizons Music® felt that their accomplishments met or exceeded their expectations.

Learning to Play Music

Learn to play music in a band or orchestra as a senior adult — even if you have no musical experience!

Playing music is a special joy and it will help you maintain mental and physical health. It is also a way of experiencing life: playing music from the past keeps us in touch with those feelings; daily practice keeps us active in the present, and striving for new goals attaches us to the future. One band member describes it as "serious fun."

As a member of the New Horizons Music®, you will meet new friends and work with them as a team to learn music for concerts and other performances in the community. New Horizons ensembles typically perform many times each year in venues ranging from formal concerts to shopping malls to parks to retirement and nursing homes.

There are also a number of annual music institutes you can attend which cater to New Horizons musicians in locations like Aspen, CO; Lake Placid, NY; Door County, WI; Sydney, Australia or Palm Springs, CA.

NEW HORIZONS MUSIC

Fill your life with music, new friends, fun, and accomplishment

(outside)

Getting Started

The first step in getting started is attending an informational meeting at which all of your questions will be answered by a music teacher and music dealer. You will also have a chance to meet some of the other people who will be participating. If you are not able to attend that meeting, contact the sponsoring music dealer, ask whatever questions you have and plan to be at the first class.

"I love making music a part of each day, new friendships, and band camps."
—A New Horizons Music® member

- Re-learn to play the instrument that you played earlier in life.
- Choose an instrument that has a sound or look that you like.
- Check with the band director to see which instrument is needed in the band.

When selecting an instrument, keep in mind that in a very small number of cases, physical characteristics may indicate that a particular instrument will be relatively easy or difficult. Options can be discussed with the music teacher.

Obtaining an Instrument

Use Your Own.
If you already have an instrument or if you'll be using an instrument that your children left behind, be sure to take it into a repair shop to make sure that it is in excellent working condition. Some music students become frustrated because they try to learn on an instrument that no one can play.

Rent an Instrument.
Music dealers in your area rent instruments for a very reasonable monthly fee. It is usually possible to exchange for another instrument if you change your mind. Talk to your New Horizons teacher and check the yellow pages. In many cases, a music dealer has been involved in planning your local New Horizons program and will understand your special needs.

Buy an Instrument.
Once you're certain of the instrument you'd like to play, purchase one at your local music store. It is recommended that you learn the basics on a particular instrument before making a purchase.

History of New Horizons Music®

The first New Horizons Band was started by professor Roy Ernst at the Eastman School of Music in 1991. It was supported by grants from NAMM, the International Music Products Association and the National Association of Band Instrument Manufacturers (NABIM). The word spread through articles in publications such as *The New York Times* and a feature spot on *The Today Show* and eventually the program expanded to include bands, orchestras and other ensembles. Today there are more than 100 New Horizons Music programs in the United States and Canada with many more in the planning phase.

Local Information

For more information on New Horizons Music, visit **www.newhorizonsmusic.org**

(inside)

Appendix 5: Policies and Procedures Example
New Horizons Band Program
Baldwin-Wallace College

Program Philosophy

The primary belief of the New Horizons Band Program is that it is never too late to learn how to play an instrument. If a person has the desire to make music, we take the responsibility to teach them very seriously. Because we believe that individuals learn in different ways and progress at different rates, we believe that individualized and small-group instruction are the means by which objectives are achieved.

Ensembles

In an effort to meet the needs of musicians of at a variety of levels, the New Horizons Band Program is divided into three bands, as follows:

Gold Band

The Gold Band is meant for those students who play at an advanced level. Very often these musicians have had previous musical experience and/or take private lessons. Musicians in the Gold Band will not have lessons of like instruments, but instead will have sectionals consisting of a variety of instruments.

Silver Band

The Silver Band is meant for students who are no longer beginners but who do not play at an advanced level. Musicians in the Silver Band will participate in full band rehearsal as well as lessons consisting of like instruments.

Beginning Band

Beginning Band is truly for those who have never played a particular instrument before, or who would like a refresher course on an instrument they played many years ago. Members of Beginning Band will participate in full band rehearsal as well as lessons consisting of like instruments.

Policies

- Students will choose which band they would like to join. A basic list of expectations can be obtained from the director.

- Due to the need for consistency in instrumentation, students should not switch bands during the semester except with permission from the director.

- In an effort to give the best possible instruction, musicians are asked not to switch instruments during a given semester. Instrument switches due to health concerns are understandable, but all switches should be done only with the consultation of the conductor.

- In the event that a member needs additional help or misses a rehearsal, Buddy Sessions are available through the Outreach Office.

Attendance Policy

Due to the fact that the bands meet only once a week, it is important that absences be minimal and that the conductors can anticipate attendance before planning each rehearsal. In the event that a member must be absent from a rehearsal, please contact the Conservatory Outreach Office, [phone number], prior to Wednesday evening.

Music Policy

Music is the property of NHB and should be marked only in *pencil*. Music must be returned to the NHB program following performances.

Performance Attire

NHB members should wear black pants or skirts, dark shoes, and a white shirt, blouse, or sweater for all performances unless otherwise instructed.

Weekly Rehearsal Procedures

- Bring all necessary materials (see below) to each rehearsal.
- Be prepared to begin rehearsal promptly at the scheduled time.
- Sit with the proper section so that the ensemble will be cohesive.
- When an instructor is teaching, it is imperative that all instruments remain silent.
- When playing, look at the conductor often so that you will stop playing immediately upon seeing a cut-off. It is very likely that important instructions will follow the cut-off!
- Please refrain from playing during transitions between pieces.
- If instructions are unclear, please make the conductor aware by raising your hand.

Materials

- Instrument
- All music and handouts from section lessons and full band rehearsal
- Band book—Beginners & Silver: *Accent on Achievement*
- Music stand
- Pencil—Please mark on your music in pencil instead of pen.
- Accessories (i.e., extra reeds, cork grease, mouthpiece, valve oil, slide grease, snare stand, practice pad)
- A positive, cooperative attitude!

Additional Information

- If you are missing any piece of music for any reason, please see a conductor or student assistant before rehearsal so that you won't miss any of the rehearsal.
- We are happy to enlarge any music to assist you with music reading.
- If you wish to sign up for a Buddy Session, a sign-up list and/or form will be made available before or after rehearsal. Please see a conductor or student assistant.

Director
Office: [phone number]
nhb@bw.edu

Appendix 6: Teaching Artists Tools

Program Proposal Form

(Please Print)
AFTA Artist Name _____ Date _____

It may be helpful to discuss your idea with the Program Director before completing this form. Please print legibly or type your proposal on this form; otherwise, you may submit your proposal on a separate sheet of paper addressing guidelines below.

Title of Program _____

Goals _____
_____
_____
_____
_____
_____

Target Group of Participants/Maximum Group Size _____
_____
_____

Location _____

Duration (check one) ❏ A single one-hour workshop
                      ❏ Ongoing project: _____ (Number of one-hour workshops)

                      ❏ Other (Please describe) _____
_____
_____

Target Start Date _____

Summary of Program _____
_____
_____
_____
_____
_____

Description of Format _____
_____
_____
_____
_____
_____

Special Considerations, Supplies or Equipment Needed _____
_____
_____
_____
_____
_____

Budget   Supplies $_____
                Other $_____

AFTA Artist Signature _____

Instructor Orientation
Program Observation Sheet

Prior to beginning your own workshop series, AFTA requires that new instructors observe three existing workshops to gain first hand insight into AFTA programs. This is a valuable time for the preparation of project ideas, and to observe the behavior and learning process of memory impaired seniors and to ascertain skill levels. Some factors to consider while observing an AFTA program:

- The diversity of the cognitive levels and fine motor skills within any group
- Group size
- Work pace and response time of senior participants
- Center staff size and number of volunteers present
- Work space and access to utilities (sink, paper towels, etc.)

First Observation

Your Name_____ Date of Observation _____

Signature _____ Location _____
AFTA Instructor _____ Subject of Program _____

What were three of the most memorable aspects of this program? _____

_____
_____
_____
_____

What tools or techniques did the AFTA instructor employ to encourage senior participation? _____

_____
_____
_____
_____

Briefly detail some observations about the seniors' responses to the program _____

_____
_____
_____
_____
_____
_____
_____
_____
_____
_____
_____
_____
_____
_____
_____

Second Observation

Your Name _____ Date of Observation _____

Signature _____ Location _____
AFTA Instructor _____ Subject of Program _____

What did you notice that was successful about this program? _____

_____
_____
_____
_____
_____

What would you have added or changed about the program? _____

_____
_____
_____
_____
_____
_____
_____

What was the observable goal of this workshop and was it accomplished? _____
_____
_____
_____
_____
_____

Third Observation
Your Name_____Date of Observation_____

Signature_____ Location_____
AFTA Instructor _____Subject of Program_____

What surprised you about this workshop?_____
_____
_____
_____
_____
_____

How was the lesson or program developed? (Look for introductions and segues, visual cues and instructions, verbal and non-verbal communication) _____
_____
_____
_____
_____
_____
_____
_____
_____
_____
_____
_____
_____
_____
_____

Appendix 7: Evaluation Tools
Memories in the Making Evaluation Instrument
Clarissa A. Rentz, M.S.M, R.N., C.S.

Domains: Positive/negative affect, self-esteem	
Indicators and ratings: 4 = always; 3 = some of the time; 2 = rarely; 1 = never	
Indicators	
Engagement	1a. The artist participant greets and socializes with other participants upon entering the art session.
	1b. The artist participant greets and socializes with other participants during the art session.
	2. While engaged in the art activity, the artist participant has sustained attention for a period of 30–45 minutes.
	3. The participant requires prompting or cueing once engaged in the art project.
Expression of pleasure	4. The artist participant has relaxed body language, smiles, and laughs during the art project.
	5. The artist participant verbalizes a sense of pleasure with phrases such as: "This feels good" or "This is relaxing."
	6. The artist participant is tense or agitated during the art project.
Self-esteem	7. The artist participant nonverbally expresses pride in participating and completing a project by smiling, nodding happily, tearfulness, clapping.
	8. The artist participant verbally expresses satisfaction by stating: "Thank you, I did that, really?"
	9. Without prompting, the artist participant offers kudos or support of another participant's work.
Expression of emotions and feelings	10. When the artist facilitator uses prompts and/or prompts and cues, the participant often paints or draws from a memory of a past experience.
	11. The artist participant responds to verbal reminiscent prompts by painting or drawing memorable past experiences.
	12. While drawing or painting, the artist participant displays nonverbal behaviors indicating comfort or discomfort in participating in the activity: (a) tears; (b) distorted facial expression; (c) grimace; (d) smiles.

Note: Read this article before administering the instrument: Jennifer M. Kinney and Clarissa A. Rentz, "Observed Well-Being Among Individuals with Dementia: Memories in the Making©, An Art Program, Versus Other Structured Activity," *American Journal of Alzheimer's Disease and Other Dementias* 20, no. 4 (2005): 220–27.

New Horizons Music Evaluation Form

Please take a few minutes to help us by giving us your evaluation.
The evaluations will be carefully considered in planning for the future.
Check your response. Add comments wherever you wish to do so.

1. Do you plan to continue? ❏ Yes ❏ No

2. Did your accomplishments this semester meet your expectations, fall short of your expectations, or exceed your expectations? ❏ Meet ❏ Fall short ❏ Exceed

3. What are your most satisfying accomplishments so far?
   _____ Playing a new instrument
   _____ Reading music
   _____ Writing music
   _____ Playing in small ensembles
   _____ Playing in the band
   _____ Playing by ear
   _____ Improvising
   _____ Starting a new area of learning and recreation
   _____ Expanding your social activities
   _____ Other: _____
   _____
   _____

4. What would you like to accomplish next? What do you want to spend more time on? _____
   _____
   _____
   _____

5. What would you like to spend less time on? _____
   _____
   _____
   _____
   _____

6. Indicate any ways in which your music listening has changed:
   ❏ Have gone to more live performances
   ❏ Enjoy listening to recordings and radio music more
   ❏ Other: _____
   _____
   _____

7. List any health problems that may have developed as a result of your participation:
   _____
   _____
   _____
   _____
   _____

8. List any ways in which your physical and mental health may have improved as a result of your participation: _____
   _____
   _____
   _____
   _____
   _____

9. Where did you obtain your instrument?
   _____ Already owned it.
   _____ It belonged to someone else in my family.
   _____ Found it through a want ad.
   _____ I purchased it at a music store.
   　　　　　If so, what store? _____
   　　　　　Reasons for selecting that store: _____
   　　　　　_____
   　　　　　_____

   　　　　　Did you purchase from the store from which you rented? ❏ Yes ❏ No
   　　　　　If no, why? _____
   　　　　　_____

10. Please list music and accessory items that you have purchased since September:
_____
_____
_____
_____
_____

My instrument teacher is _____

Your response to the following items about teachers will be confidential, but the combined responses may be used to advise teachers.

11. My teacher is willing and able to attend to my individual needs.
    ❏ Yes ❏ No
    Comment _____
    _____
    _____

12. My teacher gives me good advice on what and how to practice.
    ❏ Yes ❏ No
    Comment _____
    _____
    _____

13. Please add any additional comments about your teacher: _____
    _____
    _____
    _____
    _____
    _____

14. Please give us your general comments. What did you like best? Least? What suggestions do you have for making improvements? Sign your name at the end if you would like to, or remain anonymous. _____
    _____
    _____
    _____
    _____
    _____
    _____

Empowerment Group Care Partner Survey

	1 Not at all	2 A little bit	3 Some	4 A lot
1. Having my family member participate in the Empowerment Group helps reduce my **emotional stress**.				
2. Having my family member participate in the Empowerment Group helps me to have more **patience** with him/her.				
3. Having my family member participate in the Empowerment Group gives me more **time for other family members**.				
4. Having my family member participate in the Empowerment Group gives me some **time to relax**.				
5. Having my family member participate in the Empowerment Group gives me **time to do some things for myself** that are otherwise difficult to fit into my schedule.				
6. Having my family member participate in the Empowerment Group gives me **time to do chores** that are otherwise difficult to fit into my schedule.				
7. How much do you look forward to the time when your family member participates in the Empowerment Group?				
8. How much does your family member look forward to attending the Empowerment Group?				
9. In general, how beneficial do you think the Empowerment Group has been for your family member?				
10. In general, how satisfied are you with the Empowerment Group?				

1. What do you **like best** about the Empowerment Group? _____

_____
_____
_____
_____
_____

2. What changes could be made that would **improve** the Empowerment Group?
_____
_____
_____
_____
_____

3. Would you like your family member to continue participating in the Empowerment Group?
    ❏ Yes ❏ No
    Why or why not? _____
_____

Thank you for taking the time to help us improve our program.

Empowerment Group Survey: Initial

Respondent Name_____
Date completed_____Survey number_____

Never	**Rarely**	**Sometimes**	**Always**
1	2	3	4

1. How often do you feel part of a group of friends? _____

2. How often do you feel left out? _____

3. How often do you feel isolated from others? _____

4. How often do you feel that there are people who really understand you? _____

5. How often do you feel that there are people you can talk to? _____

6. How often do you feel useful? _____

7. How often do you feel you can help others? _____

8. How often do you feel you make a difference? _____

Empowerment Group Survey: Six Months

Respondent Name_____

Date completed_____Survey number _____

Never	**Rarely**	**Sometimes**	**Always**
1	2	3	4

1. How often do you feel part of a group of friends? _____

2. How often do you feel left out? _____

3. How often do you feel isolated from others? _____

4. How often do you feel that there are people who really understand you? _____

5. How often do you feel that there are people you can talk to? _____

6. How often do you feel useful? _____

7. How often do you feel you can help others? _____

8. How often do you feel you make a difference? _____

9. What do you like most about participating in this group? _____
_____
_____
_____
_____
_____

10. Is there anything that could be done differently to make this group better for you? _____
_____
_____
_____
_____

Adapted from the UCLA loneliness scale.

ABOUT THE PROJECT PARTNERS

National Guild of Community Schools of the Arts

520 8th Avenue, Suite 302
New York, NY 10018
Phone: 212-268-3337
Fax: 212-268-3995
kencole@nationalguild.org
www.nationalguild.org

The National Guild advances high-quality, community-based arts education so that all people may participate in the arts according to their interests and abilities. We support the creation and development of community schools of the arts by providing research and information resources, professional development and networking opportunities, advocacy, and high-profile leadership.

National Center for Creative Aging

4125 Albemarle Street, NW
Washington, DC 20016-2105
Phone: 202-895-9456
Fax: 202-895-9483
ghanna@creativeaging.org
www.creativeaging.org

The National Center for Creative Aging is dedicated to fostering an understanding of the vital relationship between creative expression and the quality of life of older people. Creative expression is important for older people of all cultures and ethnic backgrounds, regardless of economic status, age, or level of physical, emotional, or cognitive functioning.

New Jersey Performing Arts Center

One Center Street
Newark, NJ 07102
Phone: 973-297-5812
Fax: 973-642-0654
dwhite@njpac.org
www.njpac.org

The New Jersey Performing Arts Center (NJPAC) has garnered national attention in its first 10 seasons, serving as a model for its programming and audience diversity, education initiatives, and the catalytic role it has played in returning nightlife and economic activity to New Jersey's largest urban community. Arts education is at the center of NJPAC's mission, with a continuing commitment to explore new and innovative ways to serve students, educators, and parents in four different areas: performances, residencies, professional development/partnerships, and arts training.

About the Author

JMB Arts Management
702 Twin Holly Lane
Silver Spring, MD 20910
Phone/Fax: 301-589-0331
johanna@jmb-arts.com
www.jmb-arts.com

Johanna Misey Boyer is the president of JMB Arts Management, which specializes in helping clients manage programs in arts and healthcare, aging, and accessibility. She is a volunteer ombudsman for assisted living residents in Montgomery County, Maryland, and a board member of and active volunteer for PETS-DC, an organization that enables people living with HIV/AIDS or other disabling conditions to maintain and care for their pets.